RESEARCHING JUSTICE

Spaces and Practices of Justice

Series Editor: **Agatha Herman**, Cardiff University

Geographies of justice investigate the spatialities of (in)justice and its impacts on practices, relations, discourses and experiences. This book series explores and analyses the exciting nexus offered by a focus on (in)justice for interdisciplinary work and so draws on engagements from across sociology, politics, international relations, urban studies, anthropology, rural studies, cultural studies, criminology, development studies and human geography.

Scan the code below to discover new and forthcoming titles in the series, or visit:

bristoluniversitypress.co.uk/
spaces-and-practices-of-justice

RESEARCHING JUSTICE
Engaging with Questions and Spaces of
(In)Justice through Social Research

Edited by
Agatha Herman and Joshua Inwood

First published in Great Britain in 2026 by

Bristol University Press
University of Bristol
1–9 Old Park Hill
Bristol
BS2 8BB
UK
t: +44 (0)117 374 6645
e: bup-info@bristol.ac.uk

Details of international sales and distribution partners are available at bristoluniversitypress.co.uk

© Bristol University Press 2026

British Library Cataloguing in Publication Data
A catalogue record for this book is available from the British Library

ISBN 978-1-5292-2665-2 hardcover
ISBN 978-1-5292-2666-9 paperback
ISBN 978-1-5292-2667-6 ePub
ISBN 978-1-5292-2668-3 ePdf

The right of Agatha Herman and Joshua Inwood to be identified as editors of this work has been asserted by them in accordance with the Copyright, Designs and Patents Act 1988.

All rights reserved: no part of this publication may be reproduced, stored in a retrieval system, or transmitted in any form or by any means, electronic, mechanical, photocopying, recording, or otherwise without the prior permission of Bristol University Press.

Every reasonable effort has been made to obtain permission to reproduce copyrighted material. If, however, anyone knows of an oversight, please contact the publisher.

The statements and opinions contained within this publication are solely those of the editors and contributors and not of the University of Bristol or Bristol University Press. The University of Bristol and Bristol University Press disclaim responsibility for any injury to persons or property resulting from any material published in this publication.

Bristol University Press works to counter discrimination on grounds of gender, race, disability, age and sexuality.

Cover design: blu inc
Front cover image: unsplash/charlesdeluvio

Bristol University Press' authorised representative in the European Union is: Easy Access System Europe, Mustamäe tee 50, 10621 Tallinn, Estonia, Email: gpsr.requests@easproject.com

For Alina, Nicholas, Leura, Malcolm, Heidi and Heath. May you have the courage to create the worlds you deserve.

Contents

Series Editor Preface		ix
Notes on Contributors		x
Acknowledgements		xiii

1	Researching Justice: How Do You Make the Research Process 'Just'? *Agatha Herman and Joshua Inwood*	1

PART I	**Justice as Care-full Encounter**	**19**
2	Resourcing Struggles for Social Justice from the University *Kate Derickson*	21
3	Performing Timespace Encounters: Reflecting on Sharing, Voice and Justice in Qualitative Research *Elizabeth Mavroudi*	31
4	Fostering Food Justice in Academia and Beyond *Barbora Adlerova and Ana Moragues Faus*	46

PART II	**Justice as Unsettling Asymmetries**	**65**
5	Disrupting the Field? Creating Community-centred Spaces for Epistemic Justice with Rwandese Diaspora Youth *Jen Dickinson and Natasha Uwimanzi*	67
6	Researching Justice: Justice as Accountability and Justice as Collaboration *Jennifer Balint*	88
7	Approaching Energy and Climate Justice: Working Towards More Just Scholarship, Pedagogy and Praxis *Deepti Chatti*	102

PART III	**Justice as Challenge**	**119**
8	Perspectives from the Top: Justice, International Relations and the Political Geography of the Arctic *Corine Wood-Donnelly*	121

9	Justice for All? Expanding Questions and Spaces of (In)Justice through Multispecies Research, Teaching and Activism *Vegan Geography Collective (Richard J. White, Ophélie Véron, Simon Springer and Andrew McGregor)*	139
10	The Priority of Justice *Don Mitchell*	159
11	Concluding Thoughts: What Does It Mean to Do 'Just' Research? *Agatha Herman and Joshua Inwood*	176
Index		187

Series Editor Preface

Agatha Herman

Justice refers to a broad concern with fairness, equity, equality and respect. Just from the daily news, it is readily apparent how questions of justice or, in fact, the more obvious experiences of *injustice* shape our everyday lives. From global trade to our own personal consumption; living or dying through war and peace; access to education; relations in the workplace or home; how we experience life through a spectrum of identities; or the more-than-human entanglements that contextualize our environments, we need to conceptualize and analyse the intersections between spaces and practices of justice in order to formulate innovative and grounded interventions. The Spaces and Practices of Justice book series aims to do so through cutting across scales to explore power, relations and society from the local through to international levels, recognizing that space is fundamental to understanding how (in)justice is relationally produced in, and through, different temporal and geographical contexts. It is also always practised, and a conceptual focus on these 'doings and sayings' (Shove, 2014) brings a sense of the everydayness of (in)justice but also allows for analysis of the broader contexts, logics and structures within which such experiences and relations are embedded (Jaeger-Erben and Offenberger, 2014; Herman, 2018).

References

Herman, A. (2018) *Practising Empowerment in Post-Apartheid South Africa: Wine, Ethics and Development*, London: Routledge.

Jaeger-Erben, M. and Offenberger, U. (2014) A practice theory approach to sustainable consumption, *GAIA*, 23(S1): 166–174.

Shove, E. (2014) Putting practice into policy: reconfiguring questions of consumption and climate change, *Contemporary Social Science*, 9(4): 415–429.

Notes on Contributors

Barbora Adlerova is a PhD student and graduate tutor in the School of Geography and Planning at Cardiff University. She is interested in how we can create a more just participation in food governance, co-produced evaluation for food system change, and participatory and reflective approaches to research and teaching.

Jennifer Balint is Professor in Socio-Legal Studies, Criminology, and Head of School, Social and Political Sciences at the University of Melbourne. Her most recent book is *Keeping Hold of Justice: Encounters between Law and Colonialism* (University of Michigan Press, 2020, with Julie Evans, Mark McMillan and Nesam McMillan), arising out of the collaborative Minutes of Evidence project. She is the author of *Genocide, State Crime and the Law: In the Name of the State* (Routledge, 2012) and has worked extensively on accountability for state crime and access to justice.

Deepti Chatti is Assistant Professor of Climate Justice at the University of California San Diego in the Department of Urban Studies and Planning, and the Critical Gender Studies Program. A feminist scholar, ethnographer and engineer, her research critically analyses sustainable development efforts to expand clean energy access and reduce air pollution exposures in historically marginalized communities.

Kate Derickson directs the Urban Studies programme and is Associate Professor in the Department of Geography, Environment and Society at the University of Minnesota, where she conducts research on racialization and environmental change. She is also a member of the Gullah/Geechee Sustainability Think Tank.

Jen Dickinson is a political and development geographer at the University of Southampton. Her research investigates the basis on which governments, civil society and international organizations are (re)defining the role of overseas diaspora communities in development; and how diaspora communities are mobilized to contribute to creative economies, tourist landscapes and heritage sectors of their countries of origin.

Agatha Herman is Senior Lecturer in Human Geography in the School of Geography and Planning at Cardiff University. Her work engages with lived experiences and practices of ethics and social justice, raising questions around race and ethnicity, labour, community, governance, gender, land and the more-than-human through a focus on agricultural and mining production networks, and liminal communities.

Joshua Inwood is Professor of Geography and African American Studies and Senior Scientist in the Rock Ethics Institute at Pennsylvania State University. His work focuses on race and whiteness in the US South. Research interests include the US Civil Rights Movement and landscape studies in the US South.

Elizabeth Mavroudi is Reader in Human Geography in the School of Social Sciences and Humanities at Loughborough University. She is also currently Co-Director for Equity, Diversity and Inclusion for her School. Her research interests are in migration studies more broadly and in diaspora more specifically. Her qualitative research has focused on issues of identity and politics for different diasporic groups as well as on migrant perceptions of immigration policy.

Andrew McGregor is Professor of Human Geography and Director of Research and Innovation in the Macquarie School of Social Sciences at Macquarie University. His work focuses upon human-environment relations in the context of global environmental change with a view to developing more convivial and just multispecies futures. His research projects primarily examine food and forest futures in Australia and Southeast Asia, with a particular focus on the relationship between animal industries and climate change. Andrew is author of *Southeast Asian Development* (Routledge) and lead editor of the *Routledge Handbook of Southeast Asian Development*; co-editor of *Vegan Geographies: Spaces Beyond Violence, Ethics Beyond Speciesism* and former editor-in-chief of *Asia Pacific Viewpoint*. Andrew can be contacted on andrew.mcgregor@mq.edu.au.

Don Mitchell is Professor of Human Geography in the Department of Human Geography at Uppsala University and Distinguished Professor of Geography Emeritus at Syracuse University. His work focuses on historical and contemporary struggles over urban public, the relationship between capital, labour and the state in the making of geographical landscapes, and the geography of culture.

Ana Moragues Faus is Senior Research Fellow in the School of Economics and Business and Director of the Food Action and Research Observatory at the University of Barcelona, Spain. She works closely with civil society organizations and policy makers to build sustainable and just food systems, mobilizing critical analytical tools and co-productive practices.

Simon Springer's degrees, titles, awards, rank, H-Index, followers on social media and previous publications don't particularly matter ... or at least they shouldn't when reading the chapter that he contributed to and determining its worth.

Natasha Uwimanzi has over eight years' of experience in the international development management and research consulting and has worked across Africa, notably Kenya, Rwanda, South Sudan, Central African Republic and Zambia. She has extensive experience with peace education, diaspora engagement, teacher training and development programmes, and social and emotional learning in schools – and is particularly passionate about research in education and development. Natasha Uwimanzi holds two bachelor of science degrees and a master's in international development and education from the University of East Anglia.

Ophélie Véron is a Marie Skłodowska-Curie fellow at the Center for Metropolitan Studies of the Technische Universität Berlin. She is also affiliated with the Marc Bloch Centre, Berlin. Ophélie's research to date has engaged with a range of interweaving themes, including socio-ecological transformation and social justice, urban social movements, anarchist geographies and vegan geographies.

Richard J. White is Reader in Human Geography at Sheffield Hallam University, UK. Greatly influenced by anarchist praxis, his main research agenda explores a range of ethical, economic and activist landscapes rooted in questions of interspecies social justice, and the politics of total liberation. Recently edited books include *Critical Animal Studies and Activism* (Peter Lang, 2023) and *Vegan Geographies: Spaces beyond Violence, Ethics beyond Speciesism* (Lantern Press, 2022).

Corine Wood-Donnelly is Associate Professor of International Relations and the High North at the Faculty of Social Sciences at Nord University. She is also a researcher at Uppsala University where she is the Scientific Coordinator for the EU-funded project JUSTNORTH (GA 869327). Dr Wood-Donnelly is an interdisciplinary researcher in International Relations and political geography and specializes in governance and policy of the Arctic region.

Acknowledgements

No book comes together without the efforts of many, many people. This is especially true with an edited book. Researching justice would not have been possible without our contributors and their patience and generosity during this book project, as well as their critical reflections on their own experiences and practices. We also appreciate the patience of the publisher as various personal and global events kept pushing the deadline back. Josh Inwood would like to especially thank Agatha Herman for her work during this project. Quite literally this book is the result of Agatha's work and efforts and her belief in this project.

1

Researching Justice: How Do You Make the Research Process 'Just'?

Agatha Herman and Joshua Inwood

Understanding justice for many academics, practitioners and policy makers begins with questions of injustice – the way particular social, economic, political or cultural structures come to undergird exploitative conditions (Dorling, 2010; Barnett, 2017). Yet, as Sandel (2010: 10) reminds us, 'thinking about justice seems inescapably to engage us in thinking about the best way to live', which in turn requires us to consider how we engage with our day-to-day lives. As academics, spaces and practices of (in)justice may be the focus of our research although questions of the 'what', 'who' and 'how' of justice (Fraser, 2008) also shape both our working practices and everyday lives more broadly. From activist-scholars to theoreticians, ideals of justice shape how we understand and engage with our research questions and stakeholders; reflect on and practice research methodologies; and share and disseminate findings even if we are not always explicit about the reflective processes behind these approaches. Additionally, the nature and demands placed on contemporary academic outputs means that they are often focused on advancing theoretical or empirical understandings of justice or, when they are methodologically centred, reflecting on the challenges, negotiations and contradictions of doing ethical, participatory and emancipatory research. Although there have long been calls to explore how the research process itself can be a socially just endeavour (DePalma, 2010), responses have often been more critical, how-to guides rather than reflections on the role justice does, and should, play in our research praxis.

Quite simply, if we are serious about engaging in justice work, how we centralize justice within this is of vital importance to living out the broader realities of why we do what we do and the kinds of worlds we envision through our research engagements. Gaining insights into how others conceptualize, and use, justice in their work is important in encouraging discussion around contemporary research practices, opening up the 'black box' of how academics understand their own work. Furthermore, it offers a reflexive lens to engage with the variety of perspectives, ideologies, articulations, materialities and communities that connect into, and ground, justice research.

These realities are central to the goals of this edited volume and chapters. While many journal papers, book chapters and volumes have offered critical reflections on doing culturally competent and reflective research, there is a tendency to focus on specific research topics and methodological strategies. What is missing is a broader discussion about how our specific engagements themselves come to inform and direct our research methods and perspectives. As a result, this book is motivated to understand how our concepts and practices of justice shape our engagements in the field as well as the connections we make, the questions we ask and the kind of materials we come to produce through those efforts. More specifically the authors in this edited volume open for discussion the practices of justice in research and offer insights into the actual 'doings' of research. These chapters also acknowledge the tangled nature of our academic praxis and the promises and limits of justice work. Ultimately, this book presents critical engagements and reflections on the spatialities of justice and its impacts on research practices. To contextualize this, we draw on our own experiences to first conceptualize 'justice' and 'praxis' before outlining the structure of the volume.

Agatha remembers ... engaging with methods

When I was a student, research methods classes always seemed dry. During my master's I actually remember a lecturer starting a class with "[T]his isn't that interesting but we need to cover it so let's get on ...", which cemented my relationship with methods as necessary, pretty straightforward but a little dull. I think this is understandable given that my engagements were generally through lectures and literatures that dealt with data collection, analysis and management in a very practical, tick-box way. Yes, we discussed research ethics and the impact of researcher positionality, power relations in the field and developing rapport but these never really developed into discussion points. Instead, they were presented as that fairly standard existential acknowledgement that usually appears in a paragraph at the end of a dissertation methods chapter. Going from my undergraduate degree to a master's and then a PhD opened my eyes somewhat as I gained experience of doing more fieldwork in a range of places with different stakeholders; yet I still felt that most of the methods literatures I was engaging with offered me a 'recipe' rather than really capturing, explaining or helping me to process the emotional dilemmas, confusion and – in all honesty – social anxiety I felt as I stumbled from one research scenario into another. Literatures largely presented me with a serene swan of research methods, apparently conducted by calm 'grown up' researchers who didn't seem to experience things in the same way. What I really wanted was to see beneath the surface, the desperately flapping feet of nitty-gritty details and choices, and read about the sweat and tears of actions taken and their consequences.

Even now, when according to the UK research councils I am (terrifyingly) 'mid-career', I still get these feelings and concerns and, when talking to my colleagues, I know that grappling with such issues remains common. I remain slightly haunted, given my research interests in ethical geographies and social justice, with wondering to what extent I am *actually* practising the concepts and principles I write about in my research? In how I do it, the interactions, conversations, collaborations and *choices* ... are these 'just'? In my everyday life I am surrounded by such questions, concerns and reflections – in the park, in the supermarket, listening to the news ... I am constantly assessing how I define and engage with justice or, more often, injustice but have I really connected with how it plays out in my working and research practices?

This then is the setting for this edited volume – our aim is to open up that black box, disrupt the swan and hear from those researching across a variety of topics, in a range of geographical and cultural spaces and at different points in their careers to gain insights into the 'doings and sayings' of their research. How does the practice of just research actually work? How do people negotiate moral and ethical entanglements within their projects? This is clearly a big ask and, given that self-reflection in a public sphere is not the easiest, we appreciate the honesty of our contributors. The individuality of their responses offer what we hope you will find to be interesting and useful insights into *doing just research*. First, though, it is important to ground the chapters that follow by considering what do we mean by 'justice'?

Josh reflects ... what is justice?

My initial experience in graduate school was characterized by a dizzying array of ideas and concepts related to the broader idea of social justice. Lefebvre's *Production of Space* (1991) had been in English circulation for only a decade, ideas as varied as Critical Race Theory, Right to the City, and the broader cultural turn were roiling the waters of graduate seminars and the hallways of geography departments. This was a time of energized meetings and engagements across the discipline as the spatial turn in the broader social sciences and humanities opened geography to a broader appreciation. This was a time when geographic thought and ideas were at the centre for the struggle for social justice and the remaking of the world in ways that were more just and equitable; a time when the struggle for justice was going to push us towards realizing the goals of struggles that were decades in the making.

What a difference a decade and a half has made. In the wake of the Global War on (of) Terror and the vast global expansion of the US security state, the 2007 global recession triggered by the subprime mortgage market, revanchist capitals seemingly inexhaustible march to destroy the planet through unfettered consumptive practices and environmental degradation, an ascendant white nationalism and the rolling back of women's rights and assaults on non-binary peoples and it seems we are once again on the cusp of a broad and long-standing crisis. This crisis has many authors. It is in this context that we have taken up this edited book.

If this crisis has many authors, it is also true that what is needed is a multifaceted response that draws from a broad range of definitions of justice that are geographically and politically contextualized. To meet the moment also means standing outside of liberal conceptualizations of the term. Lisa Lowe in her work *The Intimacies of Four Continents* (2015) investigates the connections between the emergence of European liberalism with the expansion of settler empires, the growth of the slave trade and an expanding global empire that comes to write out myriad peoples from the idea of justice. As she notes, European conceptualizations of justice created a geography that comes to develop:

> Freedoms for 'man' in modern Europe and North America, while relegating others to geographical and temporal spaces that are constituted as backward, uncivilized, unfree. ... The social inequalities of our time are a legacy of these processes through which 'the human' is 'freed' by liberal forms, while other subjects, practices and geographies are paced at a distance from 'the human'. (Lowe, 2015: 3)

What Lowe drives at is one of the central contradictions to much of the work on justice. Namely, a reliance on liberal forms or understandings of justice predicated on a system that came to define and deny justice to untold numbers of people. As a result of these insights, we have worked to draw out a diverse set of scholars to outline various forms of justice that come to see justice beyond what has traditionally dominated the broader discussion on social justice in geography. Don Mitchell picks this theme up in his contribution and argues for a more robust debate about what exactly we mean when we come to define justice both within the discipline but also how we move forward to engage in our work and politics. Dickinson and Uwimanzi argue in their chapter on Rwanda that a starting point for approaches grounded in justice is situating them within a context of epistemic justice rooted in the communities where our work takes place. In both instances, Mitchell and Dickinson and Uwimanzi take up the position of justice as existing outside of more traditional understandings of the concept as grounded in Western notions of the individual.

What is clear from the contributions in this volume is that we need to move beyond staid definitions of justice or definitions which rely on or reify existing paradigms of exploitation. Such a move necessitates a broader discussion that is grounded in the messy and contradictory worlds of actually existing geographies. The critical engagements that are found in this volume contribute to this discussion and think through the idea of justice as praxis.

What do we mean by 'praxis' in this context?

What then do we mean by 'researching justice'? While we are both committed to research that exposes and critiques inequalities and discrimination, and advocates for and drives equitable and hopeful outcomes, there are myriad places to read past and current works doing these things to varying degrees. Here we are interested in the methodological, ethical and logistical choices that underlie all research, whether quantitative or qualitative, since 'any method "can be liberating if used by multi-culturally competent researchers and scholar-activists committed to social justice" (Cokley and Awad, 2013:26)' (Fassinger and Morrow, 2013: 70). It is the researcher, their intentions and practices that are key, and it is the latter that we particularly want to expose and unpack in this volume although this also illuminates the researcher as practitioner. We are interested in the ways a justice framework moves from being simply a tool of data analysis to informing the fundamental activities of the research process. In turn, this practice comes to structure the ways our research and writing engage with the communities we work in. In this section we first open out what we understand by praxis in this context before outlining *who* we are interested in. Finally, we reflect on some key structures that inform research practices, particularly those grounded in the Western academic tradition.

A focus on research practices recognizes the broader contexts, logics and structures within which they, and all those actants tangled up within research relationships, are embedded (Jaeger-Erben and Offenberger, 2014). Practices are therefore interconnected, emergent and dynamic 'doings and sayings' (Schatzki, 2002; Shove, 2014), which, following Herman (2018), we understand as both entities and performances, pivoting around the practitioner, who is:

> constituted through their mental and physical activities, their emotions, their knowledges and their relations with objects, which all dynamically shape what they do and what they consider possible. The practice itself is an interacting nexus of discourses, materials, skills and relations that shape its context, how the practice is understood and positioned

in society and how it is performed. This is held together as relatively stable and coherent through power operations and relations of certain, vested interests, which normalise a particular practice nexus making it acceptable and enduring. Nevertheless, this is only ever provisional and the possibility for innovation and change can come from both within or outside of the stabilised accumulation that represents a particular practice. (Herman, 2018: 20)

This highlights the multiple, contextual and contingent nature of (research) practices, which although sometimes solidifying into particular, normatively accepted formations of 'good practice' always contain the possibility for change. We shall return to consider the researcher themselves further on but this definition reminds us that to really engage with 'just' research practices, we need to reflect on the constitutive discourses, materials, skills and relations which shape them at each point in the process from idea to dissemination. Which epistemologies and ontologies shape our philosophical and methodological approaches? How do we negotiate how different knowledges are viewed or valued in and through our work, or even inside and outside the academy? Where do our topics and research questions come from? Do they spring out of literatures we've read or emerge from communities? While we are not saying here that there is necessarily a *right* answer to any of these questions, it is critical to reflect on, and engage with, the processes that ground each choice and to consider how to ensure that care infuses each relationship. As Held (2020) reflects, research relationships establish an ethical space, which requires particular skills, materials and discourses to continually engage with this unfolding and heterogeneous dialogue.

Researchers have reflected on the essential components of such non-extractive research, with Held (2020) calling for practices that are grounded in the '5 Rs' of respect, relevance, reciprocity, responsibility and relationality. Kouritzin and Nakagawa (2018) augment these with a demand for considerations of intent, integrity, a focus on process, a long-term commitment and a post-humanist outlook since 'neither value nor knowledge resides solely in human beings' (Kouritzin and Nakagawa, 2018: 684). The 'who' of research therefore needs to incorporate non-human actants as active, if unintentioning, agents within the research process, who interact with stakeholders and the researcher, inflecting those materials, skills, discourses and relations. Fassinger and Morrow (2013) argue that the researcher at the centre of this dynamic research practice needs to be culturally competent and self-reflective in order to fully and carefully engage with the 'moral considerations and ethical choices that arise as part of a researcher's daily practice' (Rossman and Rallis, 2010: 379). This needs to be a contextual and contingent process since research can never be 'a set of prescribed steps to take but [is] a complex and non-linear endeavour that will not necessarily be successful' (Held, 2020: 3). The researcher is therefore central to any endeavour to do 'just' research and it's important to remember that this is not just about, or for, researchers focusing on 'justice' topics. Justice and care need to be essential components of everyone's praxis to ensure effective, sustainable and critical research.

Within this, the research stakeholders and the relationships they have with the project and researcher are also important – where does the power lie in defining the terms of their participation? The terms of reference of the project? The ethical values underlying the research? Scholars have argued that 'researchers are expected to conform to the norms of the Western academic tradition' (Igwe et al, 2022: 454), meaning that 'research in non-Western communities may also be experienced as a form of hegemony in which the ideology of the researcher determines the research methodology' (Kouritzin and Nakagawa, 2018: 677). Decolonizing research – rebalancing through de-centring Western ideologies – is necessary for more inclusive, consultative, dialogical and diverse practices and relations. The hegemony of the Western academic tradition, and the practices that have become normalized through it, represent a key structural framing that shapes research practices in, and beyond, Western academic institutions. Efforts are being made to decolonize research – 'a process that requires learning, unlearning and relearning' (Datta, 2017 in Held, 2020: 5) – but other institutional influences may be even more challenging to navigate.

Denzin et al (2017) reflect on issues around funding and legitimacy in achieving materially engaged work, and these are joined by questions of impact in the neoliberal university. How do these interact with doing 'just' research? Fassinger and Morrow (2013) questioned whether it was possible to do genuine participatory action research in a system that does not value long-term involvement, requires stated outcomes and measures of impact, and needs projects to be finite. Conducting research that meets Held's (2020) 5 Rs, which is non-extractive within such institutional constraints is highly problematic. This is exacerbated by our drive to be 'good scholars' as defined by the hegemonic research community (Cannella and Lincoln, 2007) with Kouritzin and Nakagawa (2018) challenging us to ask whose approval is most important to us? Is it the studied group? The institution? Or other academics? Being a good researcher often comes down to meeting institutional requirements such as those set by research ethics committees but these tick-box, procedural exercises have long been deemed insufficient to respond to ethics as lived (Cannella and Lincoln, 2007). In order to engage with the moral dimensions raised by every research decision, we need constant reflection and iteration to respond in-the-moment (Rossman and Rallis, 2010). Ethics should not just be an attempt to mitigate risk (Kouritzin and Nakagawa, 2018), and so need to be engaged with throughout the research process, not confined to the completion of a form at the start of a project. The reach of these institutional structures travels beyond the Western university or research institute, and can act as constraints on practising just research whether we are researcher or stakeholder, human or non-human, in or out of academia. In order to negotiate and navigate Western and neoliberal epistemologies, we need to reflect on and scrutinize every step of our research practices and processes to work towards just and caring choices.

Book structure

In order to do research with integrity, Kouritzin and Nakagawa (2018: 683) argue that researchers need to be honest and 'disclose as much as possible about themselves, about their beliefs and assumptions, about their relationships'. They call for researchers to make themselves vulnerable – 'as they have made those they have researched vulnerable' (Kouritzin and Nakagawa, 2018: 684) – through exposing the thought processes, skills, materials and relations underlying their research decisions and choices, promoting transparency (Rossman and Rallis, 2010) and disrupting that black box of doing research (see Figure 1.1).

To this end, we invited our contributors to write a critical commentary, drawing on their own experiences, projects and relations, reflecting on:

1. the role of justice in shaping their research interests and questions;
2. how ideals of justice influence their engagements with stakeholders, choice and practice of methods and dissemination strategies;
3. what a justice perspective brings to their work over other theoretical frameworks.

Each author responded to the brief in their own way, focusing on different elements of their research process, drawing on varied spaces, places and relationships to draw out some of the mechanics, the constraints and the opportunities presented for doing research with justice. To make sense of the various ways that our contributors work with the concept of justice we have organized our book into three sections: Justice as Care-full Encounter; Justice as Unsettling Asymmetries; and Justice as Challenge. Each of these contributions reflects the political commitments of scholars and activists who are engaging in work that is focused on social change and transformation. What is unique is the way that they each come to the intersection of research and justice in deeply personal ways that reflect very

Figure 1.1: The black box of 'doing' research

seriously how each author is positioned within a diverse set of communities and socio-spatial realities.

Because of this, or perhaps in spite of the geographically grounded realities that structure each contribution, there nevertheless are certain common narratives. These have inflected all of our contributors' experiences to varying degrees or serve as ongoing question marks that they reflect on in their daily practices. First, what is the purpose of the university and how is that role changing both in terms of the institution and the individual 'intellectual'? Second, because we work across academic and activist communities, to what extent do academic spaces/practices/ideologies shape our capabilities to do just research and our relations with diverse colleagues? Third, what is the most equitable, just and caring way to engage with communities we wish to research with? Finally, and really engaging with Kouritzin and Nakagawa's (2018) call for honest disclosure, how do we manage feelings of discomfort or that we've messed up? Reflecting on these opens up broader dialogues between these diverse perspectives and experiences, as well as connecting into reflexive questions we have both long, if intermittently, been engaging with.

Agatha wonders ... how honest do you need to be in exposing your research practices?

It turns out that I've been pondering the dilemmas involved in giving a rigorous and reflective research account for years now, on and off. While reading the chapters and drafting the Introduction for this volume, I suddenly remembered writing a paper called 'Honest geographies', which never got published because I ran out of energy to deal with the reviewer comments while trying to juggle teaching commitments. Looking back at the piece, my reflections from 2013 still have relevance in opening up my then, and ongoing, reflections around how I 'do' justice within and through my engagements with research stakeholders. Coming from the time it does, it draws on my PhD experiences, which were still – naturally – very fresh in my mind having only graduated in 2010.

One thing I often wondered was, when writing about our research how transparent do we need to be? Schiellerup (2008) noted the 'black box' surrounding qualitative data analysis and writing up, arguing that more attention needs to be paid to the experiential process of doing research. So, how much of the research process or researcher should be visible? To what extent should the challenges faced in the field be explicitly acknowledged? While accepting that credibility, dependability, confirmability and transferability remain critical criteria in structuring academic research engagements (Baxter and Eyles, 1997), the standardization of academic 'integrity' masks the need for 'negotiated ethics in the field' (Sultana, 2007) and creates more of a box-ticking exercise than a reflexive engagement

(Cannella and Lincoln, 2007; Rossman and Rallis, 2010; Kouritzin and Nakagawa, 2018; Held, 2020). While autoethnography offers one way to make research more transparent through writing the researcher into their work, this has been dismissed as self-indulgent by some critics (including Sparkes, 2002; Atkinson, 2006; Delamont, 2007).

Since the 1980s, qualitative researchers have struggled with responding to the challenges surrounding the representation of research subjects. How can we write about others' experiences? Does the account reflect the research subjects or our own worldview? Whose 'issues' are we discussing? (Khan, 2007). This crisis of representation has been discussed extensively (see Noth, 2003; Besio and Butz, 2004; Crang, 2005; Butz and Besio, 2009) and yet, however prepared researchers are, the extent of this challenge is not fully visible until it emerges in one's own research.

My doctoral research was grounded in four months of qualitative fieldwork in the Western Cape, South Africa in which I investigated the ethical discourses of Fairtrade and Black Economic Empowerment (BEE) in the wine industry. My methodology was centred on semi-structured individual and group interviews with key stakeholders (farmworkers, farm owners, farm managers, promoters, exporters and non-governmental organizations) supplemented by farm visits, analysis of promotional materials and a field diary. Throughout my fieldwork, I was aware of the sensitivities of conducting research in this post-apartheid and postcolonial space, and the need to be aware of my situatedness. However, it is simple enough to recognize these dangers theoretically but less straightforward to overcome them in practice. How could I operationalize postcolonial critiques in my research practices when the latter remain saturated in remnant colonial discourses and structures (Fine, 1998)? All research contact zones are run through with power relations between researcher and researched, and these issues are not confined to 'the field' because, as Denzin and Lincoln (2005) argue, there is no difference between writing and fieldwork.

Janesick (1994) considers that 'for the researcher, the story told is the dance in all its complexity, context, originality, and passion' but while this is what, as writers, we may be hoping to achieve, there can be no final, authoritative representation (Denzin, 1994); truths are always partial and no subject position is innocent or natural. Therefore, how do we write self-other, here-there? How do we allow the stories of 'others' to be heard without colluding in the structures of domination and imperialism (Fine, 1998)? As a social researcher I cannot escape the fact that others' lives and words are my data (Besio, 2005); this necessarily entails representation since 'writing is never for itself; it is always both about and for somebody, something, somewhere, sometime ... else' (Staeheli and Nagar, 2002), and 'representational authority is dirty and ever present' (Besio, 2003). It is therefore tempting to try and forgo the whole messy process but we cannot abstain from representation (Spivak, 1988). Such representational issues were supplemented for me with dilemmas over the extent to which I should be showing the process and myself when writing about my research. Alvermann et al (1996) note that disclosures neither prove credibility nor neutralize power relations, and deliberately exposing weaknesses and foibles feels detrimental to demonstrating academic credibility and capability, especially when you are trying to gain job security. How then can we negotiate this fine line, retaining reflexivity as a critical element in acknowledging the moral and political implications of qualitative research (Crang, 2005)?

Complex interests in the South African wine industry

5 March 2008. I was finally there. On my own. In the 'field'. I had considered the issues facing my research in this postcolonial and post-apartheid space but it was only on arrival, and with some direct personal experience, that this disembodied knowledge began to make sense. I had, for example, perhaps overly optimistic hopes for the contemporary state of the wine industry. From the literatures I knew that progress in terms of social and economic transformation was slow, lagging behind other sectors due to its poor wages, grim working conditions and continuing unequal power relations (Du Toit et al, 2008). The complexity of the interests in this industry and variety of responses to the inclusion of 'ethical' discourses necessitated a multi-sited methodology focusing on four wine brands, which, given the time limits on the fieldwork, contributed to the interview based strategy (Hannerz, 2003). The nature of what I was studying – following the articulations of discourses through networks – lent itself to interviews as how Fairtrade and BEE were understood and practised by the range of stakeholders within these networks could be explored. Although the majority of interviews were one-offs, serial engagement with the networks permitted a degree of triangulation and insights into the engagements between the network nodes.

Particular insights into the relations between Fairtrade and its producers came from participating in a FLO-Cert Information Day (28 March 2008). This was run by the global Fairtrade certifying body to update producers on changes to the Fairtrade certification criteria and the role of Fairtrade-South Africa (the domestic labelling organization) within the auditing process; towards the end there were break-out groups to reflect on what we had learned. Although the rationale was understood, the way BEE was being included within Fairtrade was not universally popular as it meant more work for the producers and demanded more of South African Fairtrade producers than their international counterparts. This raised questions as to the applicability and relevance of a global discourse of 'fairness', which also emerged in later interviews with Fairtrade producers and industry stakeholders. These challenged my preconceptions of producers' attitudes towards Fairtrade (which I expected to be positive regarding its participation in South Africa's transformation agenda) and reminded me that making space for the unexpected was critical; as Crang and Cook (2007) note we never know what and in what order things are going to happen. Remaining sensitive to both the voices and feelings of my research subjects, and opportunities for gaining new insights had to, however, be balanced with ensuring that I covered the main themes that I knew I wanted to explore. I wanted to combine an informal approach to aid the development of rapport with a degree of professionalism and so, in order to present myself as 'knowledgeable as well as curious' (Crang and Cook, 2007: 63), I went into each interview with some thematic questions prepared.

Given my goal was understanding, I wanted the research subjects' own words and so it was important to hear their stories, which seemed both an expression of 'self' and of the experience (Warren and Karner, 2005). I often asked questions to which I already knew the 'official' line to create space for people to tell it from their perspective. At times I just let the flow of conversation go, which did make for some long interviews but opened up new questions and insights into areas I was unaware of or had not foreseen as being relevant. In one interview with the owner of a 'virtual winery',[1] giving her the space to talk through her experiences gave greater insights into the continuing structural constraints on BEE within the wine industry than would have emerged from keeping to the prepared questions. Her first wine brand was initially an award-winning success but over time the quality of the product decreased to such an extent that the company was forced to cease trading as the brand's reputation was destroyed. Although she subsequently started another virtual wine brand, this still suffered from a position of relative powerlessness with its supplier who refused to make a contract. Such tensions, legacy of the apartheid era, were expected but the Fairtrade information day also highlighted more unexpected strains within the farmer community between Afrikaans and English speakers. Some producers were very uncomfortable with the request to speak in English during the meeting (I think for my benefit, which further emphasized my position as an 'outsider'), suggesting a degree of separation between the communities. Stereotypes emerged throughout my research and on a number of occasions I was told that the rural Western Cape was an Afrikaans area and although farmers here were 'rough' they were also direct, in contrast to English speakers who would talk behind your back. I also had some interviewees express concern over being recorded, worrying that I would play the tapes to people back in the UK who would laugh at their accents. Although able to reassure my interviewees about the protection of their data and attempting to distance myself from broad stereotypes by treating everyone I met the same, this required thinking on my feet as neither were situations I had prepared for, demonstrating my naivety in doing research in general, and in South Africa in particular.

Wider insights into continuing structural relations within South Africa emerged throughout my research: a group interview with some BEE shareholders in a restaurant when everyone turned to stare as we walked into the formerly monochrome space; a Black vineyard owner reflecting on the poor reception he and his wife had initially received when going for wine tastings; a white farmer (acting as an interpreter) prompting a worker to tell me about all the great impacts Fairtrade had had on their farm. I constantly had to negotiate these varying power relations both within the empirical focus of my research and within the research terrain. As I reflected in my field diary (31 March 2008), 'I felt I came across as a little naïve at times, which emphasizes my position as an outsider; although it seems to inspire "guidance" rather than annoyance amongst my interviewees!'. A number of well-meaning individuals offered me advice, of varying degrees of utility, perhaps a reflection on my gender, youth and contextual disconnection. How I was positioned by my research participants, how I went about the research and the focus of the research were all shaped by interconnected ethical concerns around who/what to include and how to encourage/demonstrate stakeholder/my engagement with these spaces.

So what?

While conducting my doctoral research it was only through engaging with other PhD students and early-career researchers that I became aware that everyone struggles with various methodological issues and fears that they are not doing research 'right'. How we write ourselves into our research without succumbing to self-centred and inaction-inducing reflexivity remains an ongoing consideration of feminist scholars (McDowell, 1992; Rose, 1997; Kobayashi, 2003) but however we write, we still have to deal with '(the pleasures of) creative meaning-making as well as (the pains of) closure' (Schiellerup, 2008) and, I suggest, disclosure – negotiating responsible, accountable and *just* representation. However prepared a researcher is, these are emergent from the research although more reflexive and transparent reflections about the practices of doing research and how we write about those practices offer useful support for when other researchers are faced by these crises. Although an 'end' – a PhD, conference presentation, book chapter or paper – is undoubtedly an important element in providing a sense of direction and purpose for the researcher, the journey offers critical insights into the choices through which this outcome was constructed. As Ursula LeGuin (1969) commented, 'it is good to have an end to journey toward; but it is the journey that matters, in the end'.

Conclusions

This volume is focused on providing accounts reflecting on justice-oriented research practices that inform a range of perspectives. While geared towards early-career faculty and advanced graduate students, the volume also speaks to anyone who is interested in thinking critically about *how* concepts of justice inform their research praxis. Through our own perspectives and experiences as faculty, we have come to see justice as central to the very practices of research itself. We are on the cusp of major ecological, geopolitical and social catastrophes. As we write this, the United States and China are locked into an ever-increasing cold war that threatens the lives of untold numbers of people. Russian tanks and soldiers are locked in a deadly conflict in Ukraine that threatens the peace and stability of Europe. The continent is also locked in the grip of a 1-in-500-year drought exacerbated by climate change while tens of thousands have lost their lives, homes, communities and livelihoods in a series of earthquakes across Turkey and Syria. In the Arctic, pack ice is decreasing at nearly 13 per cent per decade and the extinction rate is many times higher than the natural baseline. In the United States, and other nation-states, democracy is arguably in crisis and the United States continues to expand its military footprint around the world. Taken together it quickly becomes apparent that centring justice is about more than ethical research practices; it also speaks to the ways our work can fundamentally address pressing planetary challenges.

Note

[1] Also known as 'buy-and-sell' operations, virtual wineries have a relationship with a vineyard or winery to buy grapes or wine and then bottle it, label it and sell it under their own brand.

References

Alvermann, D.E., O'Brien, D.G. and Dillon, D.R. (1996) On writing qualitative research, *Reading Research Quarterly*, 31(1): 114–120.

Atkinson, P. (2006) Rescuing autoethnography, *Journal of Contemporary Ethnography*, 35(4): 400–404.

Barnett, C. (2017) *The Priority of Injustice: Locating Democracy in Critical Theory*, Athens, GA: The University of Georgia Press.

Baxter, J. and Eyles, J. (1997) Evaluating qualitative research in social geography: establishing 'rigour' in interview analysis, *Transactions of the Institute of British Geographers*, 22(4): 505–525.

Besio, K. (2003) Steppin' in it: postcoloniality in northern Pakistan, *Area*, 35(1): 24–33.

Besio, K. (2005) Telling stories to hear autoethnography: researching women's lives in northern Pakistan, *Gender, Place and Culture*, 12(3): 317–331.

Besio, K. and Butz, D. (2004) The value of autoethnography for field research in transcultural settings, *The Professional Geographer*, 56(3): 350–360.

Butz, D. and Besio, K. (2009) Autoethnography, *Geography Compass*, 3(5): 1660–1674.

Cannella, G.S. and Lincoln, Y.S. (2007) Predatory vs dialogic ethics: constructing an illusion or ethical practice as the core of research methods, *Qualitative Inquiry*, 13(3): 315–335.

Crang, M. (2005) Qualitative methods (part 3): there is nothing outside the text? *Progress in Human Geography*, 29(2): 225–233.

Crang, M. and Cook, I. (2007) *Doing Ethnographies*, London: SAGE.

Delamont, S. (2007) Arguments against auto-ethnography, *Qualitative Researcher*, 4: 2–4.

Denzin, N.K. (1994) Evaluating qualitative research in the post-structural moment: the lessons James Joyce teaches us, *Qualitative Studies in Education*, 7(4): 295–308.

Denzin, N.K. and Lincoln, Y.S. (2005) Introduction, in Denzin, N.K. and Lincoln, Y.S. (eds) *The SAGE Handbook of Qualitative Research*, 3rd edn, London: SAGE, pp 1–32.

Denzin, N.K., Lincoln, Y.S., Maclure, M., Otterstand, A.M., Torrance, H., Cannella, G.S., Koro-Ljungberg, M. and McTier, T. (2017) Critical qualitative methodologies, *International Review of Qualitative Research*, 10(4): 482–498.

DePalma, R. (2010) Socially just research for social justice: negotiating consent and safety in a participatory action research project, *International Journal of Research & Method in Education*, 33(3): 215–227.

Dorling, D. (2010) *Injustice: Why Social Inequality Persists*, Bristol: Policy Press.

Du Toit, A., Kruger, S. and Ponte, S. (2008) Deracializing exploitation? 'Black economic empowerment' in the South African wine industry, *Journal of Agrarian Change*, 8(1): 6–32.

Fassinger, R. and Morrow, S.L. (2013) Towards best practice in quantitative, qualitative, and mixed-method research: a social justice perspective, *Journal for Social Action in Counseling and Psychology*, 5(2): 69–83.

Fine, M. (1998) Working the hyphens: reinventing self and other in qualitative research, in Denzin, N.K. and Lincoln, Y.S. (eds) *The Landscape of Qualitative Research: Theories and Issues*, 3rd edn, London: SAGE, pp 130–155.

Fraser, N. (2008) *Scales of Justice: Reimagining Political Space in a Globalizing World*, Cambridge: Polity Press.

Hannerz, U. (2003) Being there … and there … and there! Reflections on multi-site ehtnography, *Ethnography*, 4(2): 201–216.

Held, M.B.E. (2020) Research ethics in decolonizing research with Inuit communities in Nunavut: the challenge of translating knowledge into action, *International Journal of Qualitative Methods*, 19: 1–7.

Herman, A. (2018) *Practising Empowerment in Post-Apartheid South Africa: Wine, Ethics and Development*, Abingdon: Routledge.

Igwe, P.A., Madichie, N.O. and Rugara, D.G. (2022) Decolonising research approaches towards non-extractive research, *Qualitative Market Research: An International Journal*, 25(4): 453–468.

Jaeger-Erben, M. and Offenberger, U. (2014) A practice theory approach to sustainable consumption, *GAIA*, 23(3): 166–174.

Janesick, V.J. (1994) The dance of qualitative research design: metaphor, methodolatry, and meaning, in Denzin, N.K. and Lincoln, Y.S. (eds) *Handbook of Qualitative Research*, London: SAGE, pp 209–219.

Khan, F.R. (2007) Representational approaches matter, *Journal of Business Ethics*, 73: 77–89.

Kobayashi, A. (2003) GPC ten years on: is self-reflexivity enough? *Gender, Place and Culture: A Journal of Feminist Geography*, 10(4): 345–349.

Kouritzin, S. and Nakagawa, S. (2018) Toward a non-extractive research ethics for transcultural, translingual research: perspectives from the coloniser and the colonised, *Journal of Multilingual and Multicultural Development*, 39(8): 675–687.

Lefebvre, H. (1991) *The Production of Space*, Oxford: Wiley-Blackwell.

LeGuin, U. (1969) *The Left Hand of Darkness*, New York: Ace.

Lowe, L. (2015) *The Intimacies of Four Continents*, Durham, NC and London: Duke University Press.

McDowell, L. (1992) Doing gender: feminism, feminists and research methods in human geography, *Transactions of the Institute of British Geographers*, 17(4): 399–416.

Noth, W. (2003) Crisis of representation? *Semiotica*, 143: 9–15.

Rose, G. (1997) Situating knowledges: positionality, reflexivities and other tactics, *Progress in Human Geography*, 21(3): 305–320.

Rossman, G.B. and Rallis, S.F. (2010) Everyday ethics: reflections on practice, *International Journal of Qualitative Studies in Education*, 23(4): 379–391.

Sandel, M.J. (2010) *Justice: What's the Right Thing to Do?* London: Penguin Books.

Schatzki, T.R. (2002) *The Site of the Social: A Philosophical Account of the Constitution of Social Life and Change*, University Park: Pennsylvania State University Press.

Schiellerup, P. (2008) Stop making sense: the trials and tribulations of qualitative data analysis, *Area*, 40(2): 163–171.

Shove, E. (2014) Putting practice into policy: reconfiguring questions of consumption and climate change, *Contemporary Social Science*, 9(4): 415–429.

Sparkes, A.C. (2002) Autoethnography: self-indulgence or something more?, in Bochner, A.P. and Ellis, C. (eds) *Ethnographically Speaking: Autoethnography, Literature and Aesthetics*, Walnut Creek: AltaMira, pp 209–232.

Spivak, G.C. (1988) Can the subaltern speak?, in Nelson, C. and Grossberg, L. (eds) *Marxism and the Interpretation of Culture*, Basingstoke: Macmillan, pp 267–310.

Staeheli, L.A. and Nagar, R. (2002) Feminists talking across worlds, *Gender, Place and Culture*, 9(2): 167–172.

Sultana, F. (2007) Reflexivity, positionality and participatory ethics: negotiating fieldwork dilemmas in international research, *ACME*, 6(3): 374–385.

Warren, C.A.B. and Karner, T.X. (2005) *Discovering Qualitative Methods: Field Research, Interviews and Analysis*, Los Angeles: Roxbury.

PART I

Justice as Care-full Encounter

The three chapters in this section, written by Kate Derickson, Elizabeth Mavroudi and Barbora Adlerova and Ana Moragues Faus, reflect on, and reject, the relations of power that govern the extractive and directive neoliberal model of 'community-engaged' research that continues to hold sway within the academy. Instead, they focus on the 'more than research' nature of academic investigations, and offer frank and telling insights into the messy, contradictory and sometimes uncomfortable encounters that have shaped their research practices, relations and spaces. They call for the centring of participant voice, not just in project outcomes but throughout the everyday doing of a project, and reflect on the challenges that this can bring especially in terms of tensions between different priorities and expectations.

Justice here is grounded in the encounter, in the processes of care we should enact for our participants, colleagues and selves. These support us in negotiating the innate stresses and stressors within a project, and the academy more broadly, and remind us that words and actions matter at all points and scales. To do just research, we therefore need to practice and be enveloped within a compassionate culture of care.

2

Resourcing Struggles for Social Justice from the University

Kate Derickson

What is the relationship between scholarly knowledge and social justice? I used to believe, mistakenly, I now think, that to promote social justice I needed to develop an intimate knowledge of radical frameworks and diligently apply those frameworks to observed injustices, in order to chart their manifestations, their impacts and their entanglements. What made a framework 'radical', I thought, was the object of its critique. I used to think that knowing more in a scholarly register about racialized dispossession, for example, and publishing that knowledge in scholarly journals was a way to disrupt the processes that produced it. Much has been written about the obvious inadequacies of the 'ivory tower' and its paywalls for bringing about meaningful change that need not be rehearsed here. I am not really interested in that anti-intellectual argument (though my positions and work are sometimes interpreted that way). Instead, I want to argue that the intellectual enterprise itself *is* a site for the realization of justice, but just not, perhaps, in the way that it is often assumed.

 I used to love to debate. I grew up north of Boston in a loud extended Irish family of teachers and lawyers for whom teasing, storytelling and comedic timing are an art form. If you want to hang, you had better come armed with a thick skin, a solid point and a fast-moving story. To be effective, you have to fully commit to the argument; hesitate and you create space for your entire argument to be toppled. The point is not to persuade or be persuaded, the point is to hold the spotlight, to entertain, to show off, to win. I came to the kitchen island (and later, to social interactions and intellectual inquiry) ready to press my case, think on my feet, not take things personally (at least in public) and never back down.

This training served me well enough for a while. I came of age in the early 1990s, when the neoliberal consensus was so strong that the political space left of centre was spacious terrain. To be a middle-class white woman against racism, patriarchy and homophobia felt rather uncomplicated and morally righteous in my racially and socially homogeneous New England town. I argued my positions loudly, to my peers, to my teachers, and in the local newspaper with the same degree of certainty and commitment I developed in my kitchen island interactions. I equated winning these arguments with advancing the causes I was arguing about. My success was the movement's success.

Reading feminist theory in college complicated this assumption. Patricia Hill Collins' (1999) work on intersectionality disrupted my comfortable assumption that my own white womanhood was always already unproblematically aligned with other oppressed groups. At the same time, in my journalism courses, I was learning about the history of Black press and the importance of Black people narrating their own everyday experiences. These thinkers unsettled my assumption that I could be an unproblematic 'voice' for social justice on behalf of others.[1] They also pushed me to understand that our identities are socially constructed and made and remade through the dialectic of structures and the everyday. And that these socially constructed forms of difference in fact served to enable, explain and smooth out the pervasive structural inequalities I was so eager to dismantle. Yet somewhat counterintuitively for this young, idealistic, white woman, these identity categories become something other than just categories; they become a habitus, a subjectivity that exceeds their function and purpose. They become standpoints, places from which to know, act and live.

To be given the opportunity to learn and know this felt like a gift, but it was also disorienting. The vast spaciousness of the left that I felt as a young person came into focus as an exciting, rich, complex and fraught intellectual and political space. I was learning what is now obvious: critiques of patriarchy that positioned women as oppressed and let white women understand themselves as always already in solidarity with others who are oppressed were too coarse. For the first time, I came to understand that it wasn't all available to me. Black feminist thought, both in theory and practice, showed me that taking up space, as my kitchen island training had taught me to do, even if it was to advance arguments about oppression, might have the effect of drowning out other voices. The uneasy relationship between winning an argument about social justice and advancing social justice has become a central tension in my academic practice.

This tension is at the crux of how I engage questions of justice in my work. My scholarly practice has been oriented towards a concern with the question of how our ways of knowing position various groups and people as not only *knowable* but as *knowers themselves*. I'm informed by the work of

Kirstie Doston (2012), who has parsed the way that some forms of knowing can undermine the epistemic confidence in groups when knowledge is 'about' them, but not 'for' them. Her framework, and the work of other Black feminist philosopher, theorists and activists, has prompted me to think about what it means to produce knowledge 'for' historically marginalized groups. It doesn't always look exactly like I imagined it would.

How can I balance the way that expertise about forms of oppression can have the effect of epistemically backgrounding the very people with whom I want to be in solidarity, with the privilege, influence and responsibility that comes with being a tenured professor and researcher? To think through this question, I have explored the form that ethical collaborations can take, the assumptions embedded in ways of theorizing, and the role of scholarly research in the collective struggle for liberation. Taken together, these lines of inquiry, the questions they have raised for me, and the conclusions I have drawn add up to the question that prompted this volume: how do we engage with the concept of justice in our own work?

Nancy Fraser's theory of justice, which posits that justice has dimensions related to representation and redistribution, provides an instructive framework. In her well-known essay, 'From redistribution to recognition? Dilemmas of justice in a "post-socialist" age', Fraser (1995) argues that there are two axes of struggles for justice. Struggles for redistribution problematize the distribution of resources as both the cause and the consequence of injustice whereas, in struggles for recognition, Fraser writes:

> Injustice is rooted in social patterns of representation, interpretation, and communication. Examples include cultural domination (being subjected to patterns of interpretation and communication that are associated with another culture and are alien and/or hostile to one's own); nonrecognition (being rendered invisible by means of the authoritative representational, communicative, and interpretative practices of one's culture); and disrespect (being routinely maligned or disparaged in stereotypic public cultural representations and/or in everyday life interactions). (Fraser, 1995: 14)

Applied to the context of knowledge production and scholarly knowing, Fraser's framework highlights the two urgent dimensions of justice. The first is related to the distribution of material resources that flow through the institutions, places, communities and individuals that are involved in scholarly knowledge production. The second is related to how *recognition* functions in our scholarly knowing; who is recognized as a knower, as an actor, an agent, an expert. In my own work, I adapt this framework to operationalize a distributive conception of justice across the axes of redistribution and recognition. To do so, I begin by taking what I describe as a thick conception of the practice of knowledge production, best understood as a 'bundle of social relations'. This way of thinking about scholarly research necessarily links the ends, that is, the knowledge product, with the means, that is, the institutionally, socially and culturally embedded nature of all knowledge production processes, mediated through a range of funding agencies, institutions of higher education, institutional review boards, budgeting practices, social and cultural norms and power dynamics that comprise the field in and through which scholarly knowledge is made. This approach redirects attention away from a focus on the theoretical frameworks applied or the conclusions arrived at the place where justice is realized in scholarly work, and instead applies a procedural conception of justice concerned with how recognition and redistribution occur throughout the *process* of making knowledge. At each stage in my research and writing process, I ask myself and my collaborators two questions: what social relations are engendered in the act of knowing, and what work might this knowledge do in the world? When thought in relation to both the material distribution of resources, and the politics of recognition as laid out by Fraser, these questions locate justice in the act of knowing itself in ways that illustrate the deep entanglements between recognition and redistribution.

Distributing resources

In my scholarly practice, I have explored the distributive justice of resources in the process of scholarly knowing through a framework I have called 'resourcefulness'. This approach to scholarly knowledge production aims to use the practice of making knowledge with, about and for historically marginalized communities in ways that directs resource flows to those communities directly, and prompts a more expansive engagement with the ethical practice of scholarly research than previous iterations of feminist 'reflexivity' and other discussions around models of engaged research and scholar activism. As I have practised it, resourcefulness has three dimensions. First, it centres the needs of community-based collaborators by framing university-based researchers as *resources* for collaborators. While there is ample reason for communities who have often been the subjects of university-based research to be sceptical of the value of these institutions for their struggles for social justice, it is also true that communities, publics and movements have questions that require research to be answered. It is an oft-rehearsed mantra in some corners of social movements and research that people are experts in their own oppression and experiences. This is true enough, but my own experiences working with historically marginalized communities leads me to conclude that there is an important role for research to play in their struggle. When I have worked with community-based collaborators to identify research questions they want asked and answered, they have always had a long list of things they wanted to know more about. These include questions about how various policy changes might impact housing markets, how infrastructure projects will impact their watershed, whether property taxes are being evenly applied, and how environmental change might impact their communities. Crucially, the questions raised by collaborators is seldom about the nature of their oppression per se; they *are* experts in their own lived experiences (even if experience is always complexly mediated by ideology).

My collaborations suggest that a distributive approach to justice brings into relief the vastly uneven distribution of what I call the 'means of knowledge production'. The ability to mobilize the apparatus of the research university to ask and answer questions is concentrated in wealthy institutions, government agencies, corporations and non-governmental organizations that can fund research. This means that research disproportionately serves their needs and answers their questions and, in the process, sets the terms of disciplinary interests and research agendas. Resourcefulness, as I have practised it, aims to mobilize the resources of the research university to ask and answer questions that are a priority to those who have not historically had the opportunity to shape research agendas. In so doing, I am aiming to redistribute the means of knowledge production as one way to realize justice through scholarly research.

A second dimension of resourcefulness as I have practised it brings to the fore the issue of material resources, and emphasizes the need to focus on how resources are spent throughout the collaboration. This means that in the process of collaborating with communities, we are attentive to whose time is prioritized and compensated, whose travel is paid for, and whose priorities and needs drive the distribution of the project's resources. This practice entails thinking expansively about the resources that university-based researchers have access to, such as researcher time, student work, physical space, funding for events and speaker series, libraries, and laboratories, and considering how they can be mobilized in ways that meet the needs and answer the research questions of our community partners.

A third, and related, dimension of resourcefulness is creating a 'front door' to the research university, and thinking carefully about what institutions of higher education have to offer publics in the holistic sense. This has meant considering what the libraries, our speaker series and college-wide initiatives, our classrooms, our graduate training programmes as well as our research initiatives can provide our community collaborators.

Taken together and applied to scholarly knowledge production, Fraser's formulation of the coupling of redistribution and recognition highlights what I call the 'social relations engendered in the act of knowing'. While the distribution of material resources is a crucial dimension of these social relations, so too is recognition. Here, Kirstie Dotson's notion of 'epistemic backgrounding' is especially useful. She argues that when knowledge is made *about* a group, rather than *for* a group, it can have the effect of diminishing the epistemic confidence in that group. In my own work, I have attempted to address the politics of recognition by considering how my research practice can refuse to epistemically background my collaborators. This means sometimes *not* knowing, or not doing research about, things that are a priority to my discipline but not my collaborators. It means not using theoretical frameworks or formulations that feel unhelpful or irrelevant to my collaborators. And it means considering the dynamics involved in forms of theorizing and making knowledge that make up disciplinary forms of knowing.

Developing healthy collaborations

All of the principles and approaches to scholarly knowledge production laid out here are premised on sustained relationships and collaborations with partners beyond the academy. Based on my understanding of the uneven distribution of the means of knowledge production among historically marginalized groups, my US-based work has primarily sought to resource collaborations with communities of colour, with a focus on historically Black neighbourhoods, often, in the first instance, close to where I live and work. Developing these collaborations requires care and attention, which is intimately linked, in my practice, to a thick conception of knowledge production. In developing collaborations, I prioritize resourcing, centre community concerns and priorities, and work to establish healthy and productive relationships that can serve as the foundation for long-term collaborations.

When pursuing community-engaged research-based partnership, there is a growing awareness that the 'extractive' and 'directive' models are unacceptable. The 'directive' model is business-as-usual, in which 'best practices' emerge from university research with the expectation that communities should change their priorities and practices accordingly. Researchers who recognize the limitations of that approach may prioritize 'engagement' but can sometimes practice an 'extractive' approach, which centres questions that the researcher and their colleagues are interested in, unfolds according to university timelines, and seldom results in research findings or products that meet the needs of communities. When conducted in the name of equity and with or 'on' historically marginalized and under-resourced communities, this approach is especially problematic, as it creates additional burdens on these communities while burnishing the 'expert' credentials for researchers with unclear impacts on equity outcomes.

Researchers looking to avoid either of these can inadvertently create other modes of collaboration that are equally ineffective, unethical or likely to result in problems.

Examples of unhealthy researcher–community 'collaborations' include:

- *Proximity*: researchers attend numerous meetings, observe public activities, share spaces with activists and community members and gain credibility with other researchers as a result but do not allow them to shape or influence their research questions or approaches. It is disingenuous at best to call this 'engagement'.
- *Dependency*: researchers are wholly dependent on the community to create scholarly outputs and without community involvement at every stage the researcher has 'nothing to show for their time'. This creates undue pressure on the community partner and can cause the researcher to introduce and impose university-driven priorities and timelines on the process. This is especially problematic for graduate students and pre-tenure faculty, who have timelines and pressures to create 'outputs' that might not sync up with the needs and priorities of the community partners.
- *Imposition*: related to dependency, this is a relationship in which university priorities, values and timelines drive the engagement and substantially shape the activities that the community and/or organization are undertaking. Shaping community activities can be generative when all parties have a trusting relationship and agree that participatory action research is called for, but this should not be a default expectation of a researcher.

Healthy university–community partnerships can take a variety of forms, and should be responsive to the needs of the community, creatively mobilize the myriad resources housed in a research university, realistically take stock of the capacities of the research team, and carefully consider how the collaboration will advance the goals of the community collaborators. These can take the form of:

- *Shared interests*: researchers and community-based organizations or groups convene and converse around shared interests in topics, issues and approaches. They share findings, exchange resources and leave open the possibility of short- or long-term collaboration as opportunities arise.
- *Shared goals*: researchers and community-based collaborators have a shared and explicit theory of change, conception of justice and desired outcomes. Researchers create products for collaborators as well as products oriented towards their research communities that translate their findings to scholarly audiences.
- *Shared activities*: researchers and community members identify research processes and products that address shared interests and advance shared goals. They work together in an ongoing way to conduct research, share findings and resources.

These are just a few of the models that can be the foundation for healthy collaborations between communities and researchers that do not reproduce the extractive or directive models that have historically characterized 'engaged research'.

Putting it all together

In practice, I have actualized this resourcefulness framework through my individual research programme as well as through two research collaboratives. First is the CREATE Initiative, which I co-direct and founded with Dr Bonnie Keeler. CREATE was established to investigate the intersections of equity and the environment. Central to our programme structure is the 'policy think tank', a body supported by CREATE staff that serves as a vehicle for our community-based collaborators to share ideas and identify research products that would be of value for their communities. Think tank members receive a stipend for their participation that they can use to augment their salary or resource their organizations. The think tank in turn informs our 'synthesis team' comprised of interdisciplinary researchers whose role is to design, find funding for and conduct research that our think tank considers a priority. This approach is distinct from 'participatory action research' in which community partners participate in every stage of the research. While this model has its merits and applications, it is only one type of community-engaged research. Instead of focusing on collaboration through the process of conducting the research itself, our focus is on the topics, approaches and products we develop. Finally, we have a team of faculty and administrators interested in changing the nature of graduate education, to train students to conduct engaged, problem-oriented research in collaborative, interdisciplinary settings. This advisory team takes lessons from our policy think tank and synthesis team and applies them in their own engagement with graduate education. CREATE has trained over 20 graduate students from across the University of Minnesota in this approach to research.

We launched our initiative with a meeting of our think tank, in which we worked with to collectively identify research priorities. The group raised a number of issues, many of which graduate students addressed throughout their training and through 'externships' with our think tank partners. These included support for a curriculum project called Mni Sota Makoce, focusing on Dakota people and their relationship to the land; research on land tenure, eminent domain and infrastructure in coastal Florida; and urban development and gentrification in Minneapolis.

The overarching theme that emerged across all groups was more conceptual: how do we get out of the 'ruts' that seem to persist across space and time that result in the displacement of communities and the degradation of environments? How do we foster investment in underserved and marginalized communities without creating gentrification and displacement?

Our faculty, staff and students have worked with our community partners in Minneapolis, Atlanta and Gullah/Geechee Nation to produce a range of research products, from academic papers to public facing reports and StoryMaps. We also developed a policy toolkit to highlight policy interventions that communities have adopted to promote investment and stave off gentrification.

I have aimed to practice resourcefulness in my role as a member of the Gullah/Geechee Sustainability Think Tank. The think tank was established by Queen Quet, the Chieftess and Head of State of the Gullah/Geechee Nation and serves as a body to coordinate the activities and share information across Gullah/Geechee people who serve on the think tank and academics from a range of disciplines. The think tank provides a framework for Gullah/Geechee people to direct research activities, interpret findings of research and develop approaches to distribute findings to Gullah/Geechee people. The think tank exemplifies the commitment of resourcefulness to repurposing the research university to ask and answer questions that are a priority to Gullah/Geechee people.

Through our collaboration we have found that there are a number of knowledge problems our Gullah/Geechee collaborators want asked and answered. These questions seldom fit squarely in a single disciplinary framework. Moreover, they are often not a perfect fit for the cutting-edge questions that researchers are often trained to seek out. As a member of the think tank, I have been able to connect Gullah/Geechee people to university resources, including graduate and undergraduate research, create co-teaching opportunities for my Gullah/Geechee collaborators, and contribute to teams of researchers across disciplines and institutions to ask and answer questions that are a priority to Gullah/Geechee collaborators.

★★★

"So, what is all of this to you?" Terrion Williamson asked me from the audience of a talk to the gender and women's studies department in my home institution of the University of Minnesota. In the talk, a version of which has since been published in the *Annals of the American Association of Geographers*, I argued that if our goal is to contribute to making more just social formations, it is not enough to know 'radical things' but rather we should seek to know in radical ways. In the piece, I engage the intellectual tradition of Black feminist thought to extend and deepen an argument I had been working out for years in various publications that explores the way that forms of knowing about oppression and dispossession, even those that are motivated by a desire to undo those forms of oppression, can sometimes reproduce them in practice. I had been ruminating on the relationship between scholarly knowledge and transformative social change for my entire academic career, engaging feminist thought and Black geographies to question what seemed at times to me to be a comfortable assumption in the Marxist geographical tradition that knowledge about systems of domination and oppression was necessarily disruptive of those systems. I'm especially indebted to Clyde Woods' observation 'autopsies'.

A few months earlier, Terrion had given a talk in the very same room, which she opened with the statement about her book: "I began this project with the question 'what did my grandmother know?'" In her book she explores the socialities of everyday Black women as they butt up against both the limits of cultural stereotypes and the sometimes inaccessible politics of the academy. Her framing was immediately resonant to me: what is at stake when we engage everyday people as theorists of their own circumstances? And how can that engagement guide our scholarly inquiry?

And yet, I was not prepared to answer Terrion's question. I was accustomed to explicitly not putting myself into the frame of analysis, to step aside and let my priorities and analyses of colleagues and collaborators guide the work. Of course, as Terrion's question implied, just as feminists have shown us that it is not possible to get outside of the research process through claims of objectivity, neither is it possible through claims of 'collaboration'. To answer Terrion's question, then, what this is to me is a way of being in the academy that attempts to offer a partial, tentative way through the apparent impasse of being a white woman academic committed to making space for the cultivation of the freedom dreams of my collaborators. It is a proposition that justice requires a material and epistemological architecture to be possible, and a partial effort at making it so from my particular, embodied and situated location in relation to the struggles for justice I aim to resource.

Note
[1] I am especially indebted to David DuBois and Nick McBride, two journalism professors at University of Massachusetts Amherst who helped me learn these lessons.

References

Collins, P.H. (1999) Moving beyond gender: intersectionality and scientific knowledge, in Ferree, M.M., Lorber, J. and Hess, B.B. (eds) *Revisioning Gender*, London: Sage, pp 261–284.

Dotson, K. (2012) A cautionary tale: on limiting epistemic oppression, *Frontiers: A Journal of Women Studies*, 33(1): 24–47.

Fraser, N. (1995) From redistribution to recognition? Dilemmas of justice in a 'post-socialist' age, *New Left Review*, 212: 68.

3

Performing Timespace Encounters: Reflecting on Sharing, Voice and Justice in Qualitative Research

Elizabeth Mavroudi

This chapter focuses on the justice of sharing voices and stories, using case studies from my qualitative research. This always partial and challenging process of storytelling will be viewed through performative timespaces of encounter as a means to reflect on the potential for transformative research from the perspective of researchers and participants. Work by Coddington (2017) and others (for example, Koch, 2020) has stressed the need to unpack and critique the relationships between participant voice, authenticity and empowerment in light of feminist and anti-colonial work. Montero-Sieburth (2020), for example, stresses the need to acknowledge that researchers do not 'speak for the other' and that allowing participant voices 'to appear' does not necessarily bring about justice, change or transformation. To help counter this, Montero-Sieburth stresses the need for researchers to discover their own voices, which forms an important aspect of what this chapter attempts to do.

This body of work therefore discusses the need for critical interpretations of representation and the value and purpose of academic research in terms of how social and political justice is achieved and for whom. I aim to add to such work by viewing interviews I have been involved in as encounters through which voices can be shared, brought to a different audience and potentially be empowering. By doing so, the chapter will engage with the notion of performative timespace (Mavroudi, 2019) in order to highlight how research encounters may be seen as part of an ethical but also emotional project of justice and care. Through this, I stress the need for active reflection and negotiation of power imbalances as we navigate our own positionality as individuals and as part of a research team (Fertaly and Fluri, 2019), the positionality of our participants but also the wider frameworks of universities and ethics committees.

I argue that justice needs to be framed in broad and flexible ways and not just in terms of impact or outcome, but also through the very materiality of doing empirical research and communicating with people in mundane and 'gentle' ways (Pottinger, 2020). It is through such communication, 'deep listening' (Koch, 2020) and embodied encounters that difference is articulated and grappled with so that we can potentially learn about/from one another through timespaces. It is this encounter, then, that has the potential to be empowering and that can form part of justice seeking and justice making processes and practices, which take place within the intricacies of our everyday lives and emotions. In short, I argue that the encounter one has through conversation, through engaging and communicating with others can be transformative in small, cumulative ways. This is because they provide the chance for an encounter to occur in which we are presented with the opportunity to reflect on who we are and how we wish to perform and represent ourselves, our families and our lives.

This chapter on performative storytelling through research encounters in timespace will use case study projects on my past research on Palestinian and Greek diasporic identity and politics in Greece and Australia respectively, migrant women in Athens and immigration policy changes in the UK, as well as my recent Leverhulme funded project on young people's identity and politics in the Greek, Jewish and Palestinian diasporas in England.

Performative storytelling through timespace encounters

My research spans migration studies, diaspora, as well as human geography. I have become interested in ways to conceptualize time and space in migration studies, as have many others (for example, Griffiths, 2014; Lulle, 2014; Mavroudi et al, 2018). In particular, I have been influenced by work on the performative and the non-representational in geography and the ways in which 'doing' can be part of diaspora studies in geography (Mavroudi, 2019). In doing so, I shy away from prescriptive notions of what timespace entails, but rather engage with the politics of possibility, and hope, as enacted within and through time and space (Mavroudi, 2013). As Amelina (2021: 2) highlights: 'The third shortcoming [in migration studies work] is that they usually fail to analyse the performativity of discursive knowledge (Butler, 1993) incorporated in relevant institutional, organisational and interactional routines.'

There is, therefore, a timely need to further reflect and act upon such limitations and omissions and, in this chapter, I will be doing so through a reflection on performative storytelling in my own research. The focus here is the need to have more flexible and inclusive notions and terminologies of 'doing migration'. This is an important idea and approach which can be extended beyond migration studies to research with all potentially marginalized, ignored and under-researched groups. This is because such approaches are based more around respecting the nuances and intricacies of lives in their geopolitical context and by this we mean both the context of the research but also the context of the researcher's life and work. Rather than see a distinction and dualism between researcher and researched, I argue that by paying attention to research as performative storytelling through timespace I bring to the fore the complex ways both time and space (together and separately) are used and implicated in my research. In this way we cannot see ourselves as disconnected from those participants we work with as we are sharing certain moments through/in timespace. However, at the same time, such potentially fleeting encounters are also performative because of what they obscure as well as what they capture. In other words, these timespace encounters are at once lived and experienced in performative ways in which narratives and stories are shared. At the same time, lurking continuously in the background are the messy realities of power inequalities, emotional discomfort, sensual dis/pleasures and politics. These timespace encounters of storytelling are embodied, emotional performances in which power is negotiated.

Nina Woodrow (2017: 785) uses the following apt statement from Doreen Massey (2005) on the linkages between shared storytelling, space and politics: 'The political corollary is that a genuine, thorough, spatialisation of social theory and political thinking can force into the imagination a fuller recognition of the simultaneous coexistence of others with their own trajectories and their own stories to tell.' With this quote, and in the paper more broadly, Woodrow stresses that our encounters with others during the research process and the times and spaces created as a result, can potentially have agency and be seen as empowering. It is this process of sharing in a particular timespace and place which, although at first seems like a specific moment in time and space, is connected to other times and spaces through shared and enacted performative narratives. Such shared experiences are thus connected also to the power of speech, language, and bodily actions and emotions and imagine a world in which research encounters are transformative:

> Doing interviews is a privilege granted us, not a right that we have. Interviews are things that belong to us. Interviews are part of the dialogic conversation that connects all of us to this larger moral community. Interviews arise out of performance events. They transform information into shared experience. This reflexive project presumes

that words and language have a material presence in the world; that words have effects on people. Words matter ... I imagine a world where race, ethnicity, class, gender and sexual orientation intersect; a world where language and performance empower, and humans can become who they wish to be, free of prejudice, repression and discrimination. Those who write culture using reflexive interviews are learning to use language in a way that brings people together. (Denzin, 2001: 24)

In many ways, this is an ideal(ized) scenario but it highlights the importance of thinking through interviews and qualitative research encounters in performative ways. In a paper on the violence in qualitative research, Sabi Redwood (2008) reflects on the ways in which academic researchers try to create order through the 'taming [of] the wild profusion of data' and in doing so close down creativity and possibility, rather than encouraging performativity. Redwood stresses the need to address the inherent violence of the research process as we aim to collect data and publish our findings, often in very prescriptive ways. For me, this is reminiscent of my undergraduate and master's training in the sense that at the time, I was trying to subvert what I saw as accepted traditions in writing and this led to an undergraduate thesis on perceptions of air pollution in Athens, Greece, in 2001, which used interviews, interspersed with poetry and reflection on doing research in an age of post-modernism and the relativity of knowledge. This led onto a master's in research methods in human geography, where I vaguely remember being taught by Ian Cook who stressed to us the power and politics of academic knowledge production (see, for example, Cook, 2001); if my memory serves me correctly, I think I may have submitted a piece of work written as poetry. By the time I started my PhD, I became acutely aware of the need to strategically conform to certain ways of academic research and writing if I was to get an academic job. Yet these formative experiences have remained with me even as I played the academic game of publishing and grant applications. My approach to research remained open in the sense that I was interested in broad research ideas and did not necessarily want to be pinned down to one area. This resulted in some interesting discussions and collaborations but it also fragmented my reputation and what I was known for, I think. What has remained with me, however, is my belief in the need for flexibility in the research process and in academia/universities more broadly which I think can be incredibly rigid at times. For me, my interest in non-representation can be linked to this need to conceptualize what we do in different ways. However, rather than do away with representation, I feel that it is important to explore representational and performative worlds, narratives and experiences, while at the same time recognizing that the two go together. Representations are constantly created and this process is performative but we need to pay attention to how and why and the impacts of them on different people (see, for example, Mitchell and Elwood [2012] on the dangers of non-representational theory). Dirksmeier and Helbrecht, in a paper on intercultural interactions as 'situational places', also stress the potential of performative research, citing the work of Latham:

> [O]n the one hand it allows framing the research process differently and on the other hand the concept of performance gives space to address new questions about everyday experience that more representationally oriented approaches have failed to deal with adequately (Latham, 2003:1994). It allows insights in the reflexivity of symbolic, public and social action. (Dirksmeier and Helbrecht, 2010: 40)

Such reflection on the importance of space creating a politics of possibility does not attempt to create order or neatness out of the messy reality of research. Rather, it embeds such research as part of everyone's everyday life and, in doing so, recognizes that there will be limitations, power inequalities, emotions, challenges, silences, imperfections and so forth as so many researchers have already pointed out (England, 1994; Limb and Dwyer, 2001; Nagar and Ali, 2003). It also stresses that during this process of encounter, everyone is actively storytelling and negotiating positionalities and narratives and such reflections form part of a wider engagement with the geographies of storytelling (Cameron, 2012).

Performing emotional discomfort

I start this main section of the chapter by acknowledging the position of privilege which we have as academic researchers at different stages of our academic and employment careers. I am immensely grateful to all those who, over the years, have agreed to speak to me and engage in conversation with me, drive me and walk with me to meet others and see places, laugh with me, care for me and given their time and space to me. I can never properly repay this generosity. What I can do, though, is reflect as honestly as I can on our research experiences as often mundane, messy practices which are laden with power and emotion. To view them as performative encounters or as 'situational places' necessitates paying attention to the timespace of interactions as difference, boundaries and belonging are negotiated, often awkwardly, in our conversations. However, it also means that we must be honest about the power we have in 'pinning down' participant words and meanings as representations when in reality what we are told and what we see and experience are simply snapshots in time and space, connected and disconnected from before and after, and from here and there/transnational/ translocal/diasporic connections.

Boddy (2014: 101) stresses the 'need to "get muddy"' – to make ethical 'tensions, and ethnocentric assumptions, explicit throughout every stage and aspect of the research process' in research with children and young people from diverse ethnic backgrounds. This challenging but important issue is one that I am acutely aware of as I have a migrant background and cross-border connections to elsewhere. This is also the case for those we speak to: they have myriad connections in timespace to other people and places and this necessitates an expansive and broad understanding of such connections but also the disconnections that exist as we negotiate difference and diversity.

Such encounters with difference necessitate that we deal with our own 'unconscious bias' (Agarwal, 2020) and continuously evaluate our position, judgements, challenges and assumptions. However, it is impossible to come to qualitative research and to such encounters with a clean slate and this can have repercussions for perceptions of how such encounters pan out. In attempts to be just, do research justly and attempt to promote justice through research, we need to recognize that such encounters are not perfect and can never be, as we deal with the baggage of our own lives and those of others. We are also dealing with difference, sometimes in very abrupt and unexpected ways, but every encounter, even ones we may perceive more negatively, provides the potential for justice and change. This is why I would like to devote the next section to what I call jarring encounters: those which make us feel uncomfortable as researchers.

Jarring encounters

I will start with an example from my most recent research project on young people in the Greek, Jewish and Palestinian diasporas. I arrived at a house of a Palestinian family and was greeted by the father who had also agreed to be interviewed. I was ushered into the living room where I proceeded to discuss the research and his views. Some time into the interview a woman appeared with drink and food; it transpired that this was his wife and we smiled at each other. The husband informed me that she was very interested in the issues but didn't want to participate because her English was not good. I tried, in a friendly manner, to entice her to participate, even briefly, in case she wanted her views to be heard but she just smiled and shook her head – she didn't really speak at all. The woman proceeded to sit for a while in the sitting room and then left. After a short time, the man's teenage children arrived and sat in listening to our interview and then he listened to what they were saying.

The interviews went well and everyone was jovial, kind and generous, but I felt uncomfortable and awkward about how the interview progressed as I had imagined meeting parents and older children separately (this was the first interview for the research project). I also felt uncomfortable about the mother's silence as this was something I had not encountered before in past research in people's homes with other family members present. However, I have come to reflect that this discomfort had more to do with my own perceptions of how families operate and of women's voices and power relations. Although I tried to engage with the woman, there was a barrier between us, whether it was language or the relationship she had with her husband. The experience has taught me not to make assumptions about family relationships in interviews, but at the same time, it has taught me that I need to accept difference and not be judgemental. However, I can also reflect that with hindsight, I could have acted differently, namely by perhaps asking whether a separate interview could have been set up with her; at the same time, we also need to accept that not everyone will wish to speak to us. In this encounter, it was the silences as well as the voices that were potentially powerful as I learnt of the struggles and perceptions of some members of this family. This encounter also enabled me to ask questions to the children where it was clear that they were asserting their opinions, which were different to their father's, and it enabled us to have a frank conversation on issues of politicization. A space was created whereby the children were able to talk about an opinion that clearly their father hadn't heard before and was surprised to hear. The serendipity and unexpectedness of the research encounter thus has the potential to open up space for dialogue and negotiation but it is one that needs careful handling by the researcher so that everyone who wants to speak has the chance to do so in inclusive ways.

Another example from my most recent research project involved a Palestinian mother who was interviewed at her place of work. During the discussion on being political, the woman was adamant that she was not political and had just focused on raising children and her work, unlike her husband who she thought was political because of his advocacy work. The woman went on to discuss how she used to take her children to demonstrations supporting the Palestinian cause when they were little; I then asked her whether she saw this as political. She paused and thought for a few minutes and then acknowledged for what seemed to be the first time in her life that this could be seen as a political act and that she was political. I felt it was a powerful moment for me and possibly for her too but it only happened because of the research encounter and the discussion that we had. During these encounters, you have some questions or a guide, or you simply let participants talk but what you have to be open to is the possibility that change might occur through, for example, re-appraising beliefs. There was a period of awkwardness when I asked her whether going to demonstrations could be seen as political and I tried to ensure that I was not confrontational or judgemental about it but there is the possibility that she may have perceived the situation differently, which I also need to accept. There is a fine line between probing and confrontation in such research and we need to be mindful of what we say (and how we say it) and do. There are not only power relations and inequalities in such research encounters, but also there is power and the need for justice in how we tell participant stories.

Also in my most recent research, although the majority of encounters I had with the Jewish community were with liberal Jews, I also had some encounters with ultra-Orthodox Jews and I was interested to hear their views as well. However, on a few occasions, it became clear that some of the views being expressed towards liberal Jews and to Jews who had converted to Judaism were quite exclusionary. On one particular occasion, there was an awkward moment between myself and a participant when this person was claiming that Orthodox Judaism was superior to other forms and I felt very uncomfortable with this statement. I tried to untangle her views in a respectful way and it became clear that her thought processes and opinions were closely linked to the ways she perceived her faith and this then had a direct impact on how she lived and her relationships with others. I had to accept her way of thinking even as I acknowledged that this was unfair to non-Orthodox Jews in the UK. My gentle probing did cause her to become a little defensive and slightly prickly but I also feel that as researchers engaged with justice, we also have a responsibility to attempt to have honest discussions around issues which we feel may not be just. However, we need to do so in non-judgemental and compassionate ways which allow our participants to be heard. What is also clear is that we do not need to agree with our participants and there have been many times over the years where I have not necessarily agreed with participants. Being ethical researchers and protecting ourselves and our participants is also about ensuring that all parties feel enabled and bold enough to speak their minds. However, the reality is that this may not always be the case and we can never know exactly what participants really think. Therefore, all we have is the encounter and what is said and also what is not said (Spyrou, 2016).

Silences, or evasion, in interviews is something I have encountered quite often, especially around discussions to do with identity and politics. Sometimes, it becomes clear that participants haven't really discussed these issues before but in other cases they do not want to talk about particular things and this needs to be respected. The reality is also that some interviews feel more comfortable and easy-going than others. This is testament to the fact that these are encounters between different people, with different characters, personalities and experiences, and building trust and rapport can be hard. This can especially be the case with more elite interviews, I have found, where participants feel they should speak to you (or feel they can't say no) but don't really want to. The same can happen with non-elite participants: although the research has been explained to them and they have agreed to participate, it becomes clear during the process of talking that the participant is uncomfortable although no one has ever explicitly said that to me. In such cases, I often limit the questions and ensure the interviews ends quickly. In other cases, participants sometimes get upset which is very challenging to deal with for everyone. However, as one participant who spoke to me for my PhD research and ended up crying when discussing Palestine stressed, this was the reality for her and she couldn't help it. Through this inevitably upsetting and difficult moment, her pain was all too clear for me to see and it brought home very vividly the materiality of being Palestinian in diaspora which she wanted to share with others. This is why she continued with the interview: because she wanted her voice and the position of Palestinians to be heard. This is something I also encountered with some participants in my research on the Greek diaspora in Australia. I remember on one occasion, one participant had a great deal he wanted to tell me but was also very busy and the interview at his office got interrupted multiple times. He was very keen to get his views across but I also felt uncomfortable because in this process he was sometimes a little belittling of others who had different views. However, rather than confront him, I let him tell his story and reflected on the discomfort, which I think was now also related to gender differences. This need to set the record straight or tell me 'how things are' is, I have realized, also linked to male assumptions around female knowledge because I have never encountered this with female participants. On some occasions, I have either 'played dumb' to help make male participants feel comfortable and so that they tell me what they think as they attempt to 'educate' me, or have had very little choice but to listen to their views in what can be very one-sided conversations. The reality is that in that moment of timespace, we do whatever we can as researchers to keep ourselves safe, and to enable participants to speak to us. Although we have power as researchers, such encounters demonstrate to me that this is not always the case but that power needs to be negotiated in such encounters. For example, in some cases I have been 'tested' (by mostly men) on my knowledge of particular diasporic communities, in other words they ask me questions on what I know. In some cases, this is so they can supplement my knowledge but in other cases I have felt that it is patronizing and they don't trust my knowledge as a researcher so I have to go through these hurdles to be accepted.

Lack of trust has also meant that some potential participants have refused to speak to me. This can occur in communities where there are different sub-groups who are in opposition to each other and you have to be very careful about protecting participant anonymity because one of the first questions you get is: who else have you spoken to? Negotiating power relations, tensions and inequalities within diasporic and migrant communities can be incredibly hard because unless you are an insider, you are still learning about different sub-groups and allegiances.

Performative identities

Even being an insider is not necessarily easy as I have found during my most recent research with the Greek diaspora. I am half Greek, half British and grew up in Athens, Greece. I speak Greek although English is my first language. When I conducted research with the Greek diaspora in Australia, I found it easier to locate people willing to speak to me than I did in the UK. I am not quite sure why that was the case but it may have to do with insider/outsider relationships. My feeling is also that my Greekness is not so easy to locate in the sense that I don't perform my identity as Greek but as in-between Greece and the UK. At times, I didn't feel I was Greek enough. This is something I had had to deal with personally over the years as I have now lived in the UK for so long and my visits to the country are less frequent. This was brought home to me in one example during a visit to a Greek dance event in Melbourne, Australia where it was assumed that I knew the popular Greek folk dances, which I didn't. My lack of Greek cultural knowledge also extends to music and other cultural issues which can sometimes create distance in interviews. The same also applies to the fact that I am not Greek Orthodox, which the vast majority of Greeks are – I am no religion, which can also raise some eyebrows and mean that participants don't know where to place me in terms of my identity. Such encounters are also jarring because they are embodied and emotional, as I found out during that dance event where I couldn't physically join in because I didn't know what to do. Being asked to join in with participant activities when one hasn't set out to do ethnography (and I have never set out to do ethnography) highlights that the research process is flexible and that we need to be too where possible (but it's not always easy) and also that such unanticipated moments can cause discomfort. Another example of this was in my most recent research when I got asked to join in with a religious activity without knowing that was going to happen. I said yes and it was interesting but I felt acutely out of place and didn't really know what to do. Therefore, the momentary timespace of the interview is linked not only to other people's expectations but also our own. However, such moments can also serve to help us grow as researchers and individuals as we accept the flow of what is happening and open up to new experiences although they can also expose feelings of exclusion, inadequacy and uncertainty. We all bring our current and past anxieties to that timespace of performance even as we attempt to suppress them in the name of professionalism and respect and telling the story and narrative we wish to privilege.

The few times I have felt more of an insider was during some research with migrants in Greece from Global North countries. This research started off with men and women but progressed to women as it was much harder to find men to talk to. The women I spoke to, who had British backgrounds, had come to live in Greece and were married to Greek men, were very closely aligned to the experiences of my mother, and their children had similar experiences to me. In those interviews, there were plenty of commonalities and were among some of the longest interviews I have ever done: I remember one being three hours long. However, even in this research I encountered difference, which made me feel uncomfortable. For example, some of the women who were married to Greeks felt that sending their children to Greek school was the best idea and they were intrigued to find out that I had gone to a British-international school. I also found myself having to explain that Greek was not my first language even though I had been raised in Greece, which they found surprising. This demonstrates that insider connections also come with judgements and expectations on behalf of participants. They also asked questions on whether I was married and had a family, which at the time I didn't. This positioning of me as a researcher and now, as a mother, by participants, has been present throughout my academic research. However, it is also how we also position ourselves and I have caught myself voluntarily telling participants that I have children in an attempt to share information and build trust.

This issue of sharing and of how much to share is one that I have struggled with as a researcher. I have a tendency to over-share I think, but this may just be my perception when I look at interview transcripts and see how much my voice appears as well! However, I think that this process of sharing is important because it potentially enables you and participants to be more open and to build trust, which can lead to conversations you may not have otherwise had. However, the process of doing so can also make you feel vulnerable and Othered as a researcher.

We therefore also need to address how our own life stages change and how this also has an impact on how we reflect and negotiate our research. My identity as half-Greek, half-British has remained stable over time but my own family and working dynamics have changed. This created some interesting performative storytelling as I have tried to adapt how I position myself and have had to start narrating who I am as a mother who works part-time as an academic.

In my recent research project on young people in diaspora, I found myself at a Palestinian family home being asked about one of my daughters and her schooling. The mother was very keen to find out about me and my family and I felt I had no option but to share. I didn't want to lie so I had to tell her that my eldest daughter attends school part-time. She expressed surprise and asked why. I explained that my daughter was autistic and that she found the school environment challenging. We then had a brief conversation about home education and I could see that she was not convinced. She ended up by telling me that schools in the UK were very good and that they do wonderful things for children with disabilities and that I should send my child to school full-time because they could help her there. I didn't really know how to respond except to nod. When I reflected I could see that she was coming at this from a different cultural perspective where she positioned UK schools and education as being much better than Palestinian/Middle Eastern ones in relation to disability and neurodiversity but she was also trying to help me I think and make me feel better.

I have also experienced this Othering as an academic because I work part-time (two days a week) and have done since 2014. I have encountered understanding but there has also been inadvertent (I like to believe) marginalization and exclusion because the notion of a part-time academic seems strange to some because we are in a minority and because being an academic is seen as a profession in which you give your all, and which you live and breathe at all times. Therefore, I sometimes find that there is an implied assumption that I am less of an academic because I couldn't possibly be that way because I work part-time and because I cannot do as much as my colleagues. However, this is more to do with often gendered assumptions around academic progress and publishing and having to fit into an ideal version of what it means to be an academic and do research. This has meant having to manage other people's expectations of what I can reasonably do.

Working part-time also has many material repercussions as I found in my most recent research project where I felt I had to be available at any time to conduct interviews. With hindsight, I should have been stricter with my time as it was very stressful due to my caring responsibilities and having to find childcare often at the last minute. There were also issues when participants wanted to meet in the evening or invited me to evening events which I really wanted to go to but felt I couldn't because I needed to be home to put my children to bed. Having a child with autism also means that changes to routine are very problematic.

Therefore, I have come to reflect that although we often try our hardest, we cannot be perfect and shouldn't be expected to be so. There is an ideal attainment of excellence for academics: that we need to be excellent at everything but this is unrealistic. In reality, we all have an acute lack of time and, for me, this has meant breaking promises to stay in contact with participants as time slips by even though at the time of saying it, I meant it. All we can do is our best and the same applies to the encounter in research.

Conclusions

What does all this mean in terms of justice? I think it means that there isn't a binary between justice and injustice: that there is a spectrum and that although things are less than 'perfect' it doesn't mean that there isn't the potential for something positive to occur out of an encounter. I think a large part of this is accepting our research as part of a wider process of political actions and justice endeavours, whereby we commit to engaging with others because we want, in some small way, to facilitate change for the better, broadly defined. Through sharing and performing timespace and storytelling, the very process of meeting can act as part of a cumulative process of change. Multiple, shared encounters, reflected upon sincerely and non-judgementally, can provide hope through the very contestation and jarring that such encounters can provoke. We are all potentially out of our comfort zones when we conduct qualitative research (us and participants) and this is something we need to recognize but also potentially harness in terms of reflection and being open-minded and open-hearted. Some might say that this isn't enough and that there need to be practical and material consequences aimed at improving lives in some way. I think this raises wider questions around our role as academics and what we do, what we are able to do, what we should do, what we can reasonably do and how we see our roles as researchers.

I wouldn't say that I have ever consciously set out to do participatory action research although I have wanted to. However, in the process of writing up our research, we decide what extracts to use and how we want to frame articles and books using the data we collect. Attempting more equitable relationships with participants is very important but it is not always possible because I work part-time and have caring responsibilities that require my attention. What I try to do instead is to ensure that participant voices appear as much as possible in my writing and that the encounters I do have with them are positive for all involved. I would love to have ongoing connections with participants and in some cases I have managed this whereby they have, for example, asked for help and I have given it where I can. But when you have conducted hundreds of interviews over many years you also have to know your limits. Trying to fit research into the demands of an academic job in the UK, while also having a decent work–life balance, is hard. This is all linked to the notion of justice in academia and research: we, as academics, need to take care of ourselves as well as participants and, as a result, it is fine to sometimes be strategic in what we do and accept that we cannot do it all. For me personally, issues of diversity and inclusion are very important and I am trying to work towards more inclusive universities in my current role as a school-wide lead for equality, diversity and inclusion, a role I share with a colleague, Iris Wigger. This means addressing ongoing issues such as gender, race and disability. In short, there is no point in advocating for change in relation to our research interests and participants if where we ourselves work is exploitative and unjust in its practices and policies. For me, it's about caring at the end of the day: caring universities, caring workplaces, caring practices: 'ethics of care' (Ho et al, 2015). It's about being honest about our own limitations, feelings, insecurities and so forth, which are both bound and unbound by timespace performances in interviews as we negotiate the reality of sameness and difference. Addressing power in what we do (and don't/can't do) is part of the wider power relations which exist in academia and the multiple injustices colleagues face due to their intersectionalities of gender, race, class, disability and so forth. So our passion for creating justice in our research encounters and enabling open conversations to be had in interviews and other qualitative research is wonderful and important but we also need to continue the work in examining the injustices of where we work. Paying attention to the timespace of qualitative research encounters forms part of this wider political struggle to create inclusion and inclusive relationships for as many people as possible through our work and where we work. In relation specifically to qualitative research, this could mean that we are better enabled as researchers to find the time and space to engage deeply and meaningfully in research we feel matters. Lastly, I would like to stress the importance of optimism and hope and the need to imagine ideal worlds and scenarios which although might seem far-fetched at present can guide us to better futures and can help initiate the tools we need to initiate what we feel is just change.

References

Agarwal, P. (2020) *Sway: Unravelling Unconscious Bias*, London: Bloomsbury.

Amelina, A. (2021) After the reflexive turn in migration studies: towards the doing migration approach, *Population, Space and Place*, 27(1): e2368. https://doi.org/10.1002/psp.2368

Boddy, J. (2014) Research across cultures, within countries: hidden ethics tensions in research with children and families?, *Progress in Development Studies*, 14(1): 91–103.

Cameron, E. (2012) New geographies of story and storytelling, *Progress in Human Geography*, 36(5): 573–592.

Coddington, K. (2017) Voice under scrutiny: feminist methods, anticolonial responses, and new methodological tools, *The Professional Geographer*, 69(2): 314–320.

Cook, I.J. (2001) 'You want to be careful you don't end up like Ian. He's all over the place': autobiography in/of an expanded field, in Moss, P. (ed) *Placing Autobiography in Geography*, Syracuse: Syracuse University Press, pp 99–120.

Denzin, N.K. (2001) The reflexive interview and a performative social science, *Qualitative Research*, 1(1): 23–46.

Dirksmeier, P. and Helbrecht, I. (2010) Intercultural interaction and 'situational places': a perspective for urban cultural geography within and beyond the performative turn, *Social Geography*, 5: 39–48.

England, K.V. (1994) Getting personal: reflexivity, positionality, and feminist research, *The Professional Geographer*, 46(1): 80–89.

Fertaly, K. and Fluri, J.L. (2019) Research associates and the production of knowledge in the field, *The Professional Geographer*, 71(1): 75–82.

Griffiths, M.B. (2014) Out of time: the temporal uncertainties of refused asylum seekers and immigration detainees, *Journal of Ethnic and Migration Studies*, 40(12): 1991–2009.

Ho, E., Boyle, M. and Yeoh, B. (2015) Recasting diaspora strategies through feminist care ethics, *Geoforum*, 59: 206–214.

Koch, N. (2020) Deep listening: practicing intellectual humility in geographic fieldwork, *Geographical Review*, 110(1–2): 52–64.

Limb, M. and Dwyer, C. (2001) *Qualitative Methodologies for Geographers: Issues and Debates*, London: Arnold.

Lulle, A. (2014) *Time-space of Possibilities: Translocal Geographies of Latvians in Guernsey*, PhD thesis, University of Latvia.

Massey, D. (2005) *For Space*. London: Sage.

Mavroudi, E. (2013) Creating geographies of hope through film: performing space in Palestine-Israel, *Transactions of the Institute of British Geographers*, 38(4): 560–571.

Mavroudi, E. (2019) Revisiting diaspora as process: timespace, performative diasporas?, in Mitchell, K., Jones, R. and Fluri, J. (eds) *Handbook on Critical Geographies of Migration*, Cheltenham: Edward Elgar, pp 279–289.

Mavroudi, E., Page, B. and Christou, A. (eds) (2018) *Timespace and International Migration*, London: Edward Elgar.

Mitchell, K. and Elwood, S. (2012) Mapping children's politics: the promise of articulation and the limits of nonrepresentational theory, *Environment and Planning D: Society and Space*, 30(5): 788–804.

Montero-Sieburth, M. (2020) Who gives 'voice' or 'empowers migrants' in participatory action research? Challenges and solutions, *Migration Letters*, 17(2): 211–218.

Nagar, R. and Ali, F. (2003) Collaboration across borders: moving beyond positionality, *Singapore Journal of Tropical Geography*, 24(3): 356–372.

Pottinger, L. (2020) Treading carefully through tomatoes: embodying a gentle methodological approach, *Area*, 00: 1–7. https://doi.org/10.1111/area.12650

Redwood, S. (2008) Research less violent? Or the ethics of performative social science, *Forum: Qualitative Social Research*, 9(2): Article 60.

Spyrou, S. (2016) Researching children's silences: exploring the fullness of voice in childhood research, *Childhood*, 23(1): 7–21.

Woodrow, N. (2017) City of welcome: refugee storytelling and the politics of place, *Continuum*, 31(6): 780–790.

4

Fostering Food Justice in Academia and Beyond

Barbora Adlerova and Ana Moragues Faus

With the escalation of various food inequalities in the UK and globally, there has been a growing interest among food scholars and practitioners in working with the concept of food justice, defining it, operationalizing it (Cadieux and Slocum, 2015; Herman et al, 2018; Coulson and Milbourne, 2020) and exploring how social justice can contribute to creating more sustainable and just food systems (Moragues Faus, 2017; Maughan et al, 2020; Smaal et al, 2021). However, not all interventions include an actual commitment to the concept through performing justice in academic and more-than-research work. In this contribution we argue that to follow (food) justice scholarship, we need to go beyond using justice as a lens in our empirical and theoretical work and explore how justice is enacted (or not) in our research, in academia and beyond. To do that, we introduce our care-full participatory justice framework, mobilizing Nancy Fraser's (2009) economic, socio-cultural and political dimensions of justice, and – following Miriam Williams' (2017) concept of care-full justice – taking ethics of care as a building block of our reflection to interrogate the micro-dimension of our messy, everyday more-than-research activities. Blazek et al (2015) coined the term 'more than research' to highlight the ambivalence and in-becoming-ness of academic and non-academic outcomes to research projects, especially participatory ones. Building on this, Evans (2016) describe relationships developed with her research participants as 'more than research', motivated by ethics of care. Our use aims to extend its focus from outcomes and relationships with people in the field to capturing the complexities and relationships with other people in academia and beyond academia (colleagues, supervisors, students, practitioners, activists) as well as ourselves. Understanding our research activities are always already 'more than research' also helps to paradoxically decenter the spectacular in our research and create a space to navigate justice in all its dimensions in our more-than-research lives (and those of others) where our research is necessarily embedded. We do not endeavour to come up with a set of fool-proof techniques to achieve (food) justice in research, instead we will turn the gaze in and scrutinize our own ambiguous practices, uncomfortable contradictions and troublesome dilemmas that spill out from grant writing, interviews and analysis into our more-than-research life in the UK and beyond.

We start with outlining our reflective framework and explaining how Nancy Fraser's concept of justice is useful in shaping our interests and questions for food justice more-than-research because of its ability to capture multidimensionality and intersectionality of food deliberations, and its focus on structures as well as practices. We also incorporate ethics of care into this approach that helps to illuminate the 'how' of justice, its everyday messy practices and questions the justice dimensions of labour put in. We then go on to discuss how we apply this framework, through a preference to work with feminist and participatory methodologies, and embracing slow and care-full scholarship. In the second half of this chapter we summarize the framework and use it to reflect on our own imperfect practices in two vignettes.

Social justice lens: multidimensionality, intersectionality and care-fullness

In our work we take inspiration from the economic, socio-cultural and political dimensions of justice as outlined by Nancy Fraser (2009). She defines justice as a 'parity of participation' which requires social arrangements to permit all to participate as equals in social relations. This is underpinned by three dimensions: distribution (allocation of resources), cultural recognition (what is valued and how) and political representation (membership and practices in decision-making processes). According to Maughan et al (2020), this framework is useful in embodying multidimensionality of justice angles that are present in food deliberations around the equity of distribution and procedures, the fair distribution of resources to produce or consume food, the recognition of differential needs and cultural values in access to resources and processes as well as equity in decision making (also about the mechanisms that shape it) about one's food system. It also helps to illuminate both the equality of outputs/outcomes of food system practices, as well as the processes that shape these.

The second reason why Fraser's framework is useful in food justice research is that working with three dimensions of justice means thinking about their relationality, how they fold onto each other, and yet never completely overlap. Fraser (2009) herself identifies two kinds of intersectional obstacles to participatory parity: the lack of economic resources to engage (distributive injustice) and the institutional discrimination and hierarchies of cultural values (status inequality). To this, she adds a political dimension: who counts as a subject of justice? Who is excluded and who is included and what are the processes that shape these? In food justice and our research this means paying attention to how interlocking axes of oppression shape the differently positioned actors in the food system (Holt-Giménez and Wang, 2011) and, vice versa, how intersecting systems of class, race, gender, nationality and ethnicity produce particular foodscapes (Moragues Faus, 2019). Holding onto *all* dimensions and considering their intersections is a constant challenge for food justice studies and practices – for example, in a recent study of social-justice oriented narratives in European urban food strategies, Smaal et al (2021) found that most framings are implicit, fragmentary and unspecified, especially lacking in the political dimension where terms like 'participative' or 'inclusive' are rarely defined.

Beyond its multidimensionality and intersectionality, using this concept of justice as a lens makes visible procedures and structures of oppression which is important in a corporate agrifood system where capitalist systems of knowledge, inscription and representation enable some things to be known, while others are obfuscated. In her work on class, value and self, Beverley Skeggs (2003) details how the rhetoric of 'free market' has led to the destabilization of significance of structural forms, or 'unleashing', 'freeing' the agency from the structure. This responsibilization and individualization narrative is also widespread in the current third agricultural food regime (Friedmann, 1993) where all consumers and producers are supposedly on a flat, level playing field of exchange and expected to make rational, informed choices to maximize their 'assets' – be it health, social status or finance. Again, researching food systems through the lens of social justice brings to the fore not only the oppressive structures, but also the mechanisms through which they are assembled, negotiated and challenged. And therefore the questions of 'who' and 'what' is considered a subject of justice and what practices are shaping this has been the cornerstone of our research – such as using the framework to assess the connections between justice and food security narratives (Moragues Faus, 2017), analysing the transformative potential of food partnerships to contribute to more just and sustainable food systems (Moragues Faus, 2019; 2021) or considering the role of people with lived experience of food insecurity in transforming food governance (Barbora's PhD project).

The questions of the 'who' and 'what' of justice have been mostly used in international, national and urban levels of analysis of food systems, exploring the connections and disconnections of UK public food security narratives and their relationality (Moragues Faus, 2017), assessing how European urban food strategies deploy social justice concepts (Smaal et al, 2021) or using it as a lens to 'read for social justice' in food policy discourse in the

UK (Maughan et al, 2020). However, this framing of social justice seems to lack in its capacity to illuminate *how* justice is enacted, especially when talking about food that is experiential, embodied and deeply entangled in everyday practices; enchanting, yet mundane. Therefore, in developing our reflective framework, we take inspiration from the ethics of care approach to justice (Gilligan, 1982; Tronto, 1993; Williams, 2017) which takes the need for care at some point during our lives as the common denominator for all beings. It is an iterative, ongoing process that involves 'taking the concerns and needs of the other as the basis for action' (Tronto, 1993: 105). This is underpinned by values of being attentive to the needs of others, taking responsibility to meet them competently and creating a space for the care receiver's response as well as for caring together.

Care-full justice in particular grounds its focus on mundane practices, everyday activisms imbued with care where the 'subject of justice' is interdependent, relational. It allows us to move away from the 'spectacular' of both food and research practices (ethical approval forms, grant proposals, outputs) and instead pay attention 'to the needs of another, take responsibility for achieving fairness, recognise differences and be attuned to the relational types of political, historical, cultural and economic factors that produce injustices' (Williams, 2017: 830). What is particularly instructive about adding care-full justice to our reflective framework is how it illuminates the aspect of labour and care. It raises questions about who is doing what kind of research labour, how are the benefits and burdens distributed, how is different labour culturally valued and how are decisions about labour made and in what context. The relational aspect helps to bring into attention the 'mundane' labour which may be otherwise less visible, such as admin staff dealing with financial requests, artificial intelligence enlisted to transcribe lengthy interviews and workshops, or the emotional support given by colleagues.

Working through feminist and participatory methodologies and care-full, slow scholarship

The economic, socio-cultural and economic dimensions of social justice infused with a care-full approach not only inform our topics and research questions, but why and how we are doing our research through adopting feminist and participatory methodologies. Social justice is at the core of participatory research, where communities of researchers and participants come together to examine and change a problematic situation to improve the human and planetary wellbeing (Eikenland, 2015; Gergen and Gergen, 2015). Through co-production, which values different types of knowledge, this approach challenges epistemic injustices inherent in traditional hierarchical relationships between knowledge and action, 'knower and known' (Kindon et al, 2010). It is about co-defining with others what is relevant to study, what are the society's demands, and it allows to be attentive to the negotiation of power relationships inherent in any knowledge making (Grant et al, 2013) with the emphasis on methodological openness, responsiveness, reflexivity and relationality of research. The ethics of care approach builds on this with its attention to the interconnectivity and interdependencies which helps to guide and scrutinize research relationships (see also Figure 4.1) as it acknowledges that research is a collective, rather than individual, endeavour. Accountability is crucial – not in the form of reporting procedures or research governance, but prioritizing our responsibilities to the wider community we work with rather than our individual interests as researchers. It is about positioning ourselves as part of wider webs of relations for more than just the time it takes to collect data and considering collective interests as opposed to our individual goals. Simultaneously, collaboration cannot escape conflicts and power inequities are never erased – for example, academics are sometimes interested in a long-term social change whereas the community may be keener on quicker local benefits (Smith et al, 2010).

In our operationalization of social justice in research we go beyond recognizing injustice as the focus of our inquiry to generate general knowledge. Agreeing with Mason (2015: 500) that it is 'unethical not to take action in face of inequality', we find participatory approaches helpful in centring our research practices on the 'action', or 'usefulness' in and especially beyond academia (Taylor, 2014). What is the change in the world we want to see as a result of our research – both 'spectacular' outputs, but especially through everyday practices? We are always engaged in 'more-than-research' built on meaningful relationships, fluid participant-researcher identities, and multiple academic and non-academic outcomes (Blazek et al, 2015; Evans, 2016). As scholar-activists we prioritize dissemination techniques that are accessible to the community (part of the research or not) beyond academia, including creative outputs, such as the written submission to the House of Lords Covid-19 Committee (Adlerova et al, 2020), curator of the exhibition 'MENJA, ACTUA, IMPACTA' (EAT, ACT, IMPACT) from educational organization Fundesplai), co-written blogposts (Adlerova and Pearson, 2021), reports, toolkits or policy recommendations (co-produced guide with policy makers and civil society organizations across Europe [*Urban Food Strategies: The Rough Guide*], guide to develop food policy councils in Spanish and Catalan commissioned by civil society organizations ['Guia sobre consejos alimentarios'] or 'Sustainable food: a manual for cities' commissioned by Barcelona City Council).

Our justice framework helps us to consider not only the 'what' of outputs, but also how decisions about them are made, by whom, and especially how they are produced. Sometimes this has meant focusing on immaterial outputs and relationship building, creating spaces for reflection in the forms of workshops or meetings with participants, or taking a slow, iterative and deep approach to co-writing (Adlerova and Pearson, 2021; for example, Community of Practice created in EU Project Foodlinks whose main output was the Urban Food Strategies: The Rough Guide). In the Foodlinks project, the slow and time-consuming exercise of building trust, relationships, consisting of informal chats or participation in various events, exposed the fragility of the participatory project, as stakeholders' different interests in terms of outputs needed to be navigated, as well as their various capacities for creating them. The uncertainty, relationality and ambiguity of action-oriented methods sometimes sit uneasily with the conventional research impact frameworks since process-focused participatory research may involve a lot of collaboration, effort and work, and yet create little material impacts in future or else those impacts are unknown (Pain et al, 2011). In this way, participatory methods may 'resist auditability' (Evans, 2016), which may as a result penalize researchers within institutional frameworks of performance. For example, we have experienced how line managers and senior faculty insist on early-career researchers publishing single-authored papers and establishing an individual academic identity that will make them stand out from the rest, fostering individualism instead of collective gains and also the advantages of additional experiences and knowledges.

If we are thinking about operationalizing the concept of social justice within food justice research, we also need to consider 'who' and 'what' are the inter-relational subjects of justice outside of our imminent research project. This is where we take inspiration from the recent movement for slower (Mountz et al, 2015), gentle (Horton, 2020; Pottinger, 2020) or care-full (Care et al, 2021; Moriggi, 2021) scholarship that proposes a more care-full, slower way of working, a collective form of resistance to challenge growing injustices in neoliberal academia (Mountz et al, 2015). These calls have been reinforced in the COVID-19 pandemic that exposed the cracks and crises in academic knowledge production where unsustainable demands on performance, productivity and fashioning an enterprising, career-driven self are leading to burnout, feelings of exhaustion and alienation (Corbera et al, 2020; Plotnikof and Høg Utoft, 2022). The health crisis has laid bare injustices entrenched in European academia such as structural inequalities in research grants – for example, in gendered labour division in research, teaching and 'institutional housekeeping' where women's lives have been more adversely affected (Shalaby et al, 2021) or in funding distribution as none of the £4.3 million funding from the UKRI (UK Research and Innovation) and NHRI (National Human Rights Institution) that aimed to understand COVID-19's disproportionate impact on Black, Asian and Minority Ethnic (BAME) communities was awarded to Black academic leads (Adelaine et al, 2020).

Despite the growth of scholarship on how we can care about human and more-than-human others in our research, self-care and building collective care has been largely overlooked, with some exceptions (Care et al, 2021; Plotnikof and Høg Utoft, 2022). Therefore, we are advocating for a justice approach in academia that builds collective capacities and structures that act on intersecting gender, class and race inequalities, and prioritizes human and more-than-human wellbeing over individual productivity. Here participatory research guides us to carefully consider social justice in more-than-research relationships we are entangled in – how do we justly care for our participants, colleagues and ourselves? To what extent do academic infrastructures value different knowledges, experiences and needs of research actors? How are the benefits and burdens of research labour distributed among junior and senior research team members and how do we enact epistemic justice when writing up journal articles and other outputs, relying on the labour of our students?

Reflecting on our research with the care-full participatory justice lens

Combining social justice with ethics of care has helped us to develop a framework (Figure 4.1) to reflect on the justice dilemmas and contradictions in our more-than-research endeavours. Our framework includes reflective questions spanning three dimensions of justice (what and who) and simultaneously embedded within the ethics of care approach (how). Besides the redistributive aspect discussed earlier, the economic dimension also considers the initial position where people are coming from, how are people rewarded differently for their time, and balancing different types of benefits received. The socio-cultural dimension focuses on valuing different knowledges and needs but also understanding different cultures and integrating diversity while the political dimension asks important questions about decision-making practices. Intersections with time and space need to be explored too: who benefits from our more-than-research in the short term, in the long term and who loses out?

Furthermore, an ethics of care approach is integrated into all dimensions. Although scholars (Tronto, 2013; Moriggi, 2021) display four or five pillars of ethics of care (caring about, caring for, care giving, care receiving, caring with) in an iterative, cyclical model, this does not always recognize the imperative of the political dimension of justice in terms of decision-making. Instead of positioning care receivers as merely responding to care, creating spaces for decision making and reciprocity constitutes a backbone of our research and care practices. By specifically including researcher needs we aim to contribute to the small but growing literatures operationalizing 'self-care' in academia (Plotnikof and Høg Utoft, 2022; Gaudet et al,

Figure 4.1: Care-full participatory justice framework

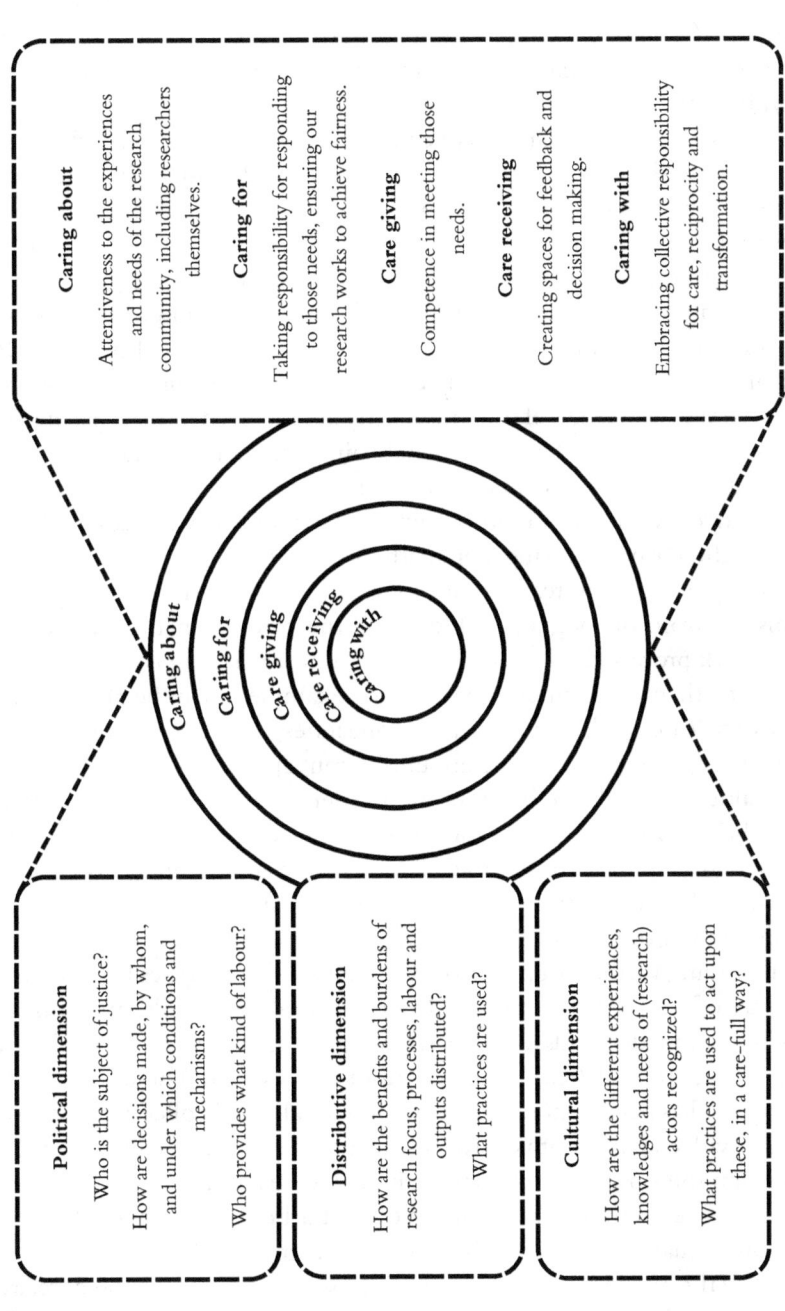

Source: Adapted from Adlerova (2024)

2022), as previously the researchers' needs (beyond honing a career-driven enterprising subjectivity) may have been decentred from methodological accounts. Nevertheless, we intend for our reflection to be less about 'writing ourselves' (Skeggs, 2003) and more about critically appraising individual, organizational and social problems with the intention to change the context in which they arise (Swan, 2008).

Applying a care-full participative justice lens to our research brings to the fore the mundane practices, which we explore alongside the 'spectacular' decisions about recruitment of participants, the choice of methods or the questions of dissemination. Instead of taking each dimension in turn, we want to embrace the messy and iterative nature of research by presenting our reflection in two vignettes which also reflect our different positionalities and stages in our academic careers. At the time of writing, Barbora was a PhD student based in the UK, working on her thesis exploring how people with experiential knowledge of food insecurity are involved in food partnerships. Ana is a senior research fellow based in Spain, conducting action research with different institutions and organizations on sustainable food, social justice and governance. We met at a British university where Ana was a research fellow and taught Barbora during her master's degree. Despite our relationship beginning as a student–teacher one, more thorough consideration of teaching is missing from our vignettes. However, the care-full participatory justice framework proposed could be used there too, as teaching is a crucial part of our more-than-research endeavours. For example, it can be about creating spaces to 'care with' students and colleagues, perhaps sharing decisions about assessments, or thinking about different approaches to teaching, what they value, their relative benefits and burdens, and their intersections with the political dimensions of justice – who ends up participating in lectures, seminars as a result of our (whose?) choices? The ambivalent gendered nature of care and meeting (non-)academic more-than-research needs has been highlighted in the COVID-19 pandemic where, on one hand, prioritizing and providing various support to our students and colleagues has been hailed as a way of performing different, less toxic academia while simultaneously making unjust demands on researcher's time and capacity (Plotnikof and Høg Utoft, 2022). Writing this contribution slowly and deliberatively over 15 months has been generative for us individually and collectively. It has not only provided an innovative lens to reflect on our academic endeavours, but also given the slow pace of working it enabled us to digest past and present injustices, see them in a different light. For Barbora, it also helped to finesse the conceptual framework in her thesis (Adlerova, 2024). Creating during the COVID-19 pandemic has tested our own framework to the core, as we sought to build a tentative space to prioritize our wellbeing and that of our families over academic excellence and meeting deadlines.

Vignette 1: Creating spaces for care receiving and caring with

Despite avowing the messiness of research where narration can be seldom linear, let me take you, reader, to the quasi-beginning of my PhD research. Inspired by my previous collaborations with Ana, as well as my brief career as a civil servant, I was considering having a 'co-inquiry group' to guide this project. This was to partially address the political injustices inherent to some extent within the existing PhD structures, where research grants and proposals are often written without the community's contribution – hence the 'quasi-beginning'. As it transpired, the political question of 'who is the subject of justice' in this project was not straightforward as I encountered different levels of access, needs and hierarchies of knowledge when it came to my research community, a diverse group of representatives from the main partner of the project, a support network for food partnerships, as well as practitioners, activists and people with lived experience embedded within those. Whose perspectives should be considered or prioritized (with some of them more easily accessible than others), to whom should I be accountable? How to balance the diverse and sometimes conflicting needs, benefits and burdens? One aim of the co-inquiry group was to ensure that people with lived experience of food insecurity can participate in decision making, to balance the access the representatives of the main organizations had through established organizational relationships. During a series of discussions with supervisors and the organizations themselves (though *not* with people with lived experience), the idea of a stable group, a formal site of accountability, morphed into creating more flexible spaces where community members who are available at any given time could reflect on the research project and allow for 'caring with'.

To start with, I ran a session at an event organized by the partner project in November 2019 for practitioners from food poverty partnerships where I aimed to explore what people are interested in, what expectations and previous experience with academic work they have, and how they prefer to work together. Despite recognizing and meeting classed needs of professionals (accommodating pressures on their time, presenting myself and the work in a professional language, within a recognizable structure of a meeting with an agenda, flipcharts and Post-it notes), reality once again proved to be a whack-a-mole game where – like the mole – a dilemma pops up, the player whacks it down one hole, and immediately, a related one pops up elsewhere (Eliasoph, 2016). A couple of months later I was reminded by the only expert by experience[1] who could attend the workshop how costly and uncomfortable the whole day was for her, being stuck on a train for four hours and then in a room with strangers, talking about topics she did not have any choice over.

Couldn't it have been done online, she pleaded over Zoom from the comfort of her living room while stroking her cat. So here it was – while focusing on the 'spectacular' structures of research governance, I forgot about the wellbeing and perspective of someone whose knowledge I paradoxically aimed to prioritize.

Slowly, through multi-spatial reflections, experimental, fluid principles emerged in fits and starts that helped to create spaces that disrupt assumptions about appropriate ways of being and behaving – who knows and who is known – ditching emails for texts and phone calls, allowing for mutual vulnerability and unstructured conversations laden with emotional, critical language, shifting focus on telling personal or organizational stories to creative methods and reflections on the conditions of their production. Similar conditions have been negotiated across a variety of research activities, including semi-structured conversations with practitioners, chats with activists, co-designed photo-competition, or reflective workshops in spring 2021 where themes emerging from the research were discussed with participants. These workshops were another attempt at creating flexible reflective spaces to democratize the research decision-making mechanism. Organizing them in a slow, care-full manner was one way of recognizing and acting on participants' needs. It meant negotiating content, date and time beforehand and eventually deciding to hold two smaller sessions that would create a space for discussion, rather than just dissemination. As social movements usually work in different/shorter timescales than academia (Kindon et al, 2010), I was not able to answer 'urgent' questions about how best to go about involving people with lived experience in their work. My intention therefore went beyond 'giving back' whatever there was from my research at that moment, and rather to facilitate an opportunity for people interested in this topic to meet, exchange learning and build relationships. On the day it meant creating a relaxed atmosphere with a limited agenda, positioning myself as a facilitator rather than 'the knower', giving time for people to talk about their work, letting the conversation take its course and not interrupting two-way chats, paying attention to people's questions and comments but also silences and breath-intakes as interruptions-to-be (more challenging online) while simultaneously attempting to 'do justice' to participants not present at the event, for example ensuring topics raised by people with lived experience as important were discussed.

Economic dimension and care-giving: responding to people's needs, valuing their knowledges and the challenges of doing so

One such key theme was the question of valuing people's diverse contributions to research and other participatory projects organized by food partnerships, a topic very familiar to all participatory researchers.

With so much work and care going around, how to ensure that the benefits and burdens of the research itself are justly distributed, when for a long time, academics have been accused of constituting their academic careers and subjectivities through establishing experience and knowledge of others as their own property (Skeggs, 2003)? As it has started to emerge from my research, a similar argument could have been made about professionals and organizations more broadly as well. In our conversations across various groups of participants different ways of recognition were discussed – from listening and acting on people's requests through offering various leisure and work experiences (travelling, training) to financial valuation. Some activists with lived experience perceived not being reimbursed or remunerated in a timely, needs-based manner as an injustice in itself, for example, recalling instances of contributing to meetings and reports where they were the only ones not paid for their time there. Going back to the economic dimension of the care-full participatory justice framework, this has informed a decision to prioritize payments to people *not* engaged in my research as part of their paid time in their jobs – meaning mostly people with lived experience of food insecurity. This redistributive practice was nevertheless limited by the university's financial infrastructure which did not allow to pay actual money to participants. Instead it relies on vouchers, which in turn limits the ability to respond fully to people's needs. On one occasion when co-designing a photo-competition with a group of participants and activists, a successful attempt was made to disrupt these infrastructures when a group of practitioners and activists took control of my personal research budget. Together, we negotiated how much to spend on craft materials as well as what they should pay themselves as a facilitation fee, which could be invoiced to the university. Despite this somewhat heroic narrative, attempting to enact justice in this was not an easy decision – rather another whack-a-mole game. Personal research budgets are traditionally aimed at enhancing personal competitiveness in neoliberal academia as they are destined to finance a researcher's needs, such as access to academic materials or enabling additional training or attendance at conferences. Is it possible that by prioritizing collective gains I penalized my future capacity for productivity, or 'academic success', such as presenting at a conventionally prestigious conference? This is again where a justice focus needs to go beyond the realm of research, into critically reflecting on the gendered, classed and raced assumptions organizational practices are based on, and actively shaping them to prioritizing 'asks' of people most affected in our work by (food and other) inequalities – especially when doing so intersects with people's access to decision-making spaces and representational practices.

Moreover, prioritizing 'immediate reciprocity' – directly helping a social movement (Cahill, 2007; Gillan and Pickerill, 2012) or 'paying forward' – was putting a strain on meeting my needs. At times it was difficult to practice care-full justice in relation to myself – becoming attentive to my needs, let alone becoming competent and responsible for meeting them; not only personal, but also academic ones, as requirements to create 'general knowledge' were pushed into the future. By negotiating deadlines and contents of mandatory assignments I was examining the edges of care present in academic performance structures, where the support of colleagues and supervisors was indispensable. 'Resisting excellence at all costs' (Corbera et al, 2020) allowed for fostering mutually attentive relationships with colleagues and students that put wellbeing and solidarity above performance and productivity. Putting ourselves in the picture as both care givers *and* care receivers is crucial for fostering just academia in a way of being and performing everyday more-than-research decisions.

Vignette 2: Making space for caring about and caring for

At the moment of writing this, I am a mom and employed by the University of Barcelona as a senior research fellow through a highly competitive programme of the Spanish Ministry of Science and Innovation. In principle, after this five-year fellowship I will have my first permanent contract in academia as an associate professor. My path up to now has been exciting, intense and hard work. I started my engagement in food system transformations as an activist supporting food sovereignty movements in Argentina and Spain, and rapidly incorporated many of those engagements and learnings into my academic practice. Since joining the university as a student I wanted to be an academic and a university lecturer, because I have always firmly believed in the public duty and potential of universities and research to transform societies and build more sustainable and just futures. I love my work, which is intrinsically linked to who I am and what I dedicate my time, energy and passion to. In this section I reflect upon some of my research experiences and use the different dimensions of justice to highlight key challenges and lessons learned.

The *economic dimension* of justice calls for a reflection on how the benefits and burdens of research focus, processes, labour and outputs are distributed. This includes considering the initial position of different research participants and how people are rewarded for their time and expertise. These different starting points are relevant and we see those inequalities emerging constantly in academia, where the labour conditions and remuneration of different positions can go as far as receiving a ten times bigger salary. Not only that, but also precarious early-career jobs mean overworking to be able to stay in the sector, which is highly normalized. I have done that on a constant basis for years, including having part-time jobs and working full-time. I recall conversations where working 50–60 hours a week was deemed as 'what it takes to make it' in the eyes of senior colleagues. This unhealthy work culture needs urgent attention to actually enact distributive justice within academia. Overworking without pay is also a luxury, for example, for those without caring responsibilities or in non-economic precarious conditions, and therefore entrenches inequalities in the system. However, distributive justice in research processes is not only about economic conditions of participants and their engagement but also about what types of outputs are generated and who they benefit. My work in Foodlinks – a European funded project based in creating communities of practice with policy makers, civil society and academics to co-produce knowledge around urban food strategies – implied collectively defining outputs and working on them. We decided to co-write a guide for different stakeholders to develop urban food strategies. The output, in the context of academic performance metrics (winning grants and publishing high impact papers) has little to no value. The consequence was that early-career researchers self-exploited themselves to produce more outputs recognized as valuable to maintain themselves in the academic world.

Socio-cultural injustices are also rampant in food systems and academia, as routinely highlighted by feminist and BAME colleagues. As a white, non-British immigrant woman in the UK, I have experienced different forms of discrimination that pushed me to 'do even better' to accomplish an academic career. The academic environment, everyday practices and performance assessments on many occasions clash with the calls for collective action, diversity, intersectional justice and complex understanding of social phenomena that scholars display in their top publications. In the literature, there are highly regarded academic pieces on justice that build upon data and work of researchers that are not recognized in terms of pay and/or authorship. The culture of individualism translated into 'building a separate identity and differentiating yourself from others' paves the ground for predatory practices along the whole academic food chain. This includes the parameter of needing international recognition for any research to be deemed as 'successful', which risks the reproduction of neocolonial attitudes by eroding the relevance of diversity of knowledges and epistemologies and calls for fostering horizontal and empowering relations with researchers worldwide rather than extractive ones.

Many of the injustices portrayed here are closely linked to the *political dimension of justice*. This dimension is partly expressed through neoliberal academia and its structures which portray success as an individual endeavour, normalize self-exploitation and perpetuate inequalities through assessment frameworks and procedures. Real participation to change the system is limited, and on many occasions, the most sensitive colleagues are early-career or precarious researchers who feel powerless or unable to confront management or senior colleagues to promote structural changes. Enacting participatory justice also requires integrating practitioners in decision-making processes. Participation is not always straightforward. It does not mean involving everyone in everything, but requires a more critical approach to needs, demands and expectations. For example, in a research-action process with buying groups in Spain we wanted to involve practitioners in all decisions and stages of the process, which included a four-hour workshop to decide the research methodology that nobody enjoyed and did not give much value to participants.

In this academic context, how can we address these injustice dynamics and develop research that is truly transformative towards more equitable futures? *A care-full approach to our work* and engagements helps to pave the way of these always conflicting transitions. A first element is the importance of *building trust* within and beyond academia. However, building trust takes time, it requires one to be accessible and also useful for practitioners. When we share high-level objectives and values (such as sustainability or food justice) these relations are easier to nurture, and also have the capacity to transform our work and the role of academia. Practitioner colleagues often openly criticize the role and attitudes of academics in front of me, for being extractive, short-term and focused on the individual interests. However, when we truly commit to action research, we experience it as a place-based and long-term process at odds with another trait of academia: short-term contracts. After leaving my latest position, I have left great colleagues outside academia and unfinished projects where different people invested their time. To sustain these collaborations and their impact, it is very important to work in teams, which links to the second element, care-fullness is a *collective endeavour*. Self-care and caring for others is challenging when you try to comply with expectations from both the academic and practitioner world. It needs a supportive environment where benefits and burdens are shared. There are an increasing number of scholars and collectives that support each other, such as the Center for Agroecology, Water and Resilience. The mundane practices of caring also need supportive structures and procedures that contribute to a change of culture towards a collective responsibility for care. Some simple experiences that I tried with others throughout my career include developing an ethical contract that recognizes the needs of early-career researchers, for example by prioritizing them as first authors in papers or including in research assistants' contracts time for them to develop their publications. To summarize, some of the key lessons learned in my 15 years as a researcher include the importance of working with people that share your core values, assess and understand different capacities and roles within your team and use them strategically (maybe someone is great in fieldwork and another one is an avid reader and writer), accept imperfection, support others and support yourself, and give yourself space to celebrate and reflect.

Conclusions

Invited by the editors, in this chapter we wanted to reflect on (in)justice from the perspective of scholar-activists working on food justice. To that end we developed a framework to examine our practices in and beyond academia, combining Nancy Fraser's conceptualization of participatory justice that enables us to focus on the structural analysis, with ethics of care that highlights the mundane, everyday, messy processes of labour, care and feelings. Threaded through our diverse vignettes is the realization that the spectacular of research and academia interacts with the mundane, and therefore both need to be hold close for inspection. The continuous framework proposed in this chapter has proven valuable to navigate the structural, procedural and spectacular with the everyday in research, academia and our communities more widely. We cannot separate our research and academic practices from the transformation we'd like to see in the food system. As food justice scholars, we often apply the critical justice lens to farmers, corporations, community organizations and governments but fail to put ourselves in the uncomfortable spotlight. Therefore we're calling for more openness to be vulnerable and critical, compassionate but not complacent with our own practices as food justice scholar-activists. How much do we *really* contribute to food justice? What role do we have beyond 'knowledge production' as actual agents in the food system? Food system as a 'system of systems' is firmly interlocked with the academic one and we are embodied 'doers' as much as 'thinkers'. We need to go beyond evidence building, critical-friendliness and evaluations, into creating spaces for collective reflection, questioning our labour, fostering horizontal relationships and generally seeing ourselves as part of the sustainable and just food systems we want to create.

Note
[1] Participant's preferred term.

References
Adelaine, A., Kalinga, C., Asani, F., Agbakoba, N.R., Smith, N., Adisa, O., Francois, J., King-Okoye, M., Williams, P. and Zelzer, R. (2020) Knowledge is power: an open letter to UKRI, *Research Professional News*, https://www.researchprofessionalnews.com/rr-news-uk-views-of-the-uk-2020-8-knowledge-is-power-an-open-letter-to-ukri/

Adlerova, B. (2024) *Cooking, caring, campaigning: making space for lived experience in food governance*, PhD Thesis, Cardiff University.

Adlerova, B. and Pearson, B. (2021) Building a community in a pandemic: engaging digitally, creatively and with care – part 1, *Covid Realities*, https://covidrealities.org/researching-poverty/building-in-a-pandemic

Adlerova, B., Pearson, B., Sowerby, M., Walters, P., Killeya, C. and Lobo, A. (2020) *Life beyond Covid: Written Evidence to the House of Lords Covid-19 Committee*, https://committees.parliament.uk/writtenevidence/10094/html/

Blazek, M., Smith, F.M., Lemešová, M. and Hricová, P. (2015) Ethics of care across professional and everyday positionalities: the (un)expected impacts of participatory video with young female carers in Slovakia, *Geoforum*, 61: 45–55.

Cadieux, K.V. and Slocum, R. (2015) What does it mean to do food justice?, *Journal of Political Ecology*, 22(1): 1–26.

Cahill, C. (2007) Repositioning ethical commitments: participatory action research as a relational praxis of social change, *ACME: An International Journal for Critical Geographies*, 6(3): 360–373.

Care, O., Bernstein, M.J., Chapman, M., Reviriego, I.D., Dressler, G., Felipe-Lucia, M.R., et al (2021) Creating leadership collectives for sustainability transformations, *Sustainability Science*, 16(2): 703–708.

Corbera, E., Anguelovski, I., Honey-Rosés, J. and Ruiz-Mallén, I. (2020) Academia in the time of COVID-19: towards an ethics of care, *Planning Theory & Practice*, 21(2): 191–199.

Coulson, H. and Milbourne, P. (2020) Food justice for all? Searching for the 'justice multiple' in UK food movements, *Agriculture and Human Values*, 38(1): 43–58.

Eikenland, O. (2015) Praxis: retrieving the roots of action research, in Bradbury, H. (ed) *The SAGE Handbook of Action Research*, 3rd edn, London: SAGE, pp 381–391.

Eliasoph, N. (2016) The mantra of empowerment talk: an essay, *Journal of Civil Society*, 12(3): 247–265.

Evans, R. (2016) Achieving and evidencing research 'impact'? Tensions and dilemmas from an ethic of care perspective, *Area*, 48(2): 213–221.

Fraser, N. (2009) *Scales of Justice: Reimagining Political Space in a Globalizing World*, Columbia: Columbia University Press.

Friedmann, H. (1993) The political economy of food: a global crisis, *New Left Review*, 197: 29–57.

Gaudet, S., Marchand, I., Bujaki, M. and Bourgeault, I.L. (2022) Women and gender equity in academia through the conceptual lens of care, *Journal of Gender Studies*, 31(1): 74–86.

Gergen, K.J. and Gergen, M.M. (2015) Social construction and research as action, in Bradbury, H. (ed) *The SAGE Handbook of Action Research*, 3rd edn, London: SAGE, pp 401–408.

Gillan, K. and Pickerill, J. (2012) The difficult and hopeful ethics of research on, and with, social movements, *Journal of Social, Cultural and Political Protest*, 11(2): 133–143.

Gilligan, C. (1982) *In a Different Voice: Psychological Theory and Women's Development*, Cambridge, MA: Harvard University Press.

Grant, J., Nelson, G. and Mitchell, T. (2013) Negotiating the challenges of participatory action research: relationships, power, participation, change and credibility, in Pearson, P. and Bradbury, H. (eds) *The SAGE Handbook of Action Research: Participative Inquiry and Practice*, 2nd edn, London: SAGE, pp 588–601.

Herman, A., Goodman, M.K. and Sage, C. (2018) Six questions for food justice, *Local Environment*, 23(11): 1075–1089.

Holt-Giménez, E. and Wang, Y. (2011) Reform or transformation? The pivotal role of food justice in the U.S. food movement, *Race/Ethnicity: Multidisciplinary Global Contexts*, 5(1): 83–102.

Horton, J. (2020) For diffident geographies and modest activisms: questioning the ANYTHING-BUT-GENTLE academy, *Area*, February. https://doi.org/10.1111/area.12610

Kindon, S., Pain, R. and Kesby, M. (eds) (2010) *Participatory Action Research Approaches and Methods: Connecting People, Participation and Place*, Abingdon: Routledge.

Mason, K. (2015) Participatory action research: coproduction, governance and care, *Geography Compass*, 9(9): 497–507.

Maughan, C., Anderson, C. and Kneafsey, M. (2020) A five-point framework for reading for social justice: a case study of food policy discourse in the context of Brexit Britain, *Journal of Agriculture, Food Systems, and Community Development*, 9(3): 1–20.

Moragues Faus, A. (2017) Problematising justice definitions in public food security debates: towards global and participative food justices, *Geoforum*, 84(August): 95–106.

Moragues Faus, A. (2019) Towards a critical governance framework: unveiling the political and justice dimensions of urban food partnerships, *The Geographical Journal*, 186(1): 73–86.

Moragues Faus, A. (2021) The emergence of city food networks: rescaling the impact of urban food policies, *Food Policy*, 103. https://doi.org/10.1016/j.foodpol.2021.102107

Moriggi, A. (2021) Practicing care-full scholarship in research, education, & collaboration: an analytical framework. Working Paper. https://doi.org/10.5281/zenodo.5095175

Mountz, A., Bonds, A., Mansfield, B., Loyd, J., Hyndman, J. and Walton-Roberts, M., et al (2015) For slow scholarship: a feminist politics of resistance through collective action in the neoliberal university, *ACME: An International Journal for Critical Geographies*, 14(4): 1235–1259.

Pain, R., Kesby, M. and Askins, K. (2011) Geographies of impact: power, participation and potential, *Area*, 43(2): 183–188.

Plotnikof, M. and Høg Utoft, E. (2022) The 'new normal' of academia in pandemic times: resisting toxicity through care, *Gender, Work & Organization*, 29(4): 1259–1271.

Pottinger, L. (2020) Treading carefully through tomatoes: embodying a gentle methodological approach, *Area*, July: 1–7. https://doi.org/10.1111/area.12650

Shalaby, M., Allam, N. and Buttorff, G.J. (2021) Leveling the field: gender inequity in academia during COVID-19, *PS: Political Science & Politics*, 54(4): 661–667.

Skeggs, B. (2003) *Class, Self, Culture*, London: Routledge.

Smaal, S.A.L., Dessein, J., Wind, B.J. and Rogge, E. (2021) Social justice-oriented narratives in European urban food strategies: bringing forward redistribution, recognition and representation, *Agriculture and Human Values*, 38: 709–727.

Smith, L., Bratini, L., Chambers, D.A., Jensen, R.V. and Romero, L.L. (2010) Between idealism and reality: meeting the challenges of participatory action research, *Action Research*, 8(4): 407–425.

Swan, E. (2008) Let's not get too personal: critical reflection, reflexivity and the confessional turn, *Journal of European Industrial Training*, 32(5): 385–399.

Taylor, M. (2014) 'Being useful' after the ivory tower: combining research and activism with the Brixton pound, *Area*, 46(3): 305–312.

Tronto, J.C. (1993) *A Political Argument for an Ethic of Care*, London: Routledge.

Tronto, J.C. (2013) *Caring Democracy: Markets, Equality, and Justice*, New York: New York University Press.

Williams, M.J. (2017) Care-full justice in the city, *Antipode*, 49(3): 821–839.

PART II

Justice as Unsettling Asymmetries

For the three chapters in this section, written by Jen Dickinson and Natasha Uwimanzi, Jennifer Balint and Deepti Chatti, justice is about action. They acknowledge the structural but also mundane, everydayness of injustice and seek to enable spaces for learning and reflection, for all participants to 'be otherwise' in an effort to disrupt and decentre Western knowledge in the academy and beyond. The projects discussed work towards a decolonizing praxis, seeking to partner with the historically marginalized and silenced to give voice to their narratives, histories and futures. Their work emphasizes the necessity for accountability and dialogical reflexivity within these partnerships in order to rebalance research spaces and relations, while acknowledging the ongoing challenges in grounding these in local and contextual understandings and interpretations.

Justice here is grounded in unsettling epistemic silencing, both through enabling spaces for testimony, collaboration and situated experiences, and in processing how you do research within – and beyond – the constraints of colonial constructions of 'fields of study' alongside the contemporary, neoliberal university context.

5

Disrupting the Field? Creating Community-centred Spaces for Epistemic Justice with Rwandese Diaspora Youth

Jen Dickinson and Natasha Uwimanzi

There is an urgent need to pluralize knowledge inquiry and production in the research about Rwanda. Conceptualized as a form of epistemicide (or, killing of knowledge), the systemic biases and highly partisan nature of Western epistemologies continues to deny the diverse ways that Rwandans make sense of their lives (Rutazibwa, 2014). Undoing epistemic injustice requires enabling individuals whose knowledge has been historically invalidated to assert their rights to contribute to, and derive benefits from, the shared knowledge pool (de Sousa Santos, 2015). In the Rwandan context, alongside including more Rwandan academic voices, epistemic justice requires reimagining research approaches, methodologies and practices so as to include and value Rwandan's lived experiences, expertise and insights as legitimate sources of knowledge (Ndahinda et al, 2022). Making such transformations to research practice is more important than ever, in the context of wider calls to dismantle epistemic injustice in Africa-centred research more widely (Ogone, 2017) and the reformulations of scholarly activity in the service of decoloniality (Esson et al, 2017; Barker and Pickerill, 2020; for example, Daley and Murrey, 2022).

This chapter reflects on our efforts to create community-centred spaces for collaborative research, as a tool for including Rwanda's multiple epistemic contributors as part of a critical and pluralized academic landscape. Destabilizing notions of 'the field' in academic research (Radcliffe, 2022), community-centric research using methods that are participatory and collaborative can facilitate the types of dialogue necessary for the urgent work of undoing academic knowledge hierarchies (Zavala, 2013; Barker and Pickerill, 2020). However, inherently intersubjective (Thambinathan and Kinsella, 2021), the researcher identities, positions, time pressures and funding deadlines that are brought to such spaces generate the power dynamics and hierarchies suffusing the practice of community-centred research. Focusing on our navigations of the competing practicalities and ethics around creating spaces for epistemic inclusion, in this chapter we surface the compromises that play out. We suggest that the potential of community-centred research for working towards epistemic justice can remain unfulfilled because of the relational nature of research spaces, where the inclusion and valuing of diverse knowledge contributions become subsumed to the pressures of academic expectations and project deadlines.

The project that forms the basis of these reflections is the Rwanda Diaspora Youth Partnership Programme (RDYPP), a collaborative research project led by Jen Dickinson seeking to understand how Rwanda diaspora youth in the UK experienced and understood ideas of engagement with post-genocide economic reconstruction. The project was funded by Jen Dickinson's then institutional Global Challenges Research Fund (GCRF) Quality Related (QR) income as a year-long project. Drawing on literature surrounding the methodological applications of epistemic justice, we explore the key practical issues and challenges that surround producing spaces for dialogue and co-learning between local and diaspora young people, academic researchers and community organizations. Recognizing that co-creating spaces for mutual learning can be generative of opportunities for epistemic justice, nonetheless we draw out the inherent tensions are built into community-centred research particularly in fraught academic and political contexts, with implications for epistemic inclusion. We conclude by emphasizing the need for a relational understanding of Rwanda's research spaces as a starting point for building generative opportunities for epistemic justice.

Rwanda's political economy of development: creating space for epistemic justice

The academic research on the political economy of development in Rwanda is highly polarized, and as such, has become the subject of extensive discussion (for example, Booth and Golooba-Mutebi, 2012; Hintjens, 2014; Chemouni, 2020). To broadly characterize the debate, since the Rwanda Patriotic Front liberated the country following the 1994 Genocide against the Tutsi, the Government of Rwanda (GoR) has embarked on a programme of political reconciliation and economic reconstruction. The academe interprets the GoR's methods either as repressive or visionary (Harrison, 2017). Within these debates, discussions about the state, its nature, legitimacy and reach in shaping Rwandan's social contexts and everyday life continues to provide a predetermined framework through which academic knowledge about Rwanda is validated. As Harrison (2017) concludes, it is precisely the over-dominance of analysis of the state's approaches and methods to post-genocide reconstruction that gives rise to such polarization, since it gets to the heart of Western academic concerns and interpretive frameworks about the role of the state in development interventions. Such a focus has resulted in the emergence of certain 'epistemic prioritizations' that silence other narratives, stories, interpretations and phenomena (Harrison, 2017: 875). For these reasons, scholars are increasingly clear that foreign researchers writing about the political economy have narrowly constructed Rwanda as a field of study (Fisher, 2015). At a more fundamental level, this can be understood as a form of epistemic injustice because it leave little room for hearing contextually specific understandings and interpretations (Rutazibwa, 2014).

In this and other scholarship on Rwanda, there is also extensive debate about how the GoR also tightly circumscribes the research space for foreign researchers (Loyle, 2016) Although grounded in legitimate concerns of ethics, protection and dignity of research participants (Park and Shema, 2019), this is often interpreted as an attempt to control knowledge production about the country. Such readings and interpretations contribute to the preservation of ideas that valid knowledge about Rwanda can only be produced through detached and objective researchers (Chemouni, 2020), thus continuing to shape not only research prioritizations and interpretive frameworks but also the systemic exclusions of Rwanda-based researchers from academic debate and knowledge production (Ndahinda et al, 2022).

An important complement to these critiques are those of Nhemachena et al (2016) and others that have surfaced the coloniality inherent in the intellectual constructions of African studies for the way foreign researchers position countries such as Rwanda as temporally and spatially distant 'fields' of study for data gathering and collection, and therefore as always other to the 'academy'. Broadly informed by recent decolonizing and Southern epistemologies, it is argued that the ongoing valuation of Western scientific detached, independent inquiry underpins the extractive, subjectifying nature of research that contributes towards epistemic silencing (Ndlovu-Gatsheni, 2018). Similarly, recent scholarship on qualitative research methods has questioned the imbalances in research design, implementation and analysis that originate from colonial research practices, which, it argued, continue to set African countries as field sites for data collection (Mwambari, 2019). In these and other calls, there remains an urgent need to continue to disrupt ideas of the 'field' by finding other methodologies so as to decentre and unsettle the self-referential frames of research that continue to define academic research on Rwanda.

Several precedents exist for developing community-centric methodologies that can enable the types of alternative entry points required for such a task.

For example, through recognition of people and places as legitimate epistemic agents (Radcliffe, 2022: 184), participatory research has long thought to have opened an opportunity to envision transformation in qualitative research methods by prioritizing people's interests and convening people/groups from different backgrounds. As a knowledge merging practice (Godrie et al, 2020), such methodologies allow the researcher to go beyond the conventional boundaries of what and who academic research is for.

Community-centric methods can offer a means of working towards epistemic justice by promoting what de Sousa Santos (2015) calls 'ecologies of knowledges'. This refers to bringing a plurality of knowers together into making contributions towards a careful, collectively owned and humanizing pool of knowledge, that starts from people's lived realities and contexts. Related to this, Fricker's (2007) concept of epistemic injustice holds that enabling communication, credibility and comprehension of the concepts and categories by which a people understand themselves and their world are necessary to realize justice. Validating epistemic materials with the context of a wider community that predominantly encompasses non-academic communities of knowledge users has the potential to disrupt the power structures that prevent participants from making sense of their own experiences (Godrie et al, 2020).

In the community-centric research led by Rwandan researchers, intellectual paradigms and interpretive frames other than the political economies of development form the key knowledge prioritizations around the state's methods of post-genocide reconstruction (see Ndahinda et al, 2022). These include intergenerational dynamics, psycho-social effects, education and everyday peace. Research foregrounding these concerns draw on a diverse range of contextually specific methodologies, such as arts and therapy based ones, to capture, interpret and theorize Rwanda's post-1994 transitions, cognisant of the sensitive, contextualized nature of post-genocide reconstruction efforts and the need for wider benefits. This stance also challenges the prevalent understandings of Rwanda as an object of study because the entry points for developing approaches, research questions and methods are determined by joint understandings and plans for action around those prioritizations.

For us, the entry points to epistemic justice in the Rwandan case involve collaborating to create space for people to have the ability to contribute knowledge in and from their own situated experiences. We concur with Zavala (2013: 57), who argues that '*where* the research grows from and who funds it matters as much as if not more than the kinds of research methods/strategies used or the theoretical frameworks that inform such work' (original emphasis). This requires researchers to build collectively constituted spaces for reciprocity and relationship building. Indeed de Sousa Santos' (2015) ecologies of knowledge approach relies on bringing together people and groups from both within and outside academia, to consolidate values, beliefs and cultures. The spaces in which co-researchers are brought together creates opportunities for surfacing alternative understandings and challenging hegemonic knowledge production. Building positive, generative spaces for research can also potentially balance out power dynamics between researchers and knowledge holders and build the capacity of co-researchers (Radcliffe, 2022). Careful attention to the construction of research spaces therefore has the potential to disrupt the idea of research taking place in a broadly constituted national context, by embedding research in the spaces, places and sites of relevance to local knowledge holders.

However, for research spaces to be understood as sites for dismantling epistemic injustices, it is also important to question their relationality to other sites, since, as Fricker (2017) argues, structural forms of injustice are embedded in practices, networks and relations. Similarly, Thambinathan and Kinsella (2021) understand epistemic justice to be an intersubjective project between different types of researchers and participants differently positioned within contexts, often working in the interstices and/or at the margins of their institutional spaces. In such contexts, community-centred methodologies such as participatory research methods can become superficially collaborative and participatory, eliding and reproducing positions of privilege, often failing to connect to the needs and interests of the communities (Cooke and Kothari, 2001). Therefore, while the use of collaborative and community orientated methodological tools may be considered to be sites for the transformation of structural forms of epistemic injustice, they nonetheless can continue to create harm. Thus it is necessary to consider the ways that a variety of 'knowledge-practices' (Casas-Cortés et al, 2008) occurring across interconnected spaces intersect to produce variegated outcomes towards knowledge pluriversality.

Situating ourselves: background and context to the study

The RDYPP occurred in the context of diverse concepts of what it means to be part of a Rwandan diaspora. Although we use the term diaspora to denote those with real or imagined links to a homeland, there are controversies surrounding the use of this label in the Rwandan case because of complex and contested migratory histories of the more than half a million Rwandese who live outside of Rwanda (European Union Global Diaspora Facility, 2021) and the estimated larger group of (mainly Francophone) settled first and second generation migrants. This latter group is composed of both genocide victims and perpetrators (and their descendants) who fled Rwanda after the 1994 Genocide against the Tutsi and have since acquired nationalities of their eventual countries of settlement. Such diversity has given rise to divided interpretations of Rwanda's political economy and support for the current government and its diaspora engagement policies.

Diaspora engagement is of major importance to the national Rwandese economic development strategy, most recently articulated in the National Strategy for Transformation 2017–2024. The very definition of diaspora as those prepared to contribute to Rwanda promulgated by the Rwandan state has been described as an attempt to elide, simplify and depoliticize these contested histories (Shindo, 2012). Others, such as Kuradusenge-McLeod (2018), argue that these narrow understandings shape the ways that those in diaspora who are critical of government are interpreted by the state, casting them as enemies of Rwanda and being prevented from participating in reconciliation processes. As is the case generally in the research about Rwanda, one can see the ongoing influence of approaches that centre the state and its methods, resulting in a prevailing view that diaspora engagement constitutes a form of governance.

Seeking to respond to the ongoing dominance of the state as the framework through which diaspora engagement efforts are interpreted, the RDYPP was an opportunity to develop a collaborative research process through which young people bound up in these divisions and the organizations that support them could foreground their own experiences of, and feelings about, the Rwandan government's diaspora mobilization efforts. This approach intended to foster dialogue among as many stakeholders as possible, explicitly including the voices of diaspora youth, community organizers and civil society actors in Rwanda, whose voices are commonly filtered through the aforementioned interpretive frameworks.

The authors of this chapter represent multiple positionalities, which are important to acknowledge in relation to the debates about the decolonization of the Rwandan research space. One of the authors (Dickinson) is a white, non-diaspora identifying academic based in the UK, who at the time of research was working in a teaching intensive university. Although she came to the research project with decolonial sensibilities, her privileged position presents certain power and knowledge differences, which as we show in what follows, resulted in discrepancies between the ideals and practices of participatory methodologies. Uwimanzi is a Rwandan researcher with previous experiences as a diaspora youth influenced by both American and British academic spaces and epistemologies. At the time of the research, she was working towards a postgraduate dissertation that was framed in the postcolonial and decolonial debates on academia; and simultaneously leading the Champion Humanity team at Aegis Trust that curated the Rwandan experience for the diasporic youth. Although she shared a similar background with the research participants, she recognized the power dynamics as a source of local knowledge and guidance for both local and diasporic participants, as well as her positionality in regards to the power and knowledge differentials between herself and her fellow researchers.

The project began with an opportunity for the two academics to spend University of Winchester QR allocation on a research project that fulfilled the objectives of the GCRF.[1] As a small teaching-focused institution with only a handful of researchers with some research experience in Overseas Development Assistance (ODA) recipient contexts, academic researchers with such experience were selected to devise projects that met the specific brief of the funding. Seeking to broaden and restructure the power relations of research (Mason, 2015) it was also an opportunity to redistribute the funding in terms of material support to organizations and youth in Rwanda and the UK working towards reconciliation and economic development.

Although broadly conceived by the academic author (Dickinson) as a piece of research on diaspora mobilization, the specificities of the project emerged through sustained professional conversations comprising Dickinson and other colleagues from the University of Winchester and the then chair of National Association of Rwandese Communities in the UK (NARC-UK). NARC-UK is an umbrella organization that co-ordinates the work of Rwandese community groups in the UK, which are active in organizing forums, meetings, dialogues and conferences around topics related to the interests of the Rwandese community abroad. Our work together included talks from the chair of NARC-UK at the university on his experiences as a refugee and the wider legacies in the diaspora; and a youth conference funded by the university exploring diaspora youth psycho-social identity dynamics, the opportunities available in Rwanda and the dilemmas around belonging and community facing young people. It also emerged from these discussions that diaspora youth needed support to contribute to reconstruction and development efforts on their own terms and using their own capacities. Seeking to respond to such concerns, the GCRF funding was an opportunity to develop a collaborative research process through which young people could develop understandings of how to contribute through practical experiences of learning from and with other young people and civil society actors in Rwanda about how to construct, design and implement small-scale interventions that addressed the material legacies of the 1994 Genocide against the Tutsi.

From these initial conversations emerged a project that would support the aspirations of the young people at the conference and fulfil the GCRF brief. The chair of NARC-UK and academic researchers designed the core of the methodology as a 10-day field visit to Rwanda with diaspora youth from the UK to collectively participate in social learning about participating in Rwanda's reconstruction efforts with academics, community members, and other youth and civil society actors in Rwanda. The intended outcomes were for participants to jointly develop micro-initiatives that diaspora youth could contribute to, work on and develop once they had returned to the UK. Building on traditions of both participant-led, place-based methods in geography (see Radcliffe, 2022), our approach concerned reconfiguring the power relations necessary for epistemic justice by locating the project in the contexts of both young diasporans' everyday lives and Rwandan youths' own concerns and agendas.

Participation in the project was approached in an epistemic justice sense as a means of recognizing the emotional and intellectual capacities of diaspora and Rwandese youth and the organizations that support them to contribute relevant lived experiences, ideas and situated expertise to engaging with Rwanda's development efforts. For example, early on in the project, overarching research questions were formulated on the basis of the youth conference, which contributed to the creation and design of learning activities and spaces on the field trip. Later in the project, the ten diaspora youth selected by application process to participate (described later in this chapter) and five youth selected by Aegis Trust contributed to research with families/communities prior to the visit, leading to the refinement of learning activities.

The role of the university researchers during the field visit was to facilitate the collaborative constitution of different research sites by bringing relevant stakeholders together at different sites around Kigali. The university researchers acted on recommendations for content and structure of the co-learning activities decided by diaspora youth and organizations in Rwanda and the UK, and offered practical guidance around what they wanted to learn and act upon as well as how to engage with Rwanda as members of diaspora. University researchers also documented meetings through audio recording when permission was given, which formed the basis of the data set that the researchers analysed, using a thematic analysis approach (Braun and Clarke, 2022). Further data came from observational notes taking in different kinds of learning spaces, where diaspora youth were learning and reflecting with community organizers and other youth in Rwanda on strategies for engaging with development, peace and reconstruction efforts. These spaces included formally convened ones such as workshops, lessons, museum visits, visits to field sites and government departments and online meetings, as well as informal spaces such as dinner and socializing. Participants were also encouraged to keep written and reflective diaries to assist them with their micro-initiatives, although these were not expected to be shared with university researchers. Ethical approval was granted by universities prior to commencing the project, and a research permit secured by Aegis Trust. Consent was sought at different points in the data collection, according to the specific context and nature of the spaces in which discussions were taking place.

Developing collaborative spaces for siting, humanizing and action

To develop a research programme that disrupted the idea of Rwanda as a distanced field within which knowledge gains legitimacy through pre-existing interpretive frameworks, it was important to develop a methodology and set of working practices that created spaces to, in de Sousa Santos's (2018: 2–3) words, expose more unequivocally 'modes of being otherwise, those of the oppressed and silenced peoples, peoples that have been radically excluded from the dominant modes of being and knowing'. In what follows, we explain how engaging with key principles of epistemic justice guided the co-curation of different formal and informal learning spaces during the research project.

Multi-situated inquiry

In epistemic justice approaches, the starting point for academics is rooting research in the communities where we work. For Ndlovu-Gatsheni (2018: 3), such a project is necessary to epistemic freedom as 'the right to think, theorise, interpret the world, develop own methodologies and write from where one is located'. Through two working practices, the RDYPP aimed to create spaces in which diaspora youth participants could pursue their own questions and contribute knowledge in the context of their multi-sited positionalities. The first working practice was to select a partner organization in Rwanda to collaborate with in designing the field visit, whom the academics gave full control to define what the learning experiences about Rwanda's histories of conflict and post-conflict reconstruction looked like. The RDYPP project began as a research project interested in diaspora youth mobilization and engagement in post-conflict reconstruction, with the academic researchers' own interest and questions initially broadly defined by fairly narrow concepts of economic development based on the GCRF brief. As the project evolved from the discussions with NARC-UK and at the youth conference, it unearthed the importance of the intergenerational silences, legacies and gaps around the 1994 Genocide against the Tutsi that affected young people's engagements with Rwandan reconstruction efforts. Therefore, a partner organization was sought based on the criteria of it having been involved in mobilizing citizens for development work in the context of working with the legacies of the 1994 genocide. Aegis Trust was contacted because it already offered established peace-education programmes for international visitors, and provided speciality long-term support for peace initiatives via Champion Humanity, its existing peer mentoring programme.

Although researchers and NARC-UK chair had pre-existing questions and objectives, Aegis Trust had considerable influence in shaping the final content, in ways that were not anticipated to the academic researchers prior to visiting Rwanda with the diaspora youth. In the context of Rwanda, becoming active citizens is rooted in and deeply shaped by an overarching goal of social cohesion, as a legacy of the colonially imposed ethnic categories that underpinned the 1994 genocide. Government efforts towards social cohesion have been widely critiqued by the Western academic literature as a form of control and repression aimed at reinforcing the ruling Rwanda Patriotic Front's power (for example, Purdeková, 2015) even though several academics highlight the limited methodological entry points on which such analyses are frequently based (Harrison, 2017; Chemouni and Mugiraneza, 2020). What became clear over the course of the discussions was that social cohesion was most important to diaspora young people's engagements with Rwanda, based on their own familial histories of exile and displacement, and experiences of ethnic divisions in their communities. Reflecting with the diaspora youth and community members, it became apparent that such histories had facilitated their potential growth into making a contribution towards reconstruction and development. These themes emerged from the creation of space for participants to research diaspora community issues and concerns prior to the trip, and to discuss, learn and debate with other young people in Rwanda the motivations and ideas for micro-initiatives.

The second working practice was to ensure that content of the field visit was tailored to the diaspora youth's specific interests and experiences, to enable us to find answers to the questions they deemed relevant. With the assistance of the chair and youth committee of NARC-UK, an advertisement for youth to join a paid-for trip to Rwanda to participate was distributed, with participants invited to complete an application form. Application questions included prior relationship to Rwanda, voluntary work undertaken either within Rwandan diaspora community settings or in other contexts, motivations for participation and what key development issues and challenges they had an interest in and why. Convenors of the trip comprising two academic researchers and the chair of NARC-UK received 18 applications, and of those ten were identified with strong motivations for participation. Given constraints around the time-bound nature of GCRF funding, where initiative building with youth in Rwanda needed to be completed within nine months, those with concrete, implementable ideas and strong motivations factored into the decision making.

Guided by collaborative research principles, we aimed to enable participants to bring to the field visit existing knowledge and experience formulated within a context of diaspora community sites, such as the home, and spaces where community convened. Following pre-departure workshops in Reading (UK), which were designed around specific prompts and questions for participants around action-based initiatives, participants were encouraged to conduct research with families and communities to learn more about the issues and concerns that mattered to the community. Diaspora participants' interests were treated as an opportunity to take young people's contextual knowledges and experiences seriously in designing the learning activities. From workshop reflections and application forms, the learning activities on the field visit were tweaked to include different topics they were interested in. Key persons working in those sectors were invited to design learning activities.

Humanizing knowledge

One of the key aspects of making space for epistemic diversity in scholarly practice is to centre and restore human notions of self, other and community, as a counterpoint to Eurocentric knowledge traditions that compound inferiorization and dehumanization (Suffla and Seedat, 2021). Although usually applied to the context of higher education curriculum development (for example, Zembylas, 2018) humanization is also a practice central to community-centred, collective research processes because it can promote critical reflection on historical realities and processes of epistemic injustices, therefore rupturing the silences that contribute to ongoing oppression. Conceptualized as a Freirean-based set of engagements between researchers and participants around problem-posing, this individual and collective process of critical reflection according to Leivas Vargas et al (2020) allows the recovery of the subjectivity of people's knowledge and experiences.

The pedagogical techniques developed by Aegis Trust's Champion Humanity education programme uses the backdrop of the historical background and the rebuilding/reconciliation journey of Rwanda in the aftermath of the 1994 Genocide against the Tutsi to build peaceful societies and the prevention of mass atrocities in Rwanda and elsewhere (Gasanabo et al, 2016). This history, and the techniques used to teach it, was considered vital to establish the relevance of diaspora youth engagement to young people's contexts. Covering a range of topics around the continuum of violence/pathways of inhumanity (Staub, 2006), learning activities progressed through increasingly interactive engagements with understanding the origins of ethnic based violence through analysing primarily the 1994 Genocide against the Tutsi; social reconstruction after human rights violations; and forgiveness as a mode of community and personal healing. Participants were enabled to consider not only the historical facts that led to the atrocities but also look at the human perspectives through testimonies of survivors and perpetrators of the genocide. Aegis Trust further provided the context for diaspora youth participants to analyse their own intercultural links, and their transferability to their lives.

Grounded in a contextualizing, dialogue-based and humanizing approach to supporting youth to orientate themselves to Rwanda's history and peace-building models, the method of content delivery developed by Aegis Trust was purposefully designed to enable the learner to recognize and explain the troubled knowledge and other concepts like reconciliation and social cohesion through engaging with other individuals who may have different perspectives (*savoir apprendre*), to reflect and empathize with the 'other' through the storytelling of difficult yet inspiring knowledge (*savoir s'engager*), to self-reflect and interculturally engage with different culturally charged scenarios through methodologies such as role-playing, active listening and sharing (*savoir etre*) and sharing of one's thoughts, emotions and perspectives through discussion forums or journaling (*savoir comprendre*). Through such interactions diaspora youth were inspired to reflect both cognitively and affectively on their own capabilities necessary to engage discussions and dialogue between stakeholders from different backgrounds, and with different positions of power.

The techniques also provided a space for Rwandan youth from the diaspora to engage in conversation with one another and with local youth, their local instructors and officials as well as the researchers they had travelled with, critically reflecting upon and potentially inspired to act on issues in their own lives and communities both in the UK and Rwanda; issues similar to those discussed during the programme such as the prevention of violence, social justice (for example, institutionalized racism, racial marginalization) and healing from violence. As one diaspora youth participant (interview, 19 July 2021) explained, such techniques equipped her with knowledge to understand her own community, affirm herself and reach understanding about the GoR's direction and choices in the context of discussions, debates and conversations within her family, a point intentionally contrasted with outsider perspectives.

Creating spaces for action

Action is a key component of achieving epistemic justice because the process of putting into practice the knowledge generated by shared/collective reasoning enhances participants' recognition of both self and others as beings with knowledge and experiences able to overcome social and environmental problems at local and global levels (Leivas Vargas et al, 2020). Operationalizing such an approach to epistemic justice meant building spaces for diaspora participants to reflect together with other Rwandese youth on the lasting economic and social legacies of the oppressions underpinning the Genocide against the Tutsi, to discuss what practical actions they had in mind to address those, and to find how they might work together to devise such an initiative.

The academic researchers did not pre-define what these initiatives would look like nor did they provide pre-scripted competency-building steps to realize these initiatives; rather, the academic researchers together with Aegis Trust built spaces for participants to identify issues of importance for each group and develop their own set of operations to achieve the goal, as a fundamental aspect of enabling participants to amplify their creative power to develop actions that reflected community concerns and knowledge. This dimension of participatory action research can make it an empowering methodology, because it involves iterative cycles of analysis-refection-action that can build self-critical investigation and analysis of participants' own reality (Gaventa and Cornwall, 2008).

This was operationalized in two ways. The first was building spaces during the field visit in which participants were provided with open-ended prompts at the end of the day's learning activities to review what they had learnt about the histories of the 1994 Genocide against the Tutsi, the steps taken towards reconciliation and ongoing legacies, and what collective and/or individual actions could be taken to address them. The second was to build spaces that could maintain the connections, collaboration, community, trust, solidarity and reciprocity that had been built when participants returned to the UK. This involved the use of digital tools such as WhatsApp and Instagram, alongside regular scheduled Zoom meetings.

The role of the academic researchers was to provide assistance to implementation of the initiatives, which ranged from sharing knowledge of educational methods, provision of materials, responding to practical questions and leveraging contacts and networks. For the academic researchers, this was designed as a method of connecting with the realities of diaspora participants, orientated towards understanding, analysing and solving the obstacles and problems they faced. Researchers were cautious, not steering or directing but ensuring views were aired, helping think though practicalities. The back and forth refection facilitated by action research revealed the barriers and challenges young people faced, underlining the continuing importance of young people's lifecourse, stages and contexts that gave shape to engagements with Rwanda, and the importance attached to young people's contexts, motivations and aspirations rather than conceiving of them as subjects to state agendas. We believe that creating such spaces makes it possible to locate research in young people's own contexts and contribute to a process of knowledge production that is formulated, deliberated and reconstructed from different contexts, cultures and processes.

Remaking the field: reflections on power relations, silence and tensions

While our practices of co-creating learning spaces, as already laid out, provided a set of tools for pluralizing epistemic contributions to knowledge production on Rwanda and elsewhere, the oppressive structures and systems embedded in academic spaces can perpetuate ongoing epistemicide (Hall and Tandon, 2017). In particular, researchers working within academic institutions in the Global North must meet project completion deadlines and academic publishing expectations, exerting practical pressures upon commitments to the praxis of epistemic justice (Perry et al, 2022). Here, we describe the academic researchers' navigation of such dynamics, providing examples of how they generate the need for compromises around epistemic justice, especially in the context of the fraught academic and political dynamics around Rwanda and the Rwandan diaspora. In so doing, we highlight the messy processes and inherent exclusions that permeate collaborative knowledge generation.

The research was funded by the University of Winchester's yearly GCRF QR allocation. The GCRF was part of the UK's ODA funding mechanism, and has been described by Noxolo (2017) as colonizing, since both individual researcher success in obtaining the funding and institutions continuing to receive their allocation was dependent on the identification of, and creation of solutions to, what were narrowly deemed 'challenges'. Although its requirements make it clear that funders expected convincing strategies for meaningful and equitable research relationships with partners and participants, the funding's framing and implementation places several institutional constraints on creating spaces for equitable collaboration, research and building partnerships. Reflecting on the GCRF in the context of refugee research, Shuayb and Brun (2021) identify these as competition, rapid turnover, limited funding and short proposal deadlines. Such conditions not only limit the ability of scholarly practice to dismantle the epistemic authority of Northern institutions but can in fact succumb to what Tuck and Yang (2012) term the 'moves to innocence' that both obscures and fails to challenge colonial complicities.

This context shaped our personal and professional motivations, roles and structural locations in the project, and the points of comprise that arose as a result. Jen Dickinson, an outsider to the community negotiating academic career trajectories and project deadlines, was dependent from the outset upon a handful of gatekeepers associated with the networks of Rwandese Community Associations in the UK. She had not negotiated the long-term trust building required to cast a wide net of participants, in content of a diaspora community comprising both supporters and opponents of the current government, as well as genocide victims, perpetrators and their families, who all have different degrees of engagement with each other and with Rwanda. This was fundamental in limiting the scope for including a diverse array of contributors since the application form was disseminated through the community WhatsApp groups, email and word-of-mouth connections of the initial gatekeepers. The academic researchers and community representatives selected the participants on basis of motivation and interest expressed on application forms, to maximize participation and success of the research project in the context of GCRF parameters, further limiting inclusion. In Fricker's terms, this created a gap in the 'collective interpretive resources', gaps that can 'put someone at a disadvantage in making sense of their own experience' (2007: 1). In the case of our project, limiting the incorporation of a diverse array of epistemic engagements, materials and contributions was a failure of acknowledgement of diaspora youths' wider corpus of knowledge about the tensions and divisions within the communities, thus harbouring potential for entrenching epistemic oppression.

Jen Dickinson's dependency on gatekeepers in the community also minimized the participative and open communication necessary for epistemic justice. The anxiety-inducing debate in the research literature around the hostile treatment of foreign researchers resulted in Jen's silences with the group around the political critiques of the government taking place across Rwanda's diasporic spaces (Kok and Rogers, 2019; Martin, 2019; Orjuela, 2020). The problem-solving requirement of GCRF meant that the deeper important discussions and trust-building that were necessary to surface these conversations became subsumed within the necessity of using the time to plan projects and initiatives. Instead, such conversations arose in the interstices and incidental conversations between formally convened spaces for deliberation during field visits, as well as in follow-up interviews with diaspora participants. This acts against epistemic justice because such silences suppress the knowledge and thoughts young people both in Rwanda and the diaspora come across in their communities, and were unable to critically reflect upon, debate and discuss these except in limited moments.

This scenario causes us to reflect upon the other tensions around knowledge sharing and dialogue in the project. For Natasha Uwimanzi, curating the project in a way that sensitized the Rwandan participants from the UK diaspora to the historical complexities around the genocide was frustrated by the lack of time in the programme. A key point in Aegis Trust's genocide education model is presenting stories of survivors and perpetrators in a way that allows participants sufficient time for exposure to the background beforehand and leaving time after to make sense of what they had heard, as a means of avoiding divisive discussions. Yet Natasha felt that the busy nature of the schedule left inadequate time for the young people to process the stories and limited dialogue with them.

We also felt that creating the means for equitable opportunities to participate was comprised by the design of the project's follow-up stage, where participants would be working in groups to implement their initiatives. The technology retaining the connection between those youth participants based in the UK and those in Rwanda following completion of the field visits (Zoom and WhatsApp) did offer an alternative forms of presence. Yet as Nadeau et al (2022) also observes in the use of such technologies, these can offer limited depth and perspective, raising questions about what should be considered 'a good enough space to ensure participants are able to voice and listen in a comfortable dialogue' within community-centric research (Nadeau et al, 2022: 11). Concerns about the limited quality of online spaces were mirrored by diaspora youth participants in follow-up interviews on their experiences. Observations of online meetings also raised the issues of equitable internet access and digital connectivity, which several of the young people also highlighted as placing Rwandese youth participations at a disadvantage.

Following the completion of the visit and the follow-up initiatives, we had hoped to develop the analysis in partnership with young people, in accordance with their interpretations and the participatory ethic guiding the research. As the grant was mainly spent on the visit to Rwanda and the preceding workshops, we lacked funds to pay for additional community and collaborator time. This was combined with pressures around the prioritization of teaching quality and student satisfaction, generating institutional barriers for us to create spaces for our research to be truly community-centric beyond our collaboration with Aegis Trust and NARC-UK in its design, objective-setting and co-analysis. This placed pressures on our ability to open up spaces for the highly needed rebalancing of power between researchers and community partners. COVID-19 exacerbated these barriers in several ways. The delayed implementations of the young people's projects focused our remaining energies on assisting young people with seeing the outcomes of their preparatory work on their initiatives. Although driven by an ethical commitment to enabling young people to use the initiatives to make the changes they wished to see, meeting institutional deadlines for measurable outcomes also remained a strong motivator for choosing to continue to focus on practicalities rather than analysis and writing. Two years on from the field visit, despite our avowed philosophy of embedding scholarly practice within transformations towards epistemic justice, our practical engagements with diaspora youth, community members and co-collaborators remain those of the conventional knowledge production: academic researchers as the knowers, theorizers and writers; and participants the data collectors and providers.

Conclusions

This chapter has put forward an analysis of the ways in which the participatory methodology of the RDYPP, built on the creation of spaces to collaborate in the creation of knowledge, is a scholarly practice aimed at resistance to the polarized hegemonic analysis of the Rwandan state and its methods. This for us is the foundation of epistemic justice because in several ways we were able to support the incorporation and valuation of participants' voices and perspectives on Rwanda's diaspora mobilization efforts within the contexts of both diaspora youths' lived, multi-sited experiences, interests and concerns. Decentring academic researcher concerns through the social learning methodology supported the development of research interactions that promoted multiple points of co-inquiry into Rwanda's genocide and peace-building histories, as an opening for diaspora youth to engage in a creative, generative process of knowing their own worlds; and to engage in solidarity with other youth, their own community, educators and government actors across different sites in the UK and Rwanda to find answers and solutions to their questions and concerns. For the academic researchers, curating learning and researching spaces together with diaspora youth and other stakeholders created opportunities to position ourselves alongside multiple knowledge holders as learners, to connect with their concerns and needs, and continue to collaborate around producing collective understandings of diaspora youths' social worlds.

Our chapter also showed that academics situated in neoliberal university spaces traverse academic careers and institutional pressures in ways that undermine commitments to epistemic justice. Reflecting on our methodology, such contexts generated compromises around the pluriversal and deliberative processes necessary. While we were able to create spaces that acted as partial entry points to the production of context-specific knowledge, their transformative potential was occluded by the pervasive effects of researching in neoliberal Northern institutional spaces. Therefore we find that Thambinathan and Kinsella's (2021) emphasis on nuanced thinking about the intersubjective and interconnected nature of the spaces created for research has much to offer in rethinking what other sites need to be thought of as enrolled in knowledge production about Rwanda, in the vein of wider feminist and decolonial theorizations of 'the field' in geography (Barker and Pickerill, 2020; Radcliffe and Radhuber, 2020).

Compared to existing approaches that approach Rwanda as a bounded object of study, seemingly geographically distant from where foreign researchers are, the challenge, following Ndahinda et al (2022), is to centre Rwanda-led and Rwanda-based scholarship, and find ways to overcome the systemic biases that exclude them from the academic research practices discourse. This requires not only addressing citational politics and locations from which we think, but as Daley and Murrey (2022) so clearly argue, the material actions taken towards addressing the racialized conditions of institutional spaces of the Global North that includes what and how we teach. The significant point here is that while academic researchers in the Global North can find methodological entry points that centre Rwandan knowledge, they are nonetheless part of a privileged group, benefiting from the continued epistemic injustices that cannot be disentangled from the institutional spaces they are a part of.

Following these principles implies rethinking the Rwandan research space not as a distant field constituted by university researchers for data extraction, but as a network of connected points where differently positioned knowledge holders commit to working together and communicate with one another. This is important to the kinds of emergent praxis at the intersection of participatory research and decolonial research because it requires researchers to think through how such points of connection are made, to what other sites they are connected, and how they shape the extent to which epistemic justice is made possible. This chapter developed these leads by reflecting on the ways thinking of sites as connected can help to engage in a critical but also generative process of collective working. Specifically, the collaborative constituted pedagogical spaces developed through RDYPP offers insights into these intersubjective dynamics of learning and un-learning, demonstrating ways that as researchers we might work towards valuing and appreciating Rwandan knowledge in the contexts where it appears. Recognizing that building collective knowledge about Rwanda cannot undo colonialities, however, we find that centring reflexive, generative and relational forms of enquiry are vital for disrupting the pre-existing frameworks that contribute to epistemic injustices in neoliberal spaces of higher education and research.

Note

[1] The GCRF was a £1.5 billion fund that forms part of the UK's Official Development Assistance (ODA) commitment to address the Sustainable Development Goals 2015, promote the economic development and welfare of developing countries, and fulfil capacity building in ODA countries. The GCRF was administered by a number of delivery mechanisms, including QR allocations to individual institutions, which managed these funds internally for the purpose of pump-priming new international collaborations.

References

Barker, A.J. and Pickerill, J. (2020) Doings with the land and sea: decolonising geographies, indigeneity, and enacting place-agency, *Progress in Human Geography*, 44(4): 640–662.

Booth, D. and Golooba-Mutebi, F. (2012) Developmental patrimonialism? The case of Rwanda, *African Affairs*, 111(444): 379–403.

Braun, V. and Clarke, V. (2022) *Thematic Analysis: A Practical Guide*, London and Thousand Oaks: SAGE.

Casas-Cortés, M.I., Osterweil, M. and Powell, D.E. (2008) Blurring boundaries: recognizing knowledge-practices in the study of social movements, *Anthropological Quarterly*, 81(1): 17–58.

Chemouni, B. (2020) Introduction to the issue: the debated research on the Rwandan state, *Politique africaine*, 4: 7–34.

Chemouni, B. and Mugiraneza, A. (2020) Ideology and interests in the Rwandan patriotic front: singing the struggle in pre-genocide Rwanda, *African Affairs*, 119(474): 115–140.

Cooke, B. and Kothari, U. (2001) *Participation: The New Tyranny?* London: Zed Books.

Daley, P.O. and Murrey, A. (2022) Defiant scholarship: dismantling coloniality in contemporary African geographies, *Singapore Journal of Tropical Geography*, 43(2): 159–176.

De Sousa Santos, B. (2015) *Epistemologies of the South: Justice against Epistemicide*, New York: Routledge.

De Sousa Santos, B. (2018) *The End of the Cognitive Empire: The Coming of Age of Epistemologies of the South*, Durham, NC: Duke University Press.

Esson, J., Noxolo, P., Baxter, R., Daley, P. and Byron, M. (2017) The 2017 RGS-IBG chair's theme: decolonising geographical knowledges, or reproducing coloniality?, *Area*, 49(3): 384–388.

European Union Global Diaspora Facility (2021) *Diaspora Engagement Mapping: Rwanda*, https://diasporafordevelopment.eu/wp-content/uploads/2021/10/CF_Rwanda-v.5.pdf

Fisher, J. (2015) Writing about Rwanda since the genocide: knowledge, power and 'truth', *Journal of Intervention and Statebuilding*, 9(1): 134–145.

Fricker, M. (2007) *Epistemic Injustice: Power and the Ethics of Knowing*, Oxford: Oxford University Press.

Fricker, M. (2017) Evolving concepts of epistemic injustice, in I. J. Kidd, J. Medina and G. Pohlhaus (eds) *The Routledge Handbook of Epistemic Injustice*, London: Routledge, pp 53–60.

Gasanabo, J.-D., Mutanguha, F. and Mpayimana, A. (2016) Teaching about the Holocaust and genocide in Rwanda, *Contemporary Review of the Middle East*, 3(3): 329–345.

Gaventa, J. and Cornwall, A. (2008) Power and knowledge, in P. Reason and H. Bradbury (eds) *The SAGE Handbook of Action Research: Participative Inquiry and Practice*, 2nd edn, London and Thousand Oaks: SAGE, pp 172–189.

Godrie, B., Boucher, M., Bissonnette, S., Chaput, P., Flores, J., Dupéré, S., et al (2020) Epistemic injustices and participatory research: a research agenda at the crossroads of university and community, *Gateways: International Journal of Community Research and Engagement*, 13(1): 1–15.

Hall, B.L. and Tandon, R. (2017) Decolonization of knowledge, epistemicide, participatory research and higher education, *Research for All*, 1(1): 6–19.

Harrison, G. (2017) Rwanda and the difficult business of capitalist development, *Development and Change*, 48(5): 873–898.

Hintjens, H. (2014) 'As if there were two Rwandas': polarised research agendas in post-genocide Rwanda, in H. Hintjens and D. Zarkov (eds) *Conflict, Peace, Security and Development*, Abingdon: Routledge, pp 145–161.

Kok, S. and Rogers, R. (2019) Social media and Rwandan migration: a moral epistemology of return, in Mitchell, K., Jones, R. and Fluri, J. (eds) *Handbook on Critical Geographies of Migration*, Cheltenham: Edward Elgar, pp 327–343.

Kuradusenge-McLeod, C. (2018) Belgian Hutu diaspora narratives of victimhood and trauma, *International Journal of Transitional Justice*, 12(3): 427–443.

Leivas Vargas, M., Fernández-Baldor, A., Maicas-Pérez, M. and Calabuig-Tormo, C. (2020) A Freirean approach to epistemic justice: contributions of action learning to capabilities for epistemic liberation, in M. Walker and A. Boni (eds) *Participatory Research, Capabilities and Epistemic Justice: A Transformative Agenda for Higher Education*, Cham: Springer International Publishing, pp 89–113.

Loyle, C.E. (2016) Overcoming research obstacles in hybrid regimes: lessons from Rwanda, *Social Science Quarterly*, 97(4): 923–935.

Martin, M. (2019) Rwandan diaspora online: social connections and identity narratives, *Crossings: Journal of Migration & Culture*, 10(2): 223–241.

Mason, K. (2015) Participatory action research: coproduction, governance and care, *Geography Compass*, 9(9): 497–507.

Mwambari, D. (2019) Local positionality in the production of knowledge in northern Uganda, *International Journal of Qualitative Methods*, 18: 1609406919864845. https://doi.org/10.1177/1609406919864845

Nadeau, L., Gaulin, D., Johnson-Lafleur, J., Levesque, C. and Fraser, S. (2022) The challenges of decolonising participatory research in indigenous contexts: the Atautsikut community of practice experience in Nunavik, *International Journal of Circumpolar Health*, 81(1): 2087846. https://doi.org/10.1080/22423982.2022.2087846

Ndahinda, F.M., Mosley, J., Palmer, N., Clark, P. and Shenge, S. (2022) Rwandan researchers are finally being centred in scholarship about their own country, *The Conversation*, http://theconversation.com/rwandan-researchers-are-finally-being-centred-in-scholarship-about-their-own-country-183142

Ndlovu-Gatsheni, S.J. (2018) *Epistemic Freedom in Africa: Deprovincialization and Decolonization*, Abingdon: Routledge.

Nhemachena, A., Mlambo, N. and Kaundjua, M. (2016) The notion of the "field" and the practices of researching and writing Africa: towards decolonial praxis, *Africology: The Journal of Pan African Studies*, 9(7): 15–36.

Noxolo, P. (2017) Decolonial theory in a time of the re-colonisation of UK research, *Transactions of the Institute of British Geographers*, 42(3): 342–344.

Ogone, J.O. (2017) Epistemic injustice: African knowledge and scholarship in the global context, in Bartels, A., L. Eckstein, N. Waller and D. Wiemann (eds) *Postcolonial Justice*, Leiden: Brill, pp 17–36.

Orjuela, C. (2020) Passing on the torch of memory: transitional justice and the transfer of diaspora identity across generations, *International Journal of Transitional Justice*, 14(2): 360–380.

Park, S. and Shema, C. (2019) Preparing for research abroad: fieldwork requirements in Rwanda, *Field Research Methods Lab*, 26 November, https://blogs.lse.ac.uk/fieldresearch/2019/11/26/preparing-for-research-abroad-fieldwork-requirements-in-rwanda/

Perry, M., Sharp, J., Aanyu, K., Robinson, J., Duclos, V. and Ferdous, R. (2022) Research partnerships across international contexts: a practice of unity or plurality?, *Development in Practice*, 32(5): 635–646.

Purdeková, A. (2015) *Making Ubumwe: Power, State and Camps in Rwanda's Unity-Building Project*, New York: Berghahn Books.

Radcliffe, S.A. (2022) *Decolonizing Geography: An Introduction*, Hoboken, NJ: John Wiley & Sons.

Radcliffe, S.A. and Radhuber, I.M. (2020) The political geographies of D/decolonization: variegation and decolonial challenges of /in geography, *Political Geography*, 78 : 102128. https://doi.org/10.1016/j.polgeo.2019.102128

Rutazibwa, O.U. (2014) Studying Agaciro: moving beyond Wilsonian interventionist knowledge production on Rwanda, *Journal of Intervention and Statebuilding*, 8(4): 291–302.

Shindo, R. (2012) The hidden effect of diaspora return to post-conflict countries: the case of policy and temporary return to Rwanda, *Third World Quarterly*, 33(9): 1685–1702.

Shuayb, M. and Brun, C. (2021) Carving out space for equitable collaborative research in protracted displacement, *Journal of Refugee Studies*, 34(3): 2539–2553.

Staub, E. (2006) *The Roots of Evil: The Origins of Genocide and Other Group Violence*, Cambridge: Cambridge University Press.

Suffla, S. and Seedat, M. (2021) Africa's knowledge archives, black consciousness and reimagining community psychology, in Stevens, G. and Sonn, C.C. (eds) *Decoloniality and Epistemic Justice in Contemporary Community Psychology*, Cham: Springer International Publishing, pp 21–38.

Thambinathan, V. and Kinsella, E.A. (2021) Decolonizing methodologies in qualitative research: creating spaces for transformative praxis, *International Journal of Qualitative Methods*, 20: 16094069211014766. https://doi.org/10.1177/16094069211014766

Tuck, E. and Yang, K.W. (2012) Decolonization is not a metaphor, *Decolonization: Indigeneity, Education & Society*, 1(1): 1–40.

Zavala, M. (2013) What do we mean by decolonizing research strategies? Lessons from decolonizing, Indigenous research projects in New Zealand and Latin America, *Decolonization: Indigeneity, Education & Society*, 9(7): 55–71.

Zembylas, M. (2018) Decolonial possibilities in South African higher education: reconfiguring humanising pedagogies as/with decolonising pedagogies, *South African Journal of Education*, 38(4): 1–11.

6

Researching Justice: Justice as Accountability and Justice as Collaboration

Jennifer Balint

How do academics know what justice means? You need to ask. And sometimes, you need to experience injustice. This is probably my main takeaway from a few decades of researching state crime. I come to this from my own lived experience, as the granddaughter of Holocaust survivors. I know this has always fueled me and my work. My father's parents were Jewish refugees from Budapest, and my mother's parents were Jewish refugees from Vienna. While this meant that we had excellent cake growing up, it also meant that there were many absences, silences and griefs. What to do when graves exist on the other side of the world, or there are no graves, just names of those taken. When close family members are murdered. When they experience isolation and discrimination in their new country. This is not unique to me or my family, or the Jewish community. But I do know that it is the reason I do what I do. I also know that because the state crime of the Holocaust has been acknowledged, and made visible, this makes a difference. There are many state crimes, past and ongoing, which have not been. Like many people, justice, and injustice, has always had an immediacy to me. How justice can be understood, and achieved, and its different meanings and shapes, is something I carry with me, and that shapes and is central to my research and work practices.

   I grew up bordering the bush of Garigal country of the Eora Nation in Sydney. I now live and work on Wurundjeri land in Naarm/Melbourne, and did my PhD on Nunnawor land in Canberra. The importance of the land on which I grew up, and the land I live and work on now, have become more evident to me in recent years. Growing up though, and through much of my earlier academic life, it was the land of East-Central Europe, that land my family had been forced to leave, and that was and continues to be a site of injustice, that was my centre. This is starting to shift.

I work in criminology, as a socio-legal scholar, in a school of social sciences, interested in the role of law in supporting, resisting and mediating justice. I work on making state crime, and structural injustice, visible and accountable. I am interested in what it means to do justice, what are the barriers to justice, what does accountability look like, and who might academics partner with in thinking through these questions. Most importantly, I am interested in what justice means to those who experience injustice.

My work has been focused on state crime, genocide and accountability. I have always been focused on the state and its institutions – and the accountability these hold for injustice, in particular state crime. My work has shifted from understanding the role that formal law plays in enabling justice, and making visible injustice – for example through courts, tribunals, truth commissions, legislation – to examining the broader informal spaces, as used and developed by communities, that may enable justice, that can include theatre and walking tours, for example, and can also be understood as means of informal or 'living law'. My collaborative work has developed this as thinking about it as a structural justice – a justice that pays attention to long-standing structures of oppression and discrimination – and about the role of peoples, institutions and states in this.

As a current Head of School, my everyday work as an academic, that occupies much of my time, is in figuring out how can I create just spaces for staff and students. How can I create a space in which all can flourish? What are the inequities, that may be hidden for some, but clear to those who experience them, that stop this? How can this be addressed? How can the university as a large and colonial institution be a space that is just and that enables just work? For many, it is not. I draw here too on my collaborative work – how can we 'keep hold' of justice? (Balint et al, 2020). When structures are unjust, how can we hold justice in sight? This also comes from my lived experiences in the institution. I am also learning every day: what I understand and have experienced as a harm may be different to someone else – listening to understand this is critical.

Justice plays a central role in determining what and why I research. And more recently, the methodologies I use. Central to my work – as a researcher and an academic leader – is that understanding the claims made, listening to people's stories and testimonies, can show clearly what the harms are. They can also show what a solution may be. My work is interested in how these sites of justice are generated – both inside and outside law. I have been interested in how justice claims – the claims of injustice that are put forward, and the alternate pathways also put forward – are made at and to particular sites and at particular times. For me, this is about making injustice visible.

Justice is a central component of all my research – what it means, how it could be attained, what it requires. What has become increasingly important in my work is who needs to be part of this conversation. Partnership in addressing these questions has become central to how I work, and how I set up any projects. I see partnership as a means of creating justice – through opening up the institution and resources of the university as public space. Making visible injustice – publicly – also becomes the justice of accountability. Accountability requires visibility. These three components – justice as accountability, justice as collaboration and justice as visibility through public spaces – are what I reflect on in this chapter.

Justice as collaboration

This is an ethical point – taking a justice perspective to research and research practice means I cannot do research without partnership. This is integral to doing research justly – what the process of research as respectful relationship requires (and here also see Boulet, 2018) – and in particular, how designing ways of having public conversations towards just outcomes, is central.

This understanding of justice, as a means of being 'in relation', is something I have learned through my work. That 'coming into relation, as a method of pursuing structural justice' (Balint et al, 2020: 134) is an ethical responsibility as well as a methodology:

> As an ethical point, it cannot be abstracted—we must practice it, through coming into relation and being exposed to new vantage points. This can be challenging and uncomfortable but can also be a method through which it becomes possible to see that there is the capacity to interact justly still. (Balint et al, 2020: 134)

Justice plays a significant role in shaping my research and my research practices. I do not have all the answers, and I am also constantly learning from those I partner with. Thinking about what we each bring, and what we can co-create. This is what I see a justice perspective brings over other theoretical frameworks. I have always taken an approach to research that it's the problem that drives the research, not the theoretical framework. Otherwise, we are playing with words and playing with concepts. A justice perspective is the rationale for the research, I believe. Maybe this comes from my Jewish heritage – 'Justice, justice shall you pursue' (Deuteronomy 16: 20). Justice is, however, necessarily relational. My justice cannot result in another's injustice.

I have become interested in how we may understand this approach as a community-engaged methodology of justice. Research methodologies are increasingly framed as 'co-production' or 'community-engaged research' or 'participatory action research' (de Sousa Santos, 2014; Bunting, 2015; Houh and Kalsem, 2015; Vaughan et al, 2016; 2019; 2020; Rowell and Hong, 2017; Kalsem, 2019). What about if we use a justice lens? If we ask 'what counts as justice' for communities, as integral to the research process? Working at the community level enables us to gain insight to the ways in which communities themselves articulate grievances *and* solutions. When I started this work, as a law student, I was heavily influenced and drew strength and meaning from Critical Race Theory. It was the 'storytelling' of this movement that made sense to me, as a means of establishing what was and is just. Using testimonies – the claims on law, in and outside the legal institution – was a means of identifying what was seen as just – what was a harm, and what was a solution. Mari Matsuda's work was particularly influential – her piece on 'looking to the bottom' has always stayed with me. As Matsuda wrote in 1987:

> This article suggests that those who have experienced discrimination speak with a special voice to which we should listen. Looking to the bottom – adopting the perspective of those who have seen and felt the falsity of the liberal promise – can assist critical scholars in the task of fathoming the phenomenology of law and defining the elements of justice. (Matsuda, 1987: 324)

Reflecting on the role that justice plays in research practices and relationships, it has become less about me as the producer of knowledge, and more about how the university, as an institution can enable a meeting point of knowledges. How the research process can be flat, not hierarchical. How power can be given up. Yet as postcolonial scholars such as Edward Said and Gayatri Chakravorty Spivak have shown us, it's not possible to transcend unequal power relations, you can only work within existing fields of power (and thank you to Charlotte Mertens for pointing this out). So we again try to 'keep hold of justice' within inequalities, we try to recognize the power of this institution, and its hierarchies, and how we can aim for just practices even so. This can include recognizing the capacity that the university can bring to this work, recognizing the knowledges that exist both in and outside, and enabling a form of meeting point through this institution that still recognizes the inequality of the power relationships and values that each bring. What we can do is consciously aim for collaboration in all work and place the university in conversation with communities and organizations and peoples of which the university is a part; the opposite of the 'ivory tower'.

I take a pluralist approach to law, as both formal – courts, tribunals – and the informal justice processes established by, and continued by, communities as sites of informal law – and how they may also be sites for change. I am interested in how communities use formal processes to claim justice. Individual testimonies and justice practices enable us to identify harms, make the invisible visible, and reveal structures and approaches that frame these harms. This became most evident when developing and conducting research on the experiences of newly arrived, migrant and refugee communities and legal and social service providers in Victoria throughout the COVID-19 pandemic, particularly during Melbourne's lockdowns over 2020 and 2021. We were interested in people's experiences, including the barriers and obstacles to accessing legal and social services, what of these were new, and what had been exacerbated (and was long-standing), and solutions and recommendations for change. We took an approach to access to justice that was interested in how justice and access were understood by those who delivered it, and those who sought it. We collaborated with a range of organizations, including social service providers with lived experience, community members, and small and larger legal service providers (see University of Melbourne et al, 2023).

What was most striking was how justice and access to justice was understood – beyond conventional legal understandings of service delivery, to a more expansive understanding of social and structural justice. Importantly, here, justice is also relational. Access to legal and social services was successful when services took a collaborative and partnership approach, that valued community knowledge and expertise. The harms perpetrated included the failure to recognize community expertise and to not include communities in decisions that directly affected them. This was most evident in the Victorian government's decision to lock down public housing towers for 14 days, without any prior warning, and the harm (and mess) that ensued, which was saved by the communities independently taking on service delivery. What has come through clearly – and we are working on a collaborative development of what was an initial project – was that communities must be involved as active, equal and paid partners in decisions that affect their lives – and that communities themselves clearly understand what best practice solutions are.

Collaboration is a means of justice. One of the most powerful moments for me was at the Aboriginal Tent Embassy in Canberra, Australia – attending the hearings of the case brought by Embassy claimants that charged genocide against the government of the day. I had sat in the Canberra courtroom over some days listening to the testimony given, had heard the powerful testimony of Elder Wadjularbinna Nulyarimma and others that showed the deep trauma of this continuing genocide, and was now at the Embassy itself, with the hearing taking place around the fire of this place set up as a continuing site of protest since 1972. Elders Wadjularbinna Nulyarimma, Isobell Coe and

Kevin Buzzacott gave their testimony around the central fire at the Embassy, situated opposite now Old Parliament House, affirming sovereignty – 'We have never relinquished sovereignty to our country' (Isobell Coe, 1998, cited in Balint et al, 2020: 112), showing how the two laws, settler and Aboriginal, while clashing, could in fact work together, and that they, the Aboriginal claimants and Aboriginal law, could 'show you a way' (Kevin Buzzacott, 1998, cited in Balint et al, 2020: 112). I was a PhD student at the time, and was alerted to the case by a fellow student, as they'd seen a short article in the *Canberra Times*. I went down to the Court, and met some of the people involved. I spoke to people internationally that also worked on conceptions of genocide, and wrote an affidavit of support, that as Embassy claimants outlined – and was the rationale for the case – the expansion of Native Title legislation was a continuing act of genocide. Having researched for years on the subject of genocide – and how we define it – it was good to put this scholarly work into useful practice with this important case. It was only many years later that I reconnected to the Embassy and discussed what had happened, through a forum brought together of scholars and activists involved in the work of the Embassy, which resulted in the book chapter (Balint, 2014), part of the collection *The Aboriginal Tent Embassy: Sovereignty, Black Power, Land Rights and the State*.

Creating spaces for justice conversations

I have been increasingly interested in creating spaces through my research and my teaching for reflections on justice. I have learnt and observed the power of this through the projects I've been involved in. The Aboriginal Embassy claimants created this themselves – a space that articulated what a justice could be, that recognized both settler and Aboriginal law, as sovereign to sovereign. In my reading of the Mau Mau case files, I also reflected on how the Kenyan claimants to the British state created a space of conversation in the UK that had not been had before – and is resurfacing again now with the death of Queen Elizabeth – the criminality of the British Empire (Balint, 2016; see also Elkins, 2005; Anderson, 2005; Bennett 2012). The affidavits of those claimants asked that their harms be recognized – and the legal hearings themselves, and the publicity that ensued – created a critical space. As one claimant, Wambugu Wa Nyingi, stated: 'I have brought this case because I want the world to know about the years I have lost and what was taken from a generation of Kenyans' (*Mutua* v *Foreign and Commonwealth Office*, [2011] EWHC 1913 (QB), cited in Balint, 2016: 272). The letter from the five claimants, delivered to the then British prime minister, noted: 'We are Kenyans in our 70s and 80s who have travelled to London from our rural villages to tell the world of the torture and trauma we lived through at the hands of the British colonial regime' (Letter from Ndiku Mutua, Paulo Nzili,

Jane Muthoni Mara, Wambugu Wa Nyingi and Susan Ngondi to Gordon Brown, 24 June 2009, cited in Balint, 2016: 272). This hearing showed me again the power of claims made to law, to generate public conversations. I have understood this as a 'limited constitutive moment', and earlier, drawing on Elizabeth Jelin's work, as 'foundational moments'. However, the ability to sustain these conversations can be limited when it remains in law – as a solely legal not a broader public conversation. Yet we have seen too how law has the power to generate and to shape and to stop.

These Mau Mau legal hearings did begin to create 'fault lines in the belief in the benevolence of Empire' and 'disrupt the celebratory narrative of the British Empire' (Balint, 2016: 285). The work of structural change, however, is yet to come – but it was these individual testimonies that prompted the searching of it out – as well as identified the borders of its possibility at present. This was most stark in the rationale given to the British public for the settlement struck (that included monetary reparations, a monument in Nairobi and a statement of regret), that was presented in the House of Commons as necessary for economic and political stability, coded as 'reconciliation', not recognition of the harms of Empire. 'We continue to deny liability', was how the then foreign secretary framed it (United Kingdom, Parliamentary Debates, House of Commons, Mau Mau Claims (Settlement), Secretary of State for Foreign and Commonwealth Affairs (Mr. William Hague), 6 June 2013, cols 1692/3.).

Legal spaces are not always the most productive spaces for justice. This was made clear through collaborative work with political survivors of the 1965 genocide in Indonesia. There had been limited success in recognition of the harms they and their families had been subject to, both through national and international legal fora. The project, that myself and a colleague were invited into, with colleagues at Universitas Gadjah Mada, sought to work with a range of communities in the city of Yogyakarta, including women survivors of 1965, members of a transgender madrassa community, and an LGBTQIA+ youth group, to make visible the violences that they had, and continued to experience, through particular sites that they chose. It was their decision that these also be sites of peace that drove the project. And it was bringing together the communities to speak to each other that was also core to the project – enabling the communities, each whom had been marginalized and discriminated against, to learn about each other and be in solidarity with each other (see Kusumaningrum et al, 2022).

It was the women survivors – the mothers – who identified that they would like to run intergenerational walking tours of the sites in the city where they had experienced violence, and seek to turn these into sites of peace. The mothers identified this themselves as a means of justice – intergenerational tours that they would lead, and take the younger generation of Indonesians on. This project highlighted new ways of doing justice through working at the local level, and focusing on changing relations, and understandings, between different generations. Watching this unfold, the questions asked, the space created, made it clear that this was justice.

This sense – of how justice is understood, by those who seek it, is what fuels me in my work. This can be through testimonies given, or conversations had. It can be both inside and outside of conventional legal means. Here, I have been influenced by Carol Smart (1989), who showed us how 'law remains a site of struggle', and can be a focal point for harms to be articulated outside of law, as law may not, will not, hear them. These walking tours of the city of Yogyakarta, that students participated in, both from Australia and from Indonesia, narrated both sites of injustice and of justice, in the city. These were not established monuments, but sites that otherwise people would walk by, or celebrate in – the tours sought to tell the otherwise hidden histories of these places. It is the spaces created both by these tours, and the interactions between generations, that is generating not just justice conversations, but a justice in the sense of an everyday practice, not just an isolated one-off legal 'grand' moment. It is also one that is generative. Here, we can see this as different to what Masha Gessen in *The New Yorker* has observed about the Holocaust memorials in Berlin:

> [A]t some point, the effort began to feel static, glassed in, as though it were an effort not only to remember history but also to insure that only this particular history is remembered—and only in this way. This is true in the physical, visual sense. Many of the memorials use glass: the Reichstag, a building nearly destroyed during the Nazi era and rebuilt half a century later, is now topped by a glass dome; the burned-books memorial lives under glass; glass partitions and glass panes put order to the stunning, once haphazard collection called 'Topography of Terror'. (Gessen, 2023)

In making justice relational, not static, individuals become responsible for changing structures – narratives that demonize, or exclude. The tours facilitate new conversations between different generations in Yogyakarta and between those viewed as 'citizens' and 'non-citizens'. For the women who sat with the students, and took them on these tours, they were not interested in the grand processes of justice, of trials and truth commissions, but in creating awareness, and through this, being reinscribed in their city (on this project, see Kusumaningrum et al, 2022).

The other justice that became so clear as well, was that the mothers were invited to participate in our joint subject at Universitas Gadjah Mada, in Yogyakarta, and the classroom was developed as a site of possibility and collaboration. They were reinscribed not only as citizens of the city, but as students at the university. These were women who as students had been thrown out of the university as alleged communists and arrested and detained, who were now able to come back and take our class.

This justice in action was both a personal justice – of being recognized, and respected – and a structural justice, through the creating of new means of relations. As we reflected:

> It is in the relations that result from coming together in space that we observed a means of tangible justice. We identify this as 'relational justice'—the justice created through establishing or reinscribing relations of responsibility to each other, compelling active engagement with the past, and consequently changing relations of the present. We suggest that relational justice is a central component of a structural justice that seeks to address not just individual harms, but ongoing structures of injustice that are both material and discursive. (Kusumaningrum et al, 2022: 316)

The importance of creating spaces for justice conversations – as a means of creating 'meeting points', was developed and made clear to me through the Minutes of Evidence project (www.minutesofevidence.com.au). This project emerged out of the desire to tell the story of the 1881 Parliamentary Coranderrk Inquiry, through its 'minutes of evidence' (transcript), alongside letters and petitions from the time. This is a story that while known to the Coranderrk community, had been invisible to the broader settler population, that of the resistance and collaboration of the Aboriginal community on Coranderrk station, outside of Melbourne, forcibly displaced from their land. The commitment to the project was to create spaces that could spark public conversations about justice. It meant that the project focused on the translation of the 'minutes of evidence' into a verbatim theatre production, *Coranderrk: We Will Show the Country*, performed in theatres in Melbourne and in regional Victoria, as well as on Country at Coranderrk (for reflections on this, see Balint et al, 2015; Balint et al 2018). It meant we designed question and answer sessions between the actors (Aboriginal and non-Aboriginal) and audience members. It meant that we developed a new curriculum for high school students, that used the testimonies from the Inquiry to consider ideas of justice.

This record of evidence – of the claims of injustice – and of just ways forward – was 'reactivated' through the verbatim theatre play. Here, we were able to hear William Barak, played by the late Uncle Jack Charles, outline a way forward:

> We want the Board and the Inspector, Captain Page, to be no longer over us. We want only one man here, and that is Mr. John Green, and

the station to be under the Chief Secretary; then we will show the country that the station could self-support itself.

We would like it if the Government leave us here, give us this ground and let us manage here and get all the money. Why not let the people do it themselves?

This testimony to the Inquiry challenged the narrative of settler colonialism. It carved out a space of resistance and of just alternatives, while placing on record the structures of injustice. It demonstrated the possibility of just relations within the unjust structure of colonialism. The performance was designed as a way to prompt new public conversations about structural and historical Indigenous injustice in Australia. Verbatim theatre became a site and an opportunity for 'new imaginings'. The 'reactivation' of the legal record – the Parliamentary Inquiry – provided a means whereby personal testimonies were brought to life, the story told of structural harm, along with the story of collaboration, of just alternatives and futures.

What became clear during the project, through the establishment of these public spaces that would enable these justice conversations, was how we can understand these as 'meeting points'. We could see that what these spaces enabled was the bringing together of different peoples, perspectives and frames. This was both through the bringing together of the different partner organizations of the project, who ranged from theatre companies, to universities, to education departments, to the encounters in the spaces, from theatres to meeting rooms. Out of this, we developed what we called a methodology of 'meeting points' that sought to create productive encounters between different peoples, perspectives and times. It was this justice that was sought – and that fuelled the project – which recognized diverse experiences and vantage points, and sought to provide spaces for this to productively come together. It enabled us to understand more fully what a structural justice – to address ongoing structural injustice – might require – that these structures of injustice become visible through these public re-tellings and the re-generation of the collaborations that surface between the past and into the present.

The collaborative work of the Minutes of Evidence project, that culminated in our book, *Keeping Hold of Justice: Encounters between Law and Colonialism*, enabled us to consider what a structural justice depends upon. Keeping hold of justice, we suggested, is about keeping hold of a justice in the face of unjust structures. What started with a focus with creating public spaces for justice conversations ended with a deeper reflection on how just relations can be generated, through the creation of 'meeting points' and encounters between peoples and communities and institutions. Structural justice thus has a relational component: 'possibilities for structural justice, we suggest, emerge through being in relation and actively engaging with the ethics, politics, and equity of broader structures in which our thoughts and actions are embedded' (Balint et al, 2020: 132). Meeting points are also contested spaces. Understanding this and accepting this is something that I have learnt. They evolve as they need to.

A structural justice lens enables us to think differently about justice, and about accountability.

Justice as accountability

The making visible of injustice – and of a justice – is a practice of creating accountability. Justice is about accountability. For me, it has been a focus on state accountability. Citizens expect that their harms are taken seriously, and accountability – state, institutional, individual – will follow. Yet states abrogate these responsibilities, particularly in relation to state crime. Doing justice reinscribes people as citizens – and this gets done inside and outside of our formal legal systems.

Through the process of my work, I am also learning how accountability stretches beyond the state. While the state is one critical space of accountability, there are others. Part of this is holding our institutions to account – how do we create structural change? My first published academic paper was titled 'Towards the anti-genocide community'. I was interested in what we may need for such a community, for genocide prevention, and what law may offer. I urged that 'we question and challenge the ethically empty institutions and norms that tolerate and perpetrate genocide' (Balint, 1994: 14).

This is a justice that is not solely focused on what an individual claim or individual redress may be, but on thinking through what it might look like for this to be addressed institutionally and structurally. In the wake of the Holocaust, there was the call 'never again'. Never again can be used as a rallying cry for so many injustices. What that requires – what may make this structural – is increasingly seen as the necessary approach. Structural justice is called for in campaigns for Sovereignty, for the Voice to Parliament, for Treaty. It is called for in a just solution to Israel-Palestine. It is called for in Black Lives Matter, and in MeToo. It is called for in a humane and just approach to refugees and migration. This goes beyond, but is grounded in individual claims – that provide reason and insight into the deep and enduring structural injustice that impacts so severely. In the 1990s, when I first started researching genocide, there was a belief that we could in fact prevent genocide. Genocide prevention – what it means to do this – was the reason that so many academics became involved in the study of this state crime. We are now, it seems, turning back to an attention to states and structures – and a hope for change.

This attention to structure is an attention to accountability. The 'everydayness' of violence is being identified as structural. Any enduring justice requires it to be structural.

Conclusions

Academic-practitioner and community collaboration becomes a methodology of justice-focused research, with an aim of identifying what a structural justice requires. This practice is not a matter of impact or output. It is part of my practice of seeking to make violence and harms visible. This includes creating public spaces that make injustices visible, and that open up spaces for conversations about what justice could be. It includes a focus on both individual harm and the structures – through both we identify the structures that enable ongoing and structural violence.

This work requires external industry and community collaboration as central to the work. Traditional academic outputs such as peer-reviewed publications are just one aspect of success and often not the most important one – they often have to come second to other outputs that are of most importance to collaborators. This is a tension I've had to navigate at the university. As a junior scholar it was very difficult. With a deeper recognition now by the university of the different types of outputs from collaborative projects, particularly in the social sciences and humanities, and of research excellence, this has become easier. Other significant outputs are that partnerships are created and sustained, that the work is successful in the ways that community partners hope it to be, that the university is seen as a trusted and valued partner, that the work is brought into teaching and teaching practice, that external and internal early-career researchers and collaborators are mentored and supported, that spaces are created at the university to support partnership research, and that public impact results from the work. Not all of these will happen for each project, nor will each project result in all measures of success. Often these come years after the official end of a project.

I don't always feel like I have succeeded or have done a good job of all of this. What I have learnt is to recognize the knowledge and expertise that resides in the organizations and communities I work with, along with my own and my colleagues; that my role can be to facilitate the work and to make it public; and that it can be non-linear and I can get it wrong. I believe that this work matters as central to the mandate of the public university. For my research, this matters for an understanding of what is a justice outcome. Collaboration enables the possibility of changing everyday structures that cause continuing harm. That justice can be and must be 'structural'. The process of this work must be just. In making injustice visible, as a matter of structure not just individual redress, accountability is justice.

Acknowledgements
My deep thanks to the many collaborators I have worked with, and who have shaped this work. Particular thanks to Nesam McMillan. Many thanks to Charlotte Mertens for research assistance and feedback on this chapter, and to the editors, Agatha Herman and Joshua Inwood, for their invitation to contribute, their encouragement and helpful comments.

References
Anderson, D. (2005) *Histories of the Hanged: Britain's Dirty War in Kenya and the End of Empire*, New York: W.W. Norton.
Balint, J. (1994) Towards the anti-genocide community: the role of law, *Australian Journal of Human Rights*, 1(1): 12–42.
Balint, J. (2014) Stating genocide in law: the Aboriginal Embassy and the ACT Supreme Court, in Foley, G., Schaap, A. and Howell, E. (eds) *The Aboriginal Tent Embassy: Sovereignty, Black Power, Land Rights and the State*, London: Routledge–Cavendish, pp 235–250.
Balint, J. (2016) The 'Mau Mau' legal hearings and recognizing the crimes of the British colonial state: a limited constitutive moment, *Critical Analysis of Law*, 3(2): 261–285.
Balint, J., Brown, L., Dullard, C., Evans, J., McMillan, N. and McMillan, M. (2018) The 'minutes of evidence' project: Doing structural justice, *State Crime Journal*, 7(2): 389–409.
Balint, J., Evans, J., McMillan, N., Nanni, G. and Reynolds-Diarra, M. (2015) The 'Minutes of Evidence' project: creating collaborative fields of engagement with the past and present, in Boucher, L. and Russell, L. (eds) *Settler Colonial Governance in Nineteenth Century Victoria*, Canberra: ANU Press, pp 203–224.
Balint, J., Evans, J., McMillan, M. and McMillan, N. (2020) *Keeping Hold of Justice: Encounters between Law and Colonialism*, Michigan: University of Michigan Press.
Bennett, H. (2012) *Fighting the Mau Mau: The British Army and Counter-Insurgency in the Kenya Emergency*, Cambridge: Cambridge University Press.
Boulet, J. (2018) Researching is relating time and space, in Kumar, M. and Pattanayak, S. (eds) *Positioning Research: Shifting Paradigms, Interdisciplinarity and Indigeneity*, London: SAGE, pp 106–141.
Bunting, A. (2015) Monitoring gender equality and violence in conditions of structural inequality and violence, in Rioux, M.H., Pinto, P.C. and Parekh, G. (eds) *Disability, Rights Monitoring and Social Change: Building Power Out of Evidence*, Toronto: Canadian Scholars' Press, pp 67–79.

De Sousa Santos, B. (2014) *Epistemologies of the South: Justice against Epistemicide*, London: Routledge.

Elkins, C. (2005) *Imperial Reckoning: The Untold Story of Britain's Gulag in Kenya*, New York: Holt.

Gessen, M. (2023) In the shadow of the Holocaust: how the politics of memory in Europe obscures what we see in Israel and Gaza today, *The New Yorker*, 9 December.

Houh, E.M.S. and Kalsem, K. (2015) 'Theorizing legal participatory action research: Critical race/feminism and participatory action research', *Qualitative Inquiry*, 21(3): 262–276.

Kalsem, K. (2019) Judicial education, private violence, and community action: a case study in legal participatory action research, *Journal of Gender, Race, & Justice*, 22(1): 41–78.

Kusumaningrum, D., Rahmawati, A.D., Balint, J. and McMillan, N. (2022) Sites of violence, sites of peace, sites of justice: transforming the relational landscape of Yogyakarta, *Space and Culture*, 25(2): 309–321.

Matsuda, M.J. (1987) Looking to the bottom: critical legal studies and reparations, *Harvard Civil Rights-Civil Liberties Law Review*, 22: 323–399.

Rowell, L.L. and Hong, E. (2017) Knowledge democracy and action research: Pathways for the twenty-first century, in Rowell, L.L., Bruce, C.D., Shosh, J.M. and Riel, M.M. (eds) *The Palgrave International Handbook of Action Research*, New York: Palgrave Macmillan, pp 63–83.

Smart, C. (1989) *Feminism and the Power of Law*, London: Routledge.

University of Melbourne and RMIT University in partnership with Foundation House, Victoria Legal Aid and Afri-Aus Care (2023) *'Under the Radar with No Support': Access to Justice for Newly Arrived, Migrant and Refugee Communities during COVID-19 in Victoria*, Melbourne: The University of Melbourne, https://events.unimelb.edu.au/live/files/94-access-to-justice-reportfinal9-octpdf

Vaughan, C., Davis, E., Murdolo, A., Chen, J., Murray, L., Quiazon, R., et al (2016) *Promoting Community-led Responses to Violence against Immigrant and Refugee Women in Metropolitan and Regional Australia*, The ASPIRE Project: Research report, ANROWS Horizons 07/2016, Australia's National Research Organisation for Women's Safety, Sydney.

Vaughan, C., Khaw, S., Katsikis, G., Wheeler, J., Ozge, J., Kasidis, V., et al (2019) 'It is like being put through a blender': inclusive research in practice in an Australian university, *Disability & Society*, 34(7–8): 1224–1240.

Vaughan, C., Chen, J., Sullivan, C., Suha, M., Sandhu, M., Hourani, J., et al (2020) *Multicultural and settlement services supporting women experiencing violence: The MuSeS project*, Research report, 11/2020, Australia's National Research Organisation for Women's Safety, Sydney.

7

Approaching Energy and Climate Justice: Working Towards More Just Scholarship, Pedagogy and Praxis

Deepti Chatti

The terms 'energy justice' and 'climate justice' are increasingly prevalent in scholarly, government and activist debates on the environment, and readers of this volume have likely encountered them in contemporary conversations about tackling climate change. The energy sector contributes significantly to global greenhouse gas emissions (US EPA, nd). The production of energy is the largest contributor to greenhouse gas emissions; in 2010 the energy supply sector accounted for 35 per cent of global emissions (Bruckner et al, 2014). Transforming the energy sector is of paramount importance to taking action on climate change. One of the main imperatives of climate action is to decarbonize the energy sector such that as a society we derive energy services from sources that do not emit carbon dioxide into the atmosphere. The energy sector is crucial for providing much-needed energy services to humanity, such as lighting, cooking, heating, cooling, communications, transportation and powering most livelihood activities, for the benefit of people all over the world. These benefits are not evenly distributed, however, as we have tremendous inequalities in the quality and quantity of energy access, such that one in ten of the global population does not have access to electricity, and 2.6 billion people rely on biomass energy sources for their subsistence needs in ways that cause premature death and disease in the most marginalized populations in the world (SEforALL, nd). The geographic and social spread of energy injustices follows a predictable pattern of other inequalities in the world such that low- and middle-income countries have a larger percentage of their populations without access to reliable and safe energy services. Furthermore, within any country or region, historically marginalized groups such as Tribes or rural populations tend to be provided fewer energy services than wealthier or more privileged groups.

Energy and climate justice are relatively new terms that emerged in the late 2000s and can mean a variety of different kinds of research and work. Scholars from various disciplines working on energy have articulated how energy, climate and justice are, or should be, related. At the outset of this chapter I provide a brief literature review for the reader to feel situated in the literature. However, this is not a chapter about the intellectual, philosophical or political history of the concept of justice and how that theoretically applies to scholarly work on energy and climate. Rather, I focus this chapter on the ways in which the concept of justice informs my research and teaching on energy and climate change, and the ways my scholarship and teaching have led me to understand the concepts of energy and climate justice. Grounded in the particularities of my work, I offer reflections on doing fieldwork on clean energy access in India and the United States, doing fieldwork as part of transnational collaborations, how justice is thought about in different geographic contexts, how different disciplinary scholars interpret what it means to do energy justice work, the role of qualitative research on these topics, how the concept of justice informs desired outcomes of community-engaged research, and the questions and concerns that students have when studying energy and climate justice, and as they plan their own scholarship and activism in the world on these topics. As I describe through the course of this chapter, these concepts in literature and in my own work are emergent and messy works-in-progress. Thus, this chapter is a self-reflexive account of me as a researcher grappling with the concept of justice while conducting research in varied collaborative contexts, teaching and advising students. Readers will note that far from being settled terms with wide agreement, these concepts are polysemic and invite many interpretations, making them fertile grounds for intellectual and political creativity.

I begin the chapter with a brief literature review of a few key terms, followed by a description of three research projects, and one pedagogical project that I have been engaged in for several years. Subsequently, I describe a few ongoing questions and takeaways for myself from my experiences in research and teaching. I conclude the chapter with some final thoughts.

How have energy justice and climate justice been discussed in the literature?

While I focus this chapter on how the concept of justice informs my own research and teaching on energy and climate change, at the outset I provide a brief summary of a few ways in which other scholars have written about these terms, as they inform my thinking.

In a recent influential commentary, the critical and feminist geographer Farhana Sultana has argued that the term climate justice helps to reorient conversations about climate change to include critical perspectives, and to open the space for a conversation about climate change that is not solely scientific and technical (Sultana, 2022). According to Sultana, climate justice scholarship 'demonstrates how climate justice is a moral and justice issue, not just a science, techno-managerial, or finance issue' (Sultana, 2022: 118). Further, according to Sultana, a climate justice approach centres questions like 'who benefits, who loses out, in what ways, where, and why'. Thus, Sultana suggests that the term allows for the focus to shift away from a techno-managerial lens to highlight ways in which climate impacts are experienced unequally, with historic and geographic differences being salient, and informed by wider structures of injustice. In this framing, a conversation about climate justice necessarily articulates with debates about colonialism, capitalism, globalization and other systemic forms of injustice that critical scholars are already engaged in. Sultana calls for a critical climate justice praxis, drawing on Paulo Freire's conceptualization of praxis as 'reflection and action upon the world in order to transform it' (Freire, as cited in Sultana, 2022: 119). In Sultana's formulation, climate justice is not an aseptic debate occurring in scholarly journals but a lively academic field that collaborates and contributes to climate activism in solidarity with social movements of many kinds, including Indigenous movements, youth movements, feminist movements, anti-racist movements and activists working to upturn injustice in its myriad forms around the world.

In another recent article conceptualizing the origins and evolution of the term climate justice, Peter Newell (2022) has described the way the term allows for questions of historical responsibility, climate debt, colonial patterns of extraction, and dominant modes of capitalist accumulation into conversations about climate justice. As Jenkins and colleagues describe, Newell draws on the philosophical traditions of justice to delineate the procedural (who gets to participate in decision making?), recognitional (who is recognized as a legitimate stakeholder with a right to participate in decisions?) and distributional aspects of justice (how are the impacts of climate change inequitably experienced and caused?).

Kirsten Jenkins and colleagues (Jenkins et al, 2016; 2020) have written about the interdisciplinary nature of energy justice scholarship, drawing from the fields of law, public health, business, religious studies and the social sciences more broadly. These scholars have articulated the different axes of justice that make up energy justice – distributional, procedural and recognitional. They also point to geographical differences in the term's interpretation, reflecting not only disciplinary but also locational (in both a spatial and geopolitical sense) differences in perspectives. For instance, while scholars writing about energy justice in the Global North have focused on participation in decision making in energy matters, scholars in the Global South have focused on questions of energy access and poverty (Jenkins et al, 2020). Sovacool and Dworkin define the concept of energy justice as 'a global energy system that fairly disseminates both the benefits and costs of energy services, and one that has representative and impartial decision making' (2015: 436). Drawing on the intellectual traditions of the discipline of philosophy, Sovacool and Dworkin (2015) describe eight aspects of an energy justice framework: availability, affordability, due process, good governance, sustainability, intergenerational equity, intra-generational equity and responsibility.

The legal scholar-activist Shalanda Baker (2021) has argued that advancing quick low-hanging fruit climate mitigation strategies with a view to tackle the urgent climate crisis can sometimes work against justice by leaving marginalized communities even more marginalized. Baker shows how renewable energy projects can propagate violence, dispossession and economic exclusion against the poor, Indigenous peoples and marginalized communities similar to the way fossil fuel powered energy can. As Baker says, 'I am not opposed to quick climate action, but I am against perpetuating injustice to save my own skin' (2021: 9).

This framing of the 'dilemma between urgency and justice' is echoed by Ankit Kumar et al (2021) while discussing energy transitions in the Global South. As they eloquently argue in the introduction to their edited volume, the climate crisis calls for meaningful, substantive and rapid collective action, and yet history, geography and politics cause us to seek recognition of individual differences. By doing so, they join several other scholars calling for conceptual clarity on identifying climate change as being caused by the actions of some humans and affecting all planetary life but not distributing responsibility and blame equally among all of humanity (see, for example, Haraway, 2015; Davis and Todd, 2017; Moore, 2017; Johnson et al, 2022).

The term 'just transitions' is worth mentioning here as well. 'Just transitions' can be used to mean a variety of concepts in which a large-scale systemic change takes into consideration social justice as well as the immediate goal of the transition (decarbonizing energy systems, climate mitigation, better labour conditions, and so on). The concept of 'just transitions' within energy studies is used to mean a systemic transformation of the energy system to using less carbon-intensive energy sources (away from fossil fuels towards renewable energy) while integrating principles of social justice, such as reducing inequality of energy access, reducing exposure to toxic pollutants in air and water, and expanding energy services to hitherto underserved communities. Just transitions also calls for paying attention to decision-making processes for energy systems such that they include 'benefits for all while remaining within environmental, natural resource, or economic constraints' (Mulvaney, 2020: 5).

While the terms 'energy justice' and 'climate justice' are relatively new and increasingly used by scholars and activists working on topics related to energy, climate and society, they flow from an older concept of environmental justice, that has a varied and rich intellectual and political history, grounded in the specific social justice struggles of different places. In India, where I am from and where I conduct a majority of my research, environmental justice scholars and activists have brought to attention the ways in which the lives and livelihoods of Adivasi (Tribal) and Dalit communities were disproportionately impacted by industrial development projects like mines, dams and power plants. On the other hand, in the United States where I currently live and work, following on the civil rights movements, early environmental justice scholars and activists analysed how Black Americans and other people of colour were disproportionately harmed by environmental toxins. (For a deeper dive into the place-based concerns animating environmental movements, see Ram Guha's *Environmentalism: A Global History*.) In short, the term environmental justice began as a way to draw attention to the social injustices and unequal harms that were integral to environmental exposures.

Approaching justice

My approach to the conceptualization of energy and climate justice in this chapter is grounded in my ongoing research and teaching on these topics. In this section, I describe three interdisciplinary, collaborative, community-based research projects that I have carried out over a period of ten years, and a seminar class that I developed and taught for four years. Engaging in these projects over the last decade has helped me analyse some ways in which the concept of justice could inform research topics, practices, collaborations, outputs and outcomes in the realm of energy and climate. These scholarly and pedagogical projects have also helped me encounter some of the challenges of conducting research on energy and climate justice, and on conducting energy and climate research in just ways. Instead of offering definitive and neatly articulated 'how tos', this chapter will engage in a reflexive analysis and offer the reader a look into the messy on-the-ground realities of conducting energy and climate justice research. By inviting the reader into my own thinking and rethinking, I hope this chapter provides a realistic primer to the imperatives for doing such work and the challenges of conducting such research. I have titled this section 'Approaching justice' with a view to embrace two meanings of the word 'approaching'. First, the word means coming closer to something. I find this appropriate because such efforts are a work in progress, and the verb *approaching* more realistically reflects the ongoing processual nature of attempting to conduct just research and research on energy justice. Second, approaching derives from 'approach', which suggests it is one pathway, perhaps out of several, that one may take to get closer to conducting research in just ways. The second meaning is crucial in the sense that I do not believe just research only takes one form, or that there is a certain formula, rubric or checklist to be followed. Rather, I offer some considerations that an engaged scholar/activist might take into account when embarking on such an endeavour.

In order to protect my collaborators' identity, and since I am not sharing research results but rather reflecting on the process of working on the projects themselves, I feel it appropriate to keep descriptions of the projects in general terms rather than specifying institutional and person names. Where necessary, I provide locational or disciplinary information as it pertains to the points I am making in this chapter about interdisciplinarity or the geographies of research. First, I will describe each of these projects, and then I will describe my insights gained from working on them over the last decade.

Research Project 1

The first research project I draw upon for my understanding of energy justice is my doctoral dissertation research that I carried out between 2013 and 2019. During this time, I was a student in an interdisciplinary environmental studies programme in the United States, being advised by multiple committee members with varying disciplinary expertise in critical geography, environmental studies, environmental anthropology, feminist studies, and science and technology studies. As part of my doctoral research, I participated in fieldwork in India along with a team of researchers from across different institutions of higher learning in North America and two non-governmental organizations (NGOs) in India in the two states of Himachal Pradesh and Karnataka. The expertise of the numerous researchers involved in the project included air pollution science, engineering, developmental economics and public policy. The research questions the project was attempting to answer were about clean cookstove adoption; including the technology preferences, cost-related behaviour, and air pollution exposure and emissions impacts, by low-income and rural families in India. Due to my own intellectual interests, and the generosity of my colleagues in India and the United States who agreed to be studied, I also critically analysed the way in which knowledge was produced about air pollution exposures to marginalized communities in rural India, and the energy technology choices made by low-income families under different scenarios. In other words, I ethnographically studied the project itself. While there are many interesting facets to this work, and

I am currently working on multiple publications (journal articles and a book manuscript) based on my dissertation (and I hope the readers, if interested, will explore those publications to learn more about the research outcomes and insights of that body of work), I rely on my experience of this research project to make a few specific points in this chapter regarding interdisciplinary collaborations, power hierarchies in fieldwork and the political economy of transnational fieldwork based research.

Research Project 2

The second research project I draw upon for my understanding of energy justice is a collaborative fieldwork based project I led and worked on with a critical human geographer in the United States and two community-based organizations in India in Himachal Pradesh and Andhra Pradesh. The research objectives of the project are to better understand the experiences of low-income families in sustaining access to clean energy, after initial access has been facilitated either by a government programme or an NGO. More specifically, we are interested in how low-income families refill their liquefied petroleum gas cylinders for cooking, with a focus on the resources and relationships required to do so. We collected both qualitative and spatial data to create richly textured 'Cylinder Stories' and bring these experiences to light. This is an ongoing project in terms of analysis and publishing. I had written the grant proposal while finishing my PhD, and carried out the research after starting work as a professor. We had envisioned this project to be extensively based in fieldwork carried out by all of us involved with the project; however, due to the COVID-19 pandemic we had to rework our project design. The pandemic meant that all research was delayed, and rightfully so. Furthermore, all the fieldwork had to be entirely carried out by local NGO staff who were based in and around the communities engaged in the project. This involved a methodological shift in the way we planned for and collected data.

Research Project 3

The third research project I describe here as a basis for my conceptualization of energy justice is an ongoing collaboration with the Karuk Tribe and Blue Lake Rancheria based in Humboldt County, California. I am a co-Principal Investigator (co-PI) along with engineering colleagues at Cal Poly Humboldt, and lead social scientist on this collaborative research programme that is studying the entangled issues of wildfires, air pollution and energy access inequities to rural and Tribal communities in California. This research project is focused on the disparities in access to the electricity grid, which makes energy a precarious service to Tribal and rural communities (Sandoval, 2018). Not having reliable electricity leads to often being unable to run air filters during times of high air pollution levels during wildfire season. Recent years have seen increasing frequency and intensity of wildfires in Northern California; in the last five years alone ten million acres have burned and 151 lives have been tragically lost (CALFIRE, 2022), not to mention the wildlife affected by raging fires, homes and landscapes burned, and the toxic smoke that accompanies such conflagrations. While California has always been a fire adapted place (Pyne, 2016; Simon, 2017), and Native Tribes have carefully tended to California's landscape using fire as a tool, centuries of settler colonial policies on the land have outlawed the cultural use of fire leading to an accumulation of a vast amount of flammable fuels in the landscapes. Add to that an ageing and snaking electricity utility grid that is quite literally falling apart and sparking fires (Blunt, 2022), and climate change creating more intense and frequent droughts, leading to several months of the year called 'fire season', leading to many communities in rural and Tribal California facing high risk of wildfires and smoke exposure. As a part of this collaborative project, I have had an opportunity to listen to a variety of Tribal and rural community members in California describe what energy justice means to them in their specific contexts. Reflecting on these varied perspectives has allowed me to expand my understanding of the concept. I draw upon these reflections in this chapter.

Pedagogical insights

The fourth intellectual project I draw upon for this chapter is pedagogical rather than scholarly in nature. Since January 2020, I have annually taught a seminar class that I developed called Energy Justice. The two main concepts underlying the class are that we need to study energy through a critical lens and not only a technical or policy lens (which is the norm when energy is taught at universities), and that understanding energy systems is crucial to understanding inequalities in the world. Through the course of the semester we study at various scales of the home, the nation, the region and the globe. We study how energy intersects with Indigenous rights, land dispossession, international development, poverty alleviation, gender, race, caste, tribe and global geopolitics. Drawing on history, geography, anthropology, Indigenous studies and gender studies, we study texts that analyse energy of different forms – oil, gas, coal, wind, solar, biomass, hydropower, lighting, cooking and electricity. I reflect on my experiences teaching this class to a combination of undergraduate and graduate students over the last four years, and how this pedagogical experience has informed my understanding of energy justice. The students who have taken this class encompass the social sciences, humanities, science and engineering.

Emergent questions and some takeaways

In this section, I describe some of the key themes, takeaways and emergent questions that animate my thinking and work on energy and climate justice. These questions have sprung from my experiences on the scholarly and pedagogical projects I have been engaged in, as described in the previous section. As I described earlier in this chapter, my aim is not to provide neatly tied up answers to these questions, but to share them as ongoing and emergent concerns in the scholarly and pedagogical endeavours of energy justice.

Who are we responsible to as scholars?

As scholars we are trained at graduate school to think carefully about research questions, methods, data collection, analysis and writing up our results. We may also be trained professionally in certain disciplines, and through formal and informal means become acculturated into the norms of certain disciplines. In particularly helpful graduate schools, we may also receive professional development training and advice on how to present one's research at conferences, find jobs, and progress within academia or other professions needing skilled knowledge workers. However, an additional question is increasingly gaining importance in conducting just research. Who are we responsible to as scholars? This question is particularly important when conducting community-engaged research, and/or when conducting research on questions of energy and climate, which are extremely pressing, contemporary socio-political-environmental challenges of our times. A simplistic answer may be that we are directly responsible to our supervisors, mentors, advisors and funding agencies who have provided resources for us to conduct our research. But I would argue that far more importantly, we are ethically, socially and politically responsible to the people and communities with whom we conduct our research, and the people and communities who we belong to outside academia as well as within academia. This means aligning our research goals, questions and outcomes to match those of our interlocutors and community partners. Needless to say, this can be extremely challenging to navigate as a scholar. If the communities we are conducting research with are economically and/or socio-politically marginalized, perhaps experiencing land dispossession, eviction, or are threatened directly or indirectly by the state, corporate or other powerful actors, it behooves us to align our scholarship to support their political claims in any manner that may be helpful (with the humble recognition that as academics our voices may carry only limited weight in wider society, but nonetheless do bring a certain legitimacy and networks of recognition and support). But furthermore, as scholars we are also obligated to think about what else we can do besides align our scholarship towards justice. Perhaps we could communicate the findings of our research to broader audiences by writing in popular magazines, newspapers, policy briefs and other venues with wider reach than academic venues of publications. Perhaps we could offer testimony in legal cases where our voices may carry heft. We could also join protests, raise funds, write grants, generate visibility and participate in other forms of direct actions in solidarity with the communities and organizations with which we conduct research.

Who gets to study what/whom/with whom?

As can be seen from the descriptions of my scholarly projects in the previous sections, I have experience with different forms of interdisciplinary energy research and have engaged with varied collaborations with a diverse set of individuals and institutional partners. Some of my research has been conducted while based in institutions far away from my research sites, while other research has been conducted in locations proximate to the institution I have been based in. Much of my research has been in India, where I am from, while some newer research has been in the United States, where I currently live and work. These experiences have allowed me to reflect on the relationship between one's identity and site of research. More specifically, they have informed my ongoing reflections on positionality and how that affects one's scholarship, pedagogy and community relationships.

Additionally, my students and I (together in our classrooms and when we are engaging in our separate scholarly projects) engage in deep reflexive work on positionality and how that affects scholarship, advocacy,and action. Critical feminist science studies scholars have long reminded us that all perspectives are partial, and there is no view from nowhere (Haraway, 1988), and critical Indigenous studies scholars have long reminded us that most research conducted with Indigenous communities has resulted in extractive modes of knowledge production that solely benefit the researcher (who is usually an outsider) and harms the communities in which the knowledge was produced (and usually *about whom* the knowledge was produced) (Smith, 2021). Thus a just approach to energy and climate research would, at a minimum, centre questions of positionality and perspective, and shun extractive knowledge production practices which create scholarship that solely (or primarily) benefits the outside researcher rather than the community in which the scholarship was conducted. Furthermore, a just approach to energy and climate scholarship would insist on resisting all modes of research which involved parachuting in scholars from 'outside' the community and external scholars creating knowledge about a community without the active participation and involvement of community members themselves. Having said that, the definitions of insider and outsider are not straightforward and unproblematic categories in themselves. How do we define who is someone from the community, and someone not from the community? Is this based on nationality, racial identity, gender identity, having a sense of solidarity, or political identity, a formal group affiliation, or a combination of both? How do we think about the complicated and multi-layered identities many of us form as scholars in the diaspora? Particularly in the context of energy which connects what we may simplistically think of as the 'local' and 'global', rendering such static definitions of scale as meaningless, categories of 'insiders' and 'outsiders' to the community need to be carefully and critically examined. I would argue that there is tremendous epistemic value in thinking across scales and with and alongside individuals and communities across the 'insider' and 'outsider' spectrum.

How should we centre reciprocity and build just relations in research?

What is the project working towards? Is it to improve understanding of certain issues, provide further evidence for normative stances towards justice, or is it also an attempt to make material transformations to the lives of people? What kinds of outcomes are seen as the goal of the collaborative endeavour? A central principle of a just collaborative process is that everyone benefits from their participation in the collaboration, hopefully equally. While power asymmetries remain regardless of people's best intentions and cannot be wished away, making these asymmetries visible and overt rather than hidden can be helpful in working towards more equitable collaborations. How should we centre reciprocity and build just relations in research? How should we account for varied outcomes that are desirable for different partners? For most academic researchers, desired project outcomes include the opportunity to publish journal articles or other forms of academic writing from their work. Additionally, developing mutually respectful relationships with community members provides an opportunity for enhancing academic understandings of energy and climate concepts. These are useful for scholarly and pedagogical aims. For most community members, academic writing is not particularly helpful in working their material and political goals. Other forms of writing such as policy memoranda and funding applications have the potential to be far more transformative in the immediate sense. Furthermore, for many community members, non-written forms of engagement and communications such as town halls, and the opportunity to verbally and publicly participate in energy and climate projects or policy making or governance processes are experienced as more impactful. Additionally, support from university researchers for protests and rallies when necessary against powerful energy corporations or policy makers can be extremely valuable for community members. And last but not least, support from legal scholars or practising lawyers from within academia can provide relief against the injustices of vastly under-resourced communities battling land or mineral dispossession or eviction.

How should we straddle epistemic divides and navigate productive tensions?

While conducting interdisciplinary energy justice research, increasingly researchers from different disciplines could find themselves on a collaborative project together. The range of interdisciplinarity can be relatively narrow, such as two engineers with different expertise areas collaborating, or wider, with critical social scientists or humanities scholars working together with engineering and natural science colleagues. The power hierarchies within interdisciplinary teams working on energy and climate topics mirror the hierarchies within wider academia, with the science, engineering and policy scholars often dominating the epistemic frameworks of collaborative endeavours. Qualitative and/or critical research, when included, is seen through the lens of how useful it is to more fully explain results from quantitative survey based methods. This often renders anodyne the more radical possibilities of critical research, when conducted in collaborative partnerships with more positivist ways of generating knowledge. Nonetheless, including critical scholars can change the frames of reference, research questions or project outcomes deemed desirable, and is a positive development on energy justice scholarship. In other words, the inclusion of critical scholars in energy research is a necessary but not sufficient development.

What is the role of critical research in energy justice scholarship?

Most research on energy and climate tends to be technical or policy oriented. In a review of energy literature, Sovacool (2014) found that sociology, history, geography, psychology and communication studies were less than 0.3 per cent of author affiliations in his analysis of energy related journal articles. In the last decade, there has been renewed attention from critical social scientists to the field of energy studies (Smith and High, 2017), leading to small but growing fields of scholarship in energy geographies, energy anthropology and the energy humanities. As scholars have argued, 'human use of energy is understood and experienced through cultural frameworks' (Strauss et al, 2013: 11). Thus, drawing on methods and disciplines of scholarship that allow the researcher to study energy questions within the context of social worlds, grounded in politics, and informed by history and place vastly expands the kinds of energy research that is possible. Questions of justice are not solely technical, they are political, and as such cannot be understood without social, cultural, historic and geographic contexts. Thus, it is imperative that research on energy justice includes critical perspectives and not solely techno-economic perspectives.

How do we account for geographic inequalities in fieldwork for international research?

When conducting international research, it is pertinent to recognize that international borders are not uniformly porous or welcoming to everybody in equal ways. A passport from the Global North provides far more ability to travel across borders for fieldwork and conferences. Travel for scholars from the Global North to the Global South is far easier than the other way around. International students and scholars from the Global South have to navigate visas, work permits and arranging funding for travel, often in ways that are far more challenging than for other scholars. Certain bodies and identities as marked by racial, national and other axes of identity are policed and surveilled at international borders far more closely than others. These differences become far more apparent when working in collaborative teams that comprise of researchers with different nationalities and other intersectional identities. While research projects cannot solve xenophobia, Islamophobia, racism, queer phobia, able-ism and subvert geopolitical hierarchies, pretending these differences don't exist often serves to further make difficult the work of building just collaborations. Furthermore, vast disparities still exist between researchers who can fly into field sites in the Global South and conduct research with communities, while community members from those same research sites cannot reciprocally travel to the universities or places where researchers come from. How do these geographic inequalities of access and travel impact the kinds of scholarship we are able to produce amidst these glaring differences?

Conclusions

In this chapter, I began with a description of the relatively new terms energy and climate justice as described in different scholarly fields. I then described four intellectual projects – three scholarly and one pedagogical – that I have been engaged in for several years in India and the United States. Using my descriptions of the projects as a way to introduce the various geographical locations, scales, community partners and questions I have been immersed in, I described emergent questions that have grown out of my experiences. My purpose in sharing these questions is not to describe a process or pathway for readers to critique or follow, but rather to invite further thinking on how one might go about doing energy and climate justice work in this contemporary moment. What kinds of research can be considered on the topic of energy justice or climate justice? Is there a distinction between doing research *on* energy and climate justice and doing research on energy and climate in just ways? Questions of justice extend beyond the topics and research questions selected, and include methods, desired outcomes, and attentiveness to the process and dynamics of the research project and the research team itself.

Readers of this chapter will note that I am not arguing for us to get caught up in boundary drawing work to delineate work on energy and climate that should constitute energy and climate justice, or not. But I do want to briefly discuss the potential consequences of us playing fast and loose with these terms. An optimistic reading of the fluidity of these terms is that energy and climate justice are inherently polysemic concepts that serve as a way for scholars and activists engaged in widely different intellectual and political projects to come together and potentially collaborate. For the contemporary 'wicked problems' that we as a society are faced with, a broad coalition of varied intellectual disciplines and political orientations may indeed be needed. On the other hand, a more sceptical reading of the way these terms are being used is that their fuzziness and capaciousness renders the radical possibilities of energy and climate justice anodyne. In other words, lumping energy and climate research that is not really focused on justice into a category of 'energy justice' or 'climate justice' blunts the possibilities of what an energy and climate just world may be. All of this academic hand-wringing is potentially moot, however, as popular terms tend to morph and get assimilated by a wide variety of users. Perhaps it is just as well to note that these concepts are emergent and highly salient today and bring together, sometimes harmoniously and at other times with contention, a wide array of actors.

To me, doing energy and climate justice scholarship, teaching and praxis means engaging not solely with techno-scientific solutions but widening one's analytical gaze conceptually to think about the historic reasons the problem is formulated the way it is, and the way solutions are framed. A common thread running through many scholarly articulations of justice in the context of energy and climate is that it is seen as being important, but also slowing down climate action. In other words, justice is framed as being opposed to a framework of urgency, in which hasty interventions are made to tackle the climate crisis from a purely technical perspective (that is, focused on reducing carbon dioxide emissions only), which often exacerbate social inequalities. Another common thread is that it is relatively new and unusual to think about justice while discussing decarbonization of energy systems and taking climate action. In this chapter, I argue that while both these claims might be true in some contexts, centring justice is about more than slowing down interventions or incorporating critical perspectives in addition to techno-managerial ones. In some contexts, centring questions of justice may call for entirely changing the framing of energy and climate research in terms of the research questions asked, methods used, collaborations forged, kinds of expertise deemed valuable, and the outcomes of the research process seen as valuable.

Acknowledgements

I am extremely grateful to the various communities, collaborators, colleagues and students with whom I have had the privilege of working with and learning alongside including in the Kullu district of Himachal Pradesh, Koppal district of Karnataka, Paderu district of Andhra Pradesh and Humboldt County in California; I am deeply indebted to many community based organizations in India, including Jagriti, Laya and Samuha; the Blue Lake Rancheria Tribe and the Karuk Tribe in California, and several colleagues I have worked with at Yale University, Cal Poly Humboldt and the University of California San Diego.

References

Baker, S. (2021) *Revolutionary Power: An Activist's Guide to the Energy Transition*, Washington, DC: Island Press.

Blunt, K. (2022) *California Burning: The Fall of Pacific Gas and Electric-And What It Means for America's Power Grid*, New York: Portfolio/Penguin.

Bruckner, T., Bashmakov, I.A., Mulugetta, Y., Chum, H., de la Vega Navarro, A., Edmonds, J., et al (2014) Energy systems, in Edenhofer, O., Pichs-Madruga, R., Sokona, Y., Farahani, E., Kadner, S., Seyboth, K., et al (eds) *Climate Change 2014: Mitigation of Climate Change. Contribution of Working Group III to the Fifth Assessment Report of the Intergovernmental Panel on Climate Change*, Cambridge and New York: Cambridge University Press.

California Department of Forestry and Fire Protection (CAL FIRE), Stats and Events, accessed here: Retrieved November 14, 2022. https://www.fire.ca.gov/.

Davis, H. and Todd, Z. (2017) On the importance of a date, or decolonizing the Anthropocene, *ACME: An International Journal for Critical Geographers*, 16(4): 761–780.

Guha, R. (2014) *Environmentalism: A Global History*. Gurgaon: Penguin Random House India.

Haraway, D. (1988) Situated knowledges: the science question in feminism and the privilege of partial perspective, *Feminist Studies*, 14(3): 575–599.

Haraway, D. (2015) Anthropocene, Capitalocene, Plantationocene, Chthulucene: Making kin, *Environmental Humanities*, 6(1): 159–165.

Jenkins, K., McCauley, D., Heffron, R., Stephan, H. and Rehner, R. (2016) Energy justice: a conceptual review, *Energy Research & Social Science*, 11: 174–182.

Jenkins, K.E., Stephens, J.C., Reames, T.G. and Hernández, D. (2020) Towards impactful energy justice research: transforming the power of academic engagement, *Energy Research & Social Science*, 67: 101510.

Johnson, A., Hebdon, C., Burow, P., Chatti, D. and Dove, M (2022) Anthropocene, in *Oxford Research Encyclopedia of Anthropology*. https://doi.org/10.1093/acrefore/9780190854584.013.295

Kumar, A., Höffken, J.I. and Pols, A. (2021) *Dilemmas of Energy Transitions in the Global South: Balancing Urgency and Justice*, London and New York: Taylor & Francis.

Moore, J.W. (2017) The Capitalocene, Part I: on the nature and origins of our ecological crisis, *The Journal of Peasant Studies*, 44(3): 594–630.

Mulvaney, D. (2020) *Sustainable Energy Transitions*, Switzerland: Palgrave Macmillan.

Newell, P. (2022) Climate justice, *The Journal of Peasant Studies*, 49(5): 915–923.

Pyne, S.J. (2016) *California: A Fire Survey*, vol. 2. Tucson: University of Arizona Press.

Sandoval, C. (2018) Energy access is energy justice: the Yurok tribe's trailblazing work to close the Native American reservation electricity gap, in Salter, R., Gonzalez, C. and Warner, E. (eds) *Energy Justice: US and International Perspectives*, Northampton, MA: Edward Elgar, pp 166–207.

SEforALL (Sustainable Energy for All) (nd) https://www.seforall.org/

Simon, G.L. (2017) *Flame and Fortune in the American West*. Oakland: University of California Press.

Smith, J. and High, M.M. (2017) Exploring the anthropology of energy: ethnography, energy and ethics, *Energy Research & Social Science*, 30: 1–6.

Smith, L.T. (2021) *Decolonizing Methodologies: Research and Indigenous Peoples*, London: Bloomsbury Publishing.

Sovacool, B.K. (2014) Diversity: energy studies need social science, *Nature*, 511(7511): 529–530.

Sovacool, B.K. and Dworkin, M.H. (2015) Energy justice: conceptual insights and practical applications, *Applied Energy*, 142: 435–444.

Strauss, S., Rupp, S. and Love, T. (2013) *Cultures of Energy: Power, Practices, Technologies*, London and New York: Routledge.

Sultana, F. (2022) Critical climate justice, *The Geographical Journal*, 188(1): 118–124.

US EPA (United States Environmental Protection Agency) (nd) https://www.epa.gov/

PART III

Justice as Challenge

The three chapters in this section, written by Corine Wood-Donnelly, the Vegan Geography Collective (VGC) and Don Mitchell, reflect on the impact, opportunities and issues of working with justice in their respective fields. Throughout it is clear that justice needs constant engagement, both theoretically and materially, in order to 'refill' it as a concept and prevent the dangers that could arise from leaving it as an empty signifier. There is therefore a need for justice to be materialized through marginal and exploited agents, spaces and relations with engaging with the more-than-human acting as one route to challenge hegemonic constructions of justice. For the VGC, just research needs to challenge anthropocentric ideals through foregrounding a fluid and embodied multispecies justice. Wood-Donnelly highlights the need for a space itself to have voice, reflecting on the necessary challenge that justice theories present to the common conceptual frameworks in International Relations, arguing that it poses critical questions of the who, why and what in a discipline where, ordinarily, the state is the unit of analysis.

Nonetheless, how justice is operationalized in these arenas is less explicit and, from their reflections, it is apparent that the practice of just research in different disciplines and epistemologies requires further consideration to continue responding to the challenge that justice does, and should, pose to us as reflexive researchers.

8

Perspectives from the Top: Justice, International Relations and the Political Geography of the Arctic

Corine Wood-Donnelly

'Perspectives from the top' is inferred as a double, or perhaps even a triple, entendre. Questions of justice in my research (to date) focus on the international politics of the Arctic and the political processes that shape the spatial and ideational structures and, in turn, how these structures influence the international politics of and in this space. To begin the contextualization of the Arctic from the top, we can begin with the placement of the region in most cartographies, both worldly and otherworldly, at the top of planet earth. Second, the Arctic features at the top – or at least the start – of many global processes; it is the weather kitchen of the world, the seeds of the food web where phytoplankton and sea algae begin the nutrient chain that sustains top predators, and even as a laboratory for norms of governance or as a frontier for the just transition. Finally, it is a commentary on the top-down character of international politics where decisions on the distribution of harms or resources, access to procedures, decision-making and the recognition of legitimate inclusion are often ultimately decided through hierarchies of power.

Conversations of justice and injustice do not come easily to discussions of International Relations theory, although they do exist within some circles, especially within discussions of global governance. While Rawls suggested that 'justice is the first virtue of international institutions' (1999: 3), this virtue does not extend to the international system as a socially constructed institution that exists only in principle. Justice appears so infrequently within the discipline, it has even been suggested that 'International Relations is insensitive to the question of justice' (Ray, 1999: 1368). Ethics, liberal values and their focus on norm-shaping interactions that create semblances of order appear more frequently than the emphasis on justice and the consequences on structures and political processes. However, within political geography — which focuses more clearly on the relationship between the people and place, there is more evaluation of geographies of injustice, such as those evident in the environmental justice discourse or, as emerges in the work of Dikeç, in looking at 'the processes that produce space, and, at the same time, the implications of these produced spaces on the dynamic processes of social, economic, and political relations' (2001: 1793). Using political geography allows for evaluation of the relationship between the state and its territory — including questioning the ways that political processes result in spatially uneven outcomes and the way that these processes and territorial organization are the products of spatial structures and the political organization of territory.

While justice theorizing is important, theory has little use unless it causes us to understand why things are the way they are, and perhaps helps us to understand how things could and should be different if injustice is removed from the system. As Kratochwil (2007) suggests, 'theory is looking out from nowhere' and justice theorizing is only a framework for organizing thoughts, patterns and questions of justice. Worse still, it may only be another form of hegemonic discourse that describes the ideal but fails to enable and facilitate ideal outcomes. In this regard, the role of justice theorizing should have less emphasis on providing the narrative of injustice and more emphasis on facilitating the removal of injustice, as suggested by Sen's suggestion to concentrate 'on reducing manifest injustices that so severely plague the world' (2009: 263). This first step is, of course, choosing to investigate questions of justice and injustice and identify how the structure of the international system and the processes of governance are reflected within conceptions of justice. After this, the course is less clear unless one happens to be in a position of power where it is easier to select and action remedies.

The task assigned to me in this chapter is divided into three parts. The first is to reflect on the role of justice in shaping my research interests and questions. The second is to explore how ideals of justice influence engagements with stakeholders, choice and practice of methods and dissemination strategies. The final task is to discuss what a justice perspective brings to my work over other theoretical frameworks. While the first and final parts of this task are relatively straightforward, the second part has revealed that as a scholar, perhaps I am not as purposeful in facilitating the removal of injustice as perhaps I should be, something that could be described in academic language as 'impact'. I conclude this piece by reflecting on how both International Relations and studies of the Arctic need more focus on justice, both in theorizing and in bringing justice into addressing issues in international society.

What is the role of justice in shaping my research interests and questions?

Research situated at the intersection of International Relations theory and political geography provides a convenient marriage of disciplinary concepts to evaluate political processes and their outcomes. The language of International Relations gives a vocabulary for explaining the development and characteristics of political processes, their structure and rules, for describing power symmetries, norms and legitimacy in state practice. Political geography gives the tools for evaluating political and temporal relationships with space and territory. However, these disciplinary frameworks fall short in providing the language to describe the impact and effects of these processes and relationships in my research agenda which has examined the longue durée political processes and norm evolution that shaped Arctic sovereignty, the structure of Arctic governance for decision-making over international spaces and even more recently in examining what may be unjust in the execution of state responsibilities by search and rescue volunteers in Arctic communities.

The study of International Relations and political geography is laced with a number of normative perspectives that are built on fundamental givens. As normative drivers, concepts of ethics emerge early in studies of International Relations from principles often now taken as givens, such as the relationship between liberal institutionalism and human rights or the even concept of justice found in studies of 'just war'. However, these normative foundations are rarely critically scrutinized for their origins or for how they enter the discourse of International Relations (Hutchings, 2019). These concepts underpin the 'is' of international ethical relationships, with the 'ought' affixed to expected behaviour in the international system established through adherence to the norms and rules of the international system, in following international legal codes and agreements.

To act as a player within the international system of states, a player must have four characteristics: a government, a territory, a people and legitimacy. While the territory is the 'where' of this, it is the government, the people and the legitimacy derived from the social contract between government and the people that give the state the mandate to act in pursuing the common good on behalf of its people in the relations between states, or International Relations. While 'the state' and the international system in which this scene plays out has a number of contradictions, not least in the narratives of its origins or the rationales for why particular peoples are included as a state's citizenry (such a language or cultural variations) or why particular swathes of territory fall within the domain of one state and not another.

For an International Relations social constructivist, injustice, rather than justice, provides the 'is' outcome for the 'ought' for the norms that have become embedded principles of the international system, 'oughts' which are themselves often riddled with characteristics of injustice from the processes that are the outcomes of participation in this social and spatial order. As a geographic space, the Arctic is a place where political processes occur and are both influenced by and create spatial structures. Long situated at the frontier for imperial expansion, resource exploitation and now the victim of climate change, it is increasingly apparent that the Arctic region is ripe with injustice inherently built into the structure from existing international norms.

In my investigations of the construction of the Arctic and its sovereignty, a number of contradictions screamed out to me. As a space brought into the sphere of interest and national boundaries of the Arctic states, the territory of the Arctic fell outside the narrative of the social contract ordinarily assumed in political legitimacy between the state and its people. This includes indigenous peoples absorbed into states through conquest and assimilation, the dislocation of indigenous peoples either through settler colonialism or by moving communities further north to 'realize' and force the effective occupation of annexed territories and, finally, the use of responsibility as a norm for spatial legitimacy. All this, without the follow through of proving or making the normative effects resulting from the assumption of responsibility a reality.

The early role of justice in shaping my research had less to do specifically with justice and was, perhaps, shaped instead by a characteristic of justice – in querying expectations of 'the good' that can be found in international legal norms. In this earlier stage of research examining the normative development of the rules of the international system that shaped territorial relationship and sovereign designation between the Arctic stage, the language of justice had yet to enter my research vocabulary. During this period, the discourse of the Arctic region frequently displayed contestation to framings of 'the good' in the delimitation of Arctic territory. Examples of these discourse debates included Canada using environmental protection clauses included in the United Nations Law of the Sea Convention to control the disputed waterway of the Northwest Passage or a Russian expedition placing a titanium tricolour at the seabed of the North Pole, causing protest from Canada that this ceremony of possession had no value in contemporary international legal frameworks. In these investigations, it was notable that questions of the social contract and responsibility for environmental safeguarding were entirely absent from questions around Arctic sovereignty. Without the language of justice, imperialism was the only word available to describe these processes and relationships.

Asymmetric power relations between a state and a colonized people, a characteristic of imperialism, has prevailed in seeping over into the new governance frameworks for the region, frameworks that emerged to coordinate to intra-state cooperation in the Arctic region on the grounds of environmental protection and to deal with transboundary environmental concerns. Notable in these frameworks is the shift in the governance arrangements to include Indigenous groups as permanent participants, sitting with the Arctic states (the eight permanent members of the Arctic Council) and while not holding any real decision-making power, still situated higher than the non-Arctic states who participate in Arctic governance processes as Observers to the proceedings. As an international institution the Arctic Council, as the pivot for Arctic governance, is extraordinary and even a progressive institution by including Indigenous participants in a position higher than some sovereignty states, ordinarily considered the highest unit in International Relations. In an earlier period, I queried whether this represented the introduction of a new and progressive norm for the international system. Yet in this arrangement, a specific hypocrisy exists. The Arctic states, who frequently claim sovereignty over the region via the social contract with Indigenous peoples as citizens of their states (and sometimes domestically have territorial devolution arrangements for self-government), made the step to exclude their Indigenous participants from the decision-making on environmental governance.

For some years, a mechanism for evaluating this relationship between Indigenous groups and states in Arctic governance evaded me until I happened upon the concept of structural injustice in the work of Iris Marion Young in her work *Responsibility for Justice*. Young details a four-part taxonomy for evaluating injustice caused by structures and structural relations, where actors behave as though the structure built in social-structural processes is real, asymmetric positions place limitations on actors' behaviour and cause resulting inequalities, repetition and performances of rules construct the system, and that these processes have real consequences for actors, including leading to vulnerability and deprivation (Young, 2011). Beyond this taxonomy, Young offers an explanation for responsibility and culpability for either causing or for perpetuating the resulting injustice. Through this, justice theory, and in particular, structural justice, has helped to show that Arctic governance is built on unjust foundations, but that a remedy is possible if agents with power accept responsibility for enabling change (Wood-Donnelly, 2023).

Another strand of research has been looking at the relationship between the assumption of responsibility by the state for search and rescue capacity in maritime spaces, which serves to extend the effective occupation of the state in extra-territorial spaces. Frequently, much of the provision of search and rescue is supplied by volunteers, who give generously of their time and other resources to save persons in distress. This provision is rarely supported by the state in financial, taxation, labour law mechanisms or mental health support. Given recent histories of migration crises in international maritime space, the refusals of a port of safety and the reliance on volunteers to provide for search and rescue capacities, several questions of injustice arise. For this topic, perspectives from the capabilities approach help to provide a frame for analysis to evaluate where injustice lies in the social contract that states agreed in the assumption of responsibility in maritime space and the limitations to human flourishing that emerge as a result of injustice.

In reflecting on the role of justice in shaping my research interests and questions, I have come to realize that the basic ambition of pursuing 'the good' isn't a sufficient target in understanding pathways and modes of interaction over space in studies of International Relations. The question, even at this level of analysis, will always return to 'whose good', and usually that is those (states) with the loudest voices or the most power. Justice theory provides the framework to evaluate the nuances of 'the good' in considering the forms of justice (that is, distribution, procedure, recognition) and the interrogations inspired by Jaggar (2009) in identifying the subject of justice, the temporal and spatial landscapes, scope of harms and methods for how injustice emerges, or can in fact be removed from the international system and the spaces in which this scene takes place.

How ideals of justice influence engagements with stakeholders, choice and practice of methods and dissemination strategies

As the scholarship of International Relations tends to focus on the state and the international system as the unit of analysis with policy, law and state practices serve as main sources of data. Depending on the subject under examination, even scholarship in political geography may result in infrequent interaction with stakeholders. Engagement with stakeholders is limited, except in the use of interviews as methodology or happenchance meetings of decision-makers at parliamentary and think tank events or at international conferences. In this regard, ideals of justice need to be converted from the ideal to the practical and from the academy to practice.

Ideals of justice, although attempting to paint pictures of what a perfectly just society might look like, can prove difficult in identifying a starting point. Rawls (1999) situates his ideals of justice from behind the veil of ignorance, where decision-makers do not understand where they are positioned in the positive and negative impacts and consequences of a decision. While this might prove an excellent remedy for eliminating problems in distributional, procedural or recognitional forms of justice, it is nearly impossible to execute from the *tabula rasa* needed to reach justice conditions. The ideals described by Nozick (1974) suggest that justice can be acquired through pure entitlement on the basis of just acquisition, transfer or of a principle of rectification, which seeks to reverse possession not gained by just acquisition or transfer. Yet, how does one in fact trace the precise lineage of unjust possession, which set of societal norms should be applied and at what point in history should rectification begin? It would be impossible to empty the Americas of all non-Indigenous persons or to return the wealth and resources that empires generated from the spice, rubber trades or mineral extraction back to the far-flung colonies.

A more practical ideal is proffered by Sen who suggests that '[w]e have reason to do what we can to remove diagnosable injustice to the extent possible' (2012: 108). Sen also suggests that it is 'hard to deny that ultimately the diagnosis of justice and injustice must depend on our values' (2012: 1), which is why Dworkin cautions that 'political decisions must be, so far as is possible, independent of any particular conception of the good life, or of what gives value to life' (2000: 127). It is Sen's suggestion to remove injustice, rather to than pursue any one specific metanarrative of justice that drives both my engagement with stakeholders and dissemination strategies for research. In part, it seems that this approach also allows for social, spatial and temporal flexibility in using specific groups of stakeholders' sense of the good life and perspectives of injustice to act as the compass for decision-making.

When viewing the Arctic through the lens of International Relations ordinarily the only stakeholder to be considered would be the primary unit of analysis in the system, the state. This positions decision-making for the region, not only from a top-down direction but also from an outside-in, with the Arctic states' decision-making centres of power often located far outside of the Arctic. However, with the advent of self-determination as a modern vehicle for effectuating the social contract, often through tacit consent, and with self-determination for Indigenous peoples rising to the fore in international discourse, the relationship of the state as the primary stakeholder in the Arctic becomes a matter of scrutiny in questions of structural injustice. Understanding these dynamics of justice and injustice, while not always resulting in direct contact with stakeholder, has a way of shaping understandings of the relationships between stakeholders in the Arctic and to watch the real-time, unfolding developments in the governance of the region with a critical eye. Accessing 'the state' as a stakeholder is complex and, in fact, means engaging with multiple actors who may have limited power to effect change.

Analysing the international system and the structure in which the politics of Arctic geography is situated means also using methods which shape meaning in the relationships and variances between stakeholders in the system. Analysing the evolution of the discourse of sovereignty legitimacy and responsibility over the Arctic requires scrutiny of the changing normative boundaries of the international structure, the way in which Arctic actors reinforce or adjust as we introduce new norms through law and practice. This involves using rather ordinary methods such as discourse analysis, policy analysis, process tracing or coding to identify themes, trends, motifs and variants against international regional norms to reveal hypocrisy, asymmetry and, in fact, injustice. Through these methods, justice becomes the measuring stick for understanding the failures of the state in these normative and governance evolutions.

The international system as we know it today is in fact a very young system. This system really emerged at the end of the Cold War with the disintegration of the Soviet bloc. Before this was a period of rapid expansion of the system of states and decolonization processes and, even before this, the 'system' was a very small and European-centric collection of states. In recent years, the system is being subjected to trends of fragmentation, where small units with stronger cultural cohesion are separating from a parent state, often formed where empires drew incongruous boundaries across maps. Examples of this fragmentation include partially recognized states, such as Kosovo or South Ossetia, fully independent states like Montenegro or South Sudan that have membership in the United Nations, and failed attempts at statehood as seen in the Scottish referendum to leave the UK, and so on. Sovereign states would have us believe their current construction and legitimacy will extend in perpetuity. However, the system is shifting and what it is evolving towards is difficult to predict.

For the foreseeable future, the best hope the state has in preventing the desire of groups to break away is to ensure 'the good' is being met and the social contract fulfilled, a reality especially palpable for the Arctic states. Where injustice exists and harm prevails, it can make it difficult for people to see how it is better to retain the status quo when there is the option to change. This places the need for the state to develop and pursue policy and governance arrangements which do not exasperate or continue the injustice created in past versions of the international system, such as the use of the Arctic as a sacrifice zone or even maintaining the injustices arising in the current version, such as issues caused by the climate crises. To do so is to ensure inequality and foster discontent and grievance. Whether this process begins from top-down action or emerges through the insistence of the citizens of the Arctic is only a matter of determining whether states will assume responsibility for justice and take action themselves or whether justice will have to be demanded, coerced and struggled for by Arctic peoples.

When the older European empires set sail for the new world in the hope of territorial expansion or resource acquisition, there were a number of necessary steps to make a successful change to their territorial volume. Step one was the discovery of new land, step two was to perform a ceremony of possession, step three was to disseminate communications of the new acquisition (that is, including it on maps) to other states who might also be seeking to discover new territories, and finally step four was to effectively occupy the new territory. It was these processes that resulted in shaping the international system and created the historical injustice that remains embedded in the Arctic today, steps which provide insights into how reaching justice can be achieved within the international system, and to reflect on engagement with stakeholders, methods and dissemination of research findings.

Removing justice from a system will also have steps. Step one is in identifying injustice. This first step of justice can be realized from the lived experiences of people and the barriers which prevent flourishing and moving towards perceptions of the good life, or through scholarship that identifies where practices of the state fail in their normative measures. However, it seems that once injustice has been identified that questions being to emerge related to responsibility for injustice, or for moving towards justice. This brings us to step two, which could involve further identification of concrete mechanisms that enable the removal of distributional, procedural and recognitional forms of injustice in substantive ways. While desk-bound researchers often fulfil these initial steps, this results in inchoate justice, which is still only injustice unresolved at best and injustice abetted at worst.

Now emerges a critical role for the scholar in step three, the communication on the identification of injustice and the tools and mechanisms for enabling the removal and rectification of injustice. In this step, it is essential that this communication reaches beyond the academy and that practices and choices of dissemination are deliberate and persistent. For my part, this happens through various dissemination methods. There are, of course, the scholarly publications which create records of the identification of and methods for removing justice. There is also the choice to be present in events and forums (that is, the Arctic Circle Conference) where it is possible to alert representatives of the Arctic states to issues of injustice, which may be in their realm to influence removal. Another important method is facilitating learning opportunities through seminars and student-teaching. However, a critical element of my overall strategy has been to facilitate the opportunity to multiply the work investigating justice and injustice in the Arctic, by coordinating workshops and research projects, such as the EU-funded climate action project JUSTNORTH or the Working Group on Justice in the Arctic, under the umbrella of the International Arctic Social Sciences Association.

We have been alerted that 'the arc of the moral universe is long, but it bends towards justice' (King 1965 in Amster, 2012: 199) and as individuals, we may never see step 4 fulfilled in the removal of injustice. It is not yet evident that the findings of my individual research findings and the dissemination strategy are facilitating the removal of injustice in the Arctic, but there is time for that yet. What is important is that the journey to remove injustice in the Arctic and to move towards the facilitation of justice for the Arctic, even if a non-ideal justice, has begun for the environment, economy and society of the region.

What a justice perspective brings to this research over other theoretical frameworks

Prior to bringing justice theory to my research, I ordinarily worked within the frameworks of three common theories for a political-scientist-cum-political-geographer researching the question of territory, the political ordering of space and the legitimacy of authority over those spaces. This includes theories of International Relations social constructivism, sovereignty and of imperialism. While informative and useful in providing explanations for the 'is', from the outcomes of my research, these theoretical frameworks are lacking normative direction in explanations of the 'ought'. It strikes me in a reflection of the many works of Arctic governance and geopolitics, that questions of justice are entirely absent, something which may be the result of the traditional theoretical frameworks not including evaluations of justice and injustice as part of their explanatory processes. These frameworks have provided a useful scaffolding for the analysis of the Arctic and its territory as a political landscape, a landscape that hosts a tension in the relationship between the domestic and international spaces.

Although deserving of a much longer exposition, the simple explanation for this tension can be attributed to the 'slow' imperialism that resulted in the division of the region into the political territories of the Arctic states – which manifested somewhat differently around the circumpolar Arctic. In the parts of the Arctic near to European centres of power, the territories and people were annexed as 'natural' extensions of the nearby states, with the ultimate result of dividing Sápmi and the Sámi people between four nations. This division was often messy and the Sámi experienced difficulties such as overlapping taxation demands from more than one state. The formal boundaries of these divisions were also subject to changing political arrangements further south with political fragmentation and conflict around Europe. The legacies of imperialism continue to be experienced in a variety of ways today, such as different political-economic rights related to cultural heritage across Sápmi, and of increasing concern, the rise of a new form of colonialism emerging from the green transition for the globalized economy.

In the parts of the Arctic flung from European centres of power, imperialism was somewhat glaciated due to the vast distances to be travelled and climatic influences, such as the Little Ice Age of the mid-19th century. For some time, the idea of a northern trading passage dominated exploration efforts of imperial nations. While Arctic territories were eventually drawn into political cartographies of states through a variety of annexation practices from 'discovery' to purchase, the absence of the practices of effective occupation left some state claims to the Arctic inchoate. This was compounded by misunderstandings of Arctic geography where it was anticipated that land, rather than frozen sea, existed nearer to the pole. When and where states pursued practical administration, this resulted in economic exploitation, settler colonialism creating competing land use and cultural assimilation policies which have left a heavy scar on Indigenous peoples in the North.

Imperialism and its theories are about the political and economic overflow of power into and onto external territories, peoples and resources, where 'power becomes precarious and artificial' (Hobson, 2005: 8). At its core, theories of imperialism give the researcher a lens to look at the exercise of power and domination over people and territory by a state with the ability to project power and to administrate over distant subjects. Although this domination came in some cases through superior technological capacities (that is, transport, weapons) of European nations, in some cases through the spreading of communicable diseases which weakened newly exposed peoples, and in other cases through unequal treaties and different understandings of territorial possession.

A primary manifestation of this domination is in the ability of imperial states to write the rules of conquest and territorial acquisition for the international system, to which assimilated peoples were subjected. Peoples experiencing processes of imperialism were incorporated into different, and often distant, political systems through a variety of administrative processes, but in most cases these were processes originating outside of the social contract, and certainly outside of democratic principles. While large parts of the world once subjected to imperialism and colonialism have experienced independence movements, this has not happened in the Arctic and, at present, Arctic territory and Indigenous peoples remain embedded within the political territory of the states that exercised imperialism to gain control over this space, an embeddedness which does not always prove beneficial for either the environment or the peoples of the high north.

Another key feature from theories of imperialism that is useful for studies of the Arctic is in considering the processes of political absorption and the identification of asymmetries of power that are manifest in core–periphery relations. This is evident in the resource extraction priorities that brought economic value and benefit to centres of power. In many cases, policies and administrative decisions influencing economic development were made in locations far outside of the Arctic, with resulting maldistribution of the flows of economic benefits, exposure to environmental harms and the experience from adverse social impacts of development. Examples of this can be found from the earliest Arctic histories, continuing until the present, such as in taxation or tribute policies, the fur trade, sealing, whaling, fishing, mining and hydrocarbon extraction.

Sovereignty as a normative operator and theories of sovereignty has also been a useful lens for understanding and explaining particular aspects of the development of the Arctic and the various political technologies that states use in the region to exercise authority and to create legitimacy. Understandings of sovereignty and the methods of exercising sovereignty have evolved throughout different periods of state engagement with the Arctic, based on what principles and norms have been produced and accepted by states wielding power in the international system. Theories of sovereignty provide the mechanisms to understand who holds legitimacy for decision-making over people and space, and also determine who has exploitation rights for the resources of a particular territory (Wood-Donnelly, 2019).

Sovereignty is often defined as 'the supreme authority within a territory' (Hobbes, 1904) and in one part includes internal authority over its people and territory, but also has external projection in its relations with other political units. In its internal features, theories of sovereignty have a variety of foundational premises, such as pure power, ecclesiastical endowment or the social contract. While the social contract, more broadly, is today understood as the foundation for popular legitimacy within democratic societies, sovereignty wielded through projections of power still features heavily within many modern states. In its external projection, the sovereignty of a state includes the government, people and territory features, but critically, it must also include a facet of international legitimization gained through recognition of sovereignty by other states within the system.

In the Arctic, theories of sovereignty have been useful for explaining the internal and external projections of legitimacy for decision-making in the region over spaces that have historically been considered by states as their territory, but in the rules of today's international system are seen as international space. In the internal projections of sovereignty, there has been an evolution of how states engage with the Arctic region in what can be termed as 'effective occupation', a rule brought to considerations of sovereignty through practices of imperialism (Wood-Donnelly, 2017). Effective occupation has been a motivating operational force in assimilation practices that sought to create popular legitimacy and consent of the governed by converting periphery residents, usually Arctic Indigenous peoples, into resembling the societal structures found in core citizens, such as religion, language and other social norms, such as conceptions of family and property.

Theories of sovereignty have been especially helpful in explaining the evolution in state legitimization of its relationship with the territory across the Arctic that lies outside of its national borders and beyond the possibility of political enfranchisement and popular legitimacy. These processes in the Arctic are possibly more peculiar than any other international space with the Arctic states seeking to legitimize their authority and decision-making practices through external recognition of legitimacy in regional governance mechanisms and international law frameworks. The first way this external legitimacy is achieved is through the Arctic Council, where the Arctic member states require non-Arctic states to recognize their sovereignty of the region to become Observers of the forum. A second way this external legitimacy is reached is through international legal frameworks, such as the law of the sea, which not only allows for states to extend their exploitation rights, which is one of the privileges of sovereignty but also allows for these states to control the actions of other states in common spaces that would otherwise have certain freedoms on the basis of concerns for environmental protection.

The other primary theoretical framework that I frequently use in my research is International Relations' social constructivism. Within the discipline, this approach is one of the most flexible and nuanced analytical tools, that is so reflective and reflexive that it is sometimes referred to as a metatheory and that to speak of only one International Relations social constructivism is problematic (Kubálková, 2001). While other International Relations theories can have quite targeted focus points – such as different forms of cooperation or material manifestations of power, social constructivism suggests that the international system and its rules are co-constituted and that the process by which society and its rules 'constitute each other [is] continuous and reciprocal' (Onuf in Kubálková et al, 1998: 59). More pronounced in International Relations social constructivism is the role of identity and its intersubjective realization as a key feature of order within the international system and in framing the interests of states.

International Relations social constructivism is built around four pillars: rules, interests, agents and identity (Klotz and Lynch, 2007). Rules create the normative impulse guiding actions and suggest how agents, or states, within the system ought to behave in relation to one another. Where and how these four pillars are constituted, mobilized, reciprocated and reproduced create the intersubjective realities of international politics and of the international system. In this regard, IR social constructivism gives meaning to explaining how imperialism in the Arctic worked beyond the simple terms of power and domination. Constructivism makes it possible to see how the rules of imperialism with regard to territorial annexation were introduced, constituted and communicated through repetition and shared interest. This approach also gives meaning to explaining how sovereignty and exploitation rights associated with extra-territorial spaces in the Arctic have developed over time within the international system through repetition or codification.

The pillar of identity provides curious insight into theorizing Arctic International Relations and geopolitics, both in the context of watching the unfolding development of states as 'Arctic states' and in relation to the establishment of decision-making legitimacy. The identification of the eight states who are full members of the Arctic Council is situated somewhere between their histories of imperialism in the Arctic and their contemporary interests in resource exploitation and other forms of securitization, premised on the legitimizing of their sovereignty over the region in both internal and external forms. This identity-building has been apparent in a variety of political technologies, in the domestic realm including exhibits at national museums, postage stamps and arms of bureaucracy dedicated to the region. In the external realm, this is evident in creating Arctic policies, participating in Arctic-focused multi-lateral agreements with other Arctic states and accepting responsibility for environmental protection and safety provision (that is, search and rescue) in the international spaces of the Arctic. What is especially curious about the Arctic policies and strategies of the Arctic states is that they blur the lines between domestic policy and foreign policy, frequently focusing on four areas of economic development, environmental protection, sovereignty and security.

Theories of imperialism, in their identification of power asymmetry, domination and maldistribution of harms and benefits, seem a likely lens for conducting research on the resulting justice or injustice of these processes and their impacts. However, theories of imperialism, outside of some radical work on imperialism, are void of normative frameworks. Theories of sovereignty are extremely useful in understanding why and how the state derives its authority and legitimacy for the benefits and privileges of territorial occupation and exploitation. There are strong relationships between theories of imperialism and of sovereignty, where the latter often provides the normative justifications for the former, however without considering 'the good' beyond what is deemed good and essential for the state, even when sovereignty and legitimacy are premised on the social contract between the state and its citizens. Despite the normative force of rules in International Relations social constructivism in informing how states ought to behave within the international system and in their relationship with other states in the community, it does not provide evaluations of benefit or harm and the pursuit of interests beyond the level of the state. In this regard, despite the explanatory power and usefulness of all of these theoretical approaches, they are missing evaluations of what decision-making 'ought' to be made in respect to what facilitates fairness, equity and flourishing.

What is missing in these theories is 'the good' and the 'ought' that makes for good governance. In this regard, theories of justice bring depth for understanding how the distribution of harms and benefits could be made in respect of resource exploitation, how procedures could be designed that bring recognition to the voices and livelihoods of those most affected by decision-making and how retribution for past practices of domination can be recognized as preventing flourishing for peoples and creatures living in the Arctic. In my study of Arctic governance, the work of Young's taxonomy for structural injustice has been particularly enlightening in understanding how the current structure of Arctic governance as it is promoted in the Arctic Council, while although an advance on earlier forms of international governance, falls short by perpetuating asymmetry and domination within the structure. In this regard, the theories of imperialism, sovereignty, International Relations social constructivism together with structural justice form an enlightening partnership.

By developing a movement towards studies of justice in and for the Arctic, justice theory and theorizing have expanded my research horizons in significant ways. Through the JUSTNORTH project, which is funded by the EU as a climate action project, the research team has been investigating how past and existing practices in economic exploitation and decision-making around economic development results in injustice for Arctic citizens and, in some cases, for the entire globe. In this, the research team has used injustice to identify barriers to sustainable development and what prevents Arctic economic development from facilitating a just transition for the European climate action agenda – an agenda which relies heavily on the extraction of Arctic resources or for housing technologies of the future (that is, wind farms, data centres). In this work, we have used a taxonomy of realms, forms, aspects and fields of justice to analyse the project data set. In the realms we find concepts such as temporality or scale, in forms, we find modes such as distribution or recognition. In the aspects, we have drawn from Jaggar's (2009) who, what, when, where and how of justice and, finally, in the fields of justice the work can be framed with a special focus (that is, climate, spatial or environmental justice). In this work, justice theorizing has supported the study in moving beyond utilitarian decision-making and making decisions that enable a just transition.

In recent decades there has been a debate in Arctic discourse about whether states should create an Arctic Treaty, establishing the region as a global commons and protecting the environment from economic exploitation and degradation. Theories of imperialism, sovereignty and International Relations social constructivism can explain why this is not in states' interests and why it is not likely to happen on the basis of rules and interests. As the global debate about responsibility for climate action intensifies, justice theory brings light to how this matters in the Arctic and whom it matters for. Still missing in questions of environmental justice is whether nature should be included as a subject of justice or whether the Arctic is simply a sacrifice zone for the economic development ambitions of the Arctic states or as a landscape irretrievably damaged by climate change. While the work on justice and the Arctic is growing, there is still much to be done.

Conclusions

In reflecting on the contribution and role of justice in informing 'perspectives from the top' it is clear that justice theorizing stands to bring significant contributions to studies of the Arctic, and in particular, to studies of Arctic International Relations and the political geography of the region. Until bringing theories of justice into my research agenda, it seemed to lack normative perspective that went beyond explaining how things are to thinking about how things could be. Justice theory brings this element to the discussion because justice is a vector. As a vector, justice theory brings magnitude to understanding the scale and substance of injustice and it brings direction in identifying what should be removed or changed to bring about more justice conditions.

Perspectives of justice are multi-layered, multi-faceted and frequently subjective. My own research agenda, even when factoring in the contributions from the JUSTNORTH project, does not come close to identifying the many causes and conditions of injustice in the Arctic, nor does it provide all the answers to removing injustice. In this area, there remains a substantial need for further research. There is a need for a thorough analysis of justice and injustice from Indigenous perspectives and scholars, for analysis from the various schools of justice, such as feminist or cosmopolitan justice. There is also a need to understand the implications of justice and injustice for the Arctic in connection to the environment, ecosystems and nature as the subject of justice. Finally, there is the need to bring justice theory to studies in the connection of the Arctic to processes of global climate change, including just transition in climate action, globalized economies and responsibility for climate reparations.

The moral arc towards justice may be long, but it begins with a single spark. It begins with the identification of injustice through perspectives found in justice theory while the remedy for injustice can begin through identifying pathways for the removal of injustice in its distribution, procedure and recognition features that seek to rebalance power asymmetries and to flatten horizontal decision-making hierarchies. While communicating facts about injustice and opportunities for change is important in promoting the removal of injustice, this is not the end. Achieving justice is not a linear process towards creating an ideal society because notions of 'the good' and what constitutes an ideal society will change with every generation.

Justice, as a normative operator, is a reiterative and co-constitutive precept that should spiral towards flourishing with justice and just conditions as the ultimate condition of 'the good'. Given this, we can see that the pursuit of justice in and for the Arctic is the pathway towards the best of perspectives from the top. To reach this vantage point, it is important to continue bringing the theoretical perspective of justice into studies of International Relations and political geography – not just of the Arctic – but for all of the international system.

Acknowledgements
This research has received funding from the European Union's Horizon 2020 research and innovation programme under grant agreement No 869327.

References
Amster, R. (2012) Just, in time: cultivating the long arc of justice, *Contemporary Justice Review*, 15(2): 197–202.
Dikeç, M. (2001) Justice and the spatial imagination, *Environment and Planning A: Economy and Space*, 33(10): 1785–1805.
Dworkin, R. (2000) *A Matter of Principle*, Cambridge, MA: Harvard University Press.
Hobbes, T. (1904) *Leviathan: Or, The Matter, Forme & Power of a Commonwealth, Ecclesiastical and Civil*, London: C.J. Clay and Sons.
Hobson, J.A. (2005) *Imperialism: A Study*, New York: Cosimo.
Hutchings, K. (2019) Decolonizing global ethics: thinking with the pluriverse, *Ethics & International Affairs; New York*, 33(2): 115–125.
Jaggar, A.M. (2009) The philosophical challenges of global gender justice, *Philosophical Topics*, 37(2): 1–15.
Klotz, A. and Lynch, C. (2007) *Strategies for Research in Constructivist International Relations*. International Relations in a Constructed World. Abingdon, Oxon: Routledge.
Kratochwil, F. (2007) Looking back from somewhere: reflections on what remains 'critical' in critical theory, *Review of International Studies*, 33(S1): 25–45.
Kubálková, V. (ed) (2001) *Foreign Policy in a Constructed World*, Armonk: M.E. Sharpe.
Kubálková, V., Onuf, N.G. and Kowert, P. (eds) (1998) *International Relations in a Constructed World*, Armonk: M.E. Sharpe.
Nozick, R. (1974) *Anarchy, State, and Utopia*, Oxford: Blackwell.
Rawls, J. (1999) *A Theory of Justice*, revised edn, Cambridge: Belknap Press.
Ray, A.K. (1999) The concept of justice in international relations, *Economic and Political Weekly*, 34(22): 1368–1374.
Sen, A. (2009) *The Idea of Justice*, Cambridge, MA: Harvard University Press.
Sen, A. (2012) Values and justice, *Journal of Economic Methodology*, 19(2): 101–108.

Wood-Donnelly, C. (2017) Messages on Arctic policy: effective occupation in the postage stamps of the United States, Canada and Russia, *Geographical Review*, 107(1): 236–257.

Wood-Donnelly, C. (2019) *Performing Arctic Sovereignty: Policy and Visual Narratives*, Abingdon: Routledge.

Wood-Donnelly, C. (2023) Responsibility of and for structural (in)justice in Arctic governance, in Wood-Donnelly, C. and Ohlsson, J. (eds) *Arctic Justice: Society, Environment and Governance*, Bristol: Bristol University Press, pp 25–35.

Young, I.M. (2011) *Responsibility for Justice*, New York: Oxford University Press.

9

Justice for All? Expanding Questions and Spaces of (In)Justice through Multispecies Research, Teaching and Activism

Vegan Geography Collective (Richard J. White, Ophélie Véron, Simon Springer and Andrew McGregor)

A great swathe of the rapidly expanding fields of critical animal geographies and vegan geographies (Hodge et al, 2022) are driven by a desire to better articulate, conceptualize and respond to a range of complex themes and questions rooted in *multispecies* justice (MSJ). In contrast, when considering broader (inter)disciplinary 'critical' geographies narratives of social justice, the appeal for multispecies accounts of justice to come to the fore is still seen to be a deeply contentious and 'radical' or extreme position to take. Yet, if there is one thing that the ongoing crises and injustice evident within our world(s) might teach us – from climate catastrophe, species extinction and zoonotic diseases, to the normalized (racist, casteist, colonial, classist, capitalist) geographies of the meat, egg and dairy industries – it is that anthropocentric narratives of justice 'for us' are not fit for purpose. In this sense we stand in complete agreement with Celermajer et al's arguments as to why a MSJ politics is so important now, more so than ever:

> An account of MSJ is required to rectify false assumptions and longstanding misconceptions in justice theory. Principal amongst these is the fictitious idea of human beings as individual, isolated, unattached and unencumbered, and the correlative presumption that more-than-human nature is mere passive background. Beyond rejecting the belief that humans alone merit ethical or political consideration, multispecies justice rejects three related ideas central to human exceptionalism: a)

that humans are physically separate or separable from other species and non-human nature, b) that humans are unique from all other species because they possess minds (or consciousness) and agency and c) that humans are therefore more important than other species. (Celermajer et al, 2021: 120)

While acknowledging and welcoming a multispecies praxes that is diverse, contingent and ephemeral in nature, this chapter considers what 'justice *for all*' means in the context of our experiences across a variety of settings and roles: as 'scholars', as 'activists', as 'parents' and so on. One of the common threads that link these experiences together is the question of 'How can we more justly share [and help shape] space?' (Gillespie and Collard, 2015: 8). Recognizing the importance of social and spatial specificities when talking about MSJ, and embracing the international scholarship and activism of this Vegan Geography Collective, the main body of the chapter is composed of a combination of four case studies, commentaries and reflections. In particular we hope to impress upon the reader the importance of embracing a vegan praxis in informing MSJ; a praxis rooted across a range of (everyday) contested geographies, in ways that might be taken forward to inform and animate future MSJ research, teaching and activism.

In terms of structure, first, Andrew McGregor reflects on MSJ in the context of food systems transition. He explores how meat and dairy industries are increasingly scrutinized for their impacts on climate change and environmental sustainability rather than on their impacts on the lives of the human and non-human animals entrapped within exploitative food systems. His concern is that technological solutions to climate change that do not have principles of MSJ at their fore may further accentuate the violence inflicted on farmed animals and human workers. However there is now an opportunity and imperative for environmental and animal activists to work together to bring about more just and desirable food systems.

The second set of reflections is given by Simon Springer. Reflecting on his own children, all lifelong vegans, and their experiences with family and friends in negotiating the everyday realities of pervasive carnism, Springer illuminates a sense of justice that extends beyond the human realm. By bringing the experiences of children to the fore, veganism becomes a conduit to understanding justice in non-anthropocentric terms. Children are often undeterred by 'polite' social protocols and will challenge speciesism head on, taking to task one of the last remaining systemic prejudices that continues to enjoy widespread support.

Third, Richard White focuses on his lecturing experiences at university as opening up a vital 'activist' space with which to challenge dominant narratives of justice, and raise consciousness among students around MSJ. Drawing largely on his own experiences of teaching vegan geographies to undergraduate students, White pays particular attention to the contrasting relationships between companion animals and farmed animals among his students – which mirror those across contemporary society. Here he talks about how these two contrasting perspectives and references can be brought together to create a powerful argument for a MSJ praxis to come forward.

Finally, Ophélie Véron reflects on the use of militant (auto)ethnography in the context of community food spaces. Drawing on her experience of fieldwork in both vegan and non-vegan activist groups as a vegan scholar-activist, Véron reflects on the ethical dilemmas, potential tensions and critical transformations that such engagement entails, and what it can contribute to understandings of MSJ.

Multispecies justice in the context of food systems transition (Andrew McGregor)

As the planet enters a new epoch, one marked by widespread environmental instability, it is clear that the anthroprivilege (Springer, 2022) that has historically informed many approaches to justice needs to be rethought. Pursuing more just human worlds is vitally important, but not enough. The planetary boundaries that support human and non-human life are being eroded, the biosphere may already have begun a mass extinction event, and non-humans are being intentionally incarcerated, tortured and killed for human use at unimaginable scales. Work in animal ethics, eco-feminism, post-humanism, Indigenous knowledges and more-than-human geographies have all stressed the multiple agencies, interests and relational interdependence of humans and non-humans and the urgent need to do better. As biophysical and conceptual worlds evolve, so too must ethics and understandings of justice.

Much of my own work has focused on environmental concerns and issues, particularly as they relate to climate change, while my personal life, politics and practices have also been informed by veganism. Until recently I have considered the justice dimensions of environmentalism and veganism as mostly aligned, both seeking to create more just worlds for human and non-human others in different ways. However, as my research has become more focused on food–environment relations the tensions between these approaches have become more apparent (see McGregor, 2022). As I will describe in this section, environmentalism is unnecessarily limited in terms of both space and species in its pursuit of more just worlds. In contrast, concepts like MSJ (Tschakert, 2020) and total liberation (Glasser, 2015) align well with veganism and can provide conceptual tools that can bolster environmental outcomes.

Currently I work on the nexus of animal agriculture and climate, exploring the challenges of just food transitions. Animal agriculture is implicated in a multitude of environmental calamities, including climate change, deforestation, biodiversity crises and extinction, land and water degradation, food security, and a host of other issues (FAO, 2006). And yet, until recently most forms of environmentalism have had little to say about animal agriculture. Mainstream Western environmentalism has tended to prioritize the protection of romantic but now thoroughly debunked and racialized concepts of 'wilderness' (Cronon, 1996) or promoted greener policies and technologies to protect the earth. The just transitions movement has focused primarily on the fossil fuel sector, developing pathways for workers and communities to move into cleaner industries. Southern environmentalism and environmental justice movements have focused on the racialized and classed unequal distribution of environmental benefits and hazards, stressing the interdependence of human communities with their environments in efforts to improve both.

All this is important work. However, it has left a large gap in activism and research when it comes to animal agriculture. Pig farming only matters when it pollutes rivers; cattle farming matters when it causes deforestation; chicken farming matters when it causes air pollution; fish farming matters when it pollutes marine habitats. The approach has been fragmented, seeking to address anthropocentric and ecocentric environmental issues as they arise. The lives of the animals being farmed, the chickens, ducks, turkeys, pigs, cattle, goats, minks, dogs, and many other species are insignificant, hovering outside the moral scope and concerns of environmentalism. Even now, when the global scale of terrestrial animal slaughter exceeds well over a billion animals a week, it is the cumulative environmental impacts of the industry, rather than the scale of death and suffering, that has propelled animal agriculture to become a matter of concern.

The two primary justice frames for analysing animal agriculture within environmentalism are environmental justice and climate justice. Environmental justice has highlighted the classed and racialized geographic distribution of environmental harms associated with animal agriculture, such as the placement and pollution associated with battery farms and slaughterhouses among low-income communities, as well as the impacts of the difficult and violent working conditions on often migrant, poorly paid and/or precariously employed workers (see Emel and Neo, 2015). Climate justice advocates are more likely to focus on global scale inequalities, highlighting the uneven environmental burdens associated with the overconsumption of animal products amongst richer countries and communities.

In both these framings the lives of the farmed animals don't matter in and of themselves. Environmentalism does not seek the end of animal agriculture, but to minimize its environmental impacts. At a local scale this may mean better regulations and enforcement to minimize pollution and run-off from agricultural industries and better conditions and pay for workers. At a global scale it involves techno-science communities racing to develop technologies and farm management strategies that can decrease animal emissions and impacts as well as lukewarm efforts to reduce meat consumption amongst high consumption societies. The priority is to reduce environmental impacts by producing more environmentally friendly animal products.

The problem with these approaches is that environmentally friendly animal products generally require making and growing animals more efficiently (FAO, 2006: 120). This often equates to inflicting more violence within already violent production systems to further control breeding and movement so that environmental externalities can be constrained and controlled. Some research suggests, for example, that intensively farmed animals may emit less emissions per kilo of product as they grow more quickly than grazing animals (Swain et al, 2018). Similarly, much touted animal feed supplements to reduce methane emissions from cattle can more easily be distributed to feedlot cattle than grazing cattle, creating a further incentive to restrict movements and animal lives. Such approaches are likely to favour larger, more capital-intensive corporate farms over smaller family farms, enhancing the likelihood of worker exploitation (McGregor et al, 2021). The unwanted and unanticipated outcome from growing environmental interest in animal agriculture may well be an increase in animal suffering.

It is for this reason that concepts like MSJ need fleshing out. The question should not be how can humans further exploit farm animals to minimize environmental impacts, but how can humans more justly share space and engage with our non-human kin (Gillespie and Collard, 2015)? It makes no sense for environmental concerns for humans, non-humans and environments to stop at the farm gate. In doing so the one-third of the earth's non-ice surface devoted to animal agriculture escapes environmental scrutiny, as does the bulk of life on earth. By an order of magnitude there are more chickens on the planet than any other bird, so numerous that their bones are being considered a marker of the Anthropocene (Bennett et al, 2018), and the combined weight of farmed animals weighs more than 20 times that of wild animals (Appleby, 2008). The lives of these animals matter not only because the resources that go into their production are destroying the homes, habitats and planetary conditions that sustain life on earth, but because their suffering is unnecessary, avoidable and unjust. Principles of MSJ and total liberation can breach arbitrary spatial and speciesist environmentalist blindspots and bring the lives of all animals, inside and outside the farm, into consideration and focus. It enables animal agriculture to go from a matter of concern that can be brutally managed for minor environmental gains, to a matter of care in which the lives and interests of all those involved inform ways forward (Puig de la Bellacasa, 2011).

It is through the lens of MSJ that I now approach food systems transitions research. When developing research projects I choose topics that will shed light into how the lives of non-human animals, mostly farm animals, are likely to be impacted by initiatives oriented at developing more sustainable food systems. I am interested in MSJ as it relates to the new technologies and forms of governance oriented at reducing emissions from farm animals, the shifting economies, actors, landscapes and products associated with 'plant-based capitalism' (Giraud, 2021), and the more intersectional ethics and activism of veganism. Data analysis of industry documents and websites explores how farm animals are constructed and considered, which more often highlights a lack of recognition, evident in absences and silences, rather than any clear engagement with the concerns of MSJ. During interviews and workshops participants are asked about their motivations and probed to consider the significance and impacts of their initiatives on the lives of human and non-human animals. This can be difficult and, in some cases, an obvious absence of concern or consideration for animal lives can lead to awkwardness, when the rhythm of the discussion shifts momentarily into less comfortable ground before moving on to other topics. I am hopeful such pauses bring non-human animals into view and consideration, even if only for a moment, and have them recognized in a way that may trigger later reflection about animal lives, however I have no evidence of this. In contrast, when vegan activists and some vegan businesses are asked about similar issues the conversation flows in interesting ways and shows that concerns about MSJ are prominent, active and alive within these communities. The challenge is to bring these activist perspectives and the lives of animals into the foreground during this moment when food systems are reimagined and reshaped in the context of planetary change.

The justice of suffering? Raising ethical vegan children (Simon Springer)

My children are vegan. Born and raised. Non-vegan friends and relatives have often opined that one day they will rebel against my partner, Marni, and I to become ardent carnivores. The awkward laughter that follows suggests that this is said partially in jest, as though there is anything at all funny about the horror and tragedy of murdering animals to consume their dismembered body parts. Yet in part this is something they also seem to truly believe. Such sentiments are profoundly mistaken. My children were raised to think and act for themselves in ways that are compatible with their own sense of right and wrong. We have always encouraged them to think critically and for themselves, as opposed to simply toeing the line and following the status quo (Springer, 2016). The act of rebellion is a counter to authoritarian tendencies, but my children have always been treated as equals, respected in every measure of their autonomy. Stopping a child from walking into traffic is different than ensuring that they capitulate to your beliefs, whether vegan or otherwise. Care and protection are set apart from demanding respect when it is not reciprocated. Sadly, authoritarian parenting is so ingrained in our society that it is often taken for granted. But that is an approach my partner and I have actively pushed back on since our first day of becoming parents. More importantly, however, is that this assertion of a future revolution towards eating meat is rooted in carnist beliefs, wherein the consumption of deceased animals is considered normative (Joy, 2020). The extension of that assumption is that my children are being raised in a state of privation. As my sister-in-law framed it, "How can you justify forcing your kids not to eat meat?", to which Marni responded, "How can you justify forcing children to eat meat?". The normativity of my sister-in-law's position was not something she was able to see beyond, and nor was she able to appreciate veganism as a deep and uncompromising ethical commitment for parents (Alvaro, 2020). Such reflexivity is not an issue for my kids.

Justice for my children is to be found in the idea that all sentient creatures, big and small, are deserving of meaningful and fulfilling lives free from both violence and suffering (Singer, 2009). Just as I developed a deep sense that something was wrong with our food systems once I learned the truth about the euphemization of dead bodies as 'meat' when I was a child, so too do my children consider eating the corpses of murdered animals to be a transgression of what is fair, what is right and what is just. The difference for my children, then, is that they have been free to explore the ethical implications of consuming slaughtered animal carcasses through the encouragement of their critical reflections, as opposed to being redirected and lied to. In fact, most children are acutely aware of the problems with eating cadavers. When watching a film like *Bambi* and seeing the mother deer shot, it typically elicits a deeply empathetic response. The child recognizes that a child has lost its mother and they put themselves into that frame of reference. Parents will often console their children in such situations, offering emotional support, and reassuring them that it is just a story. Yet in the next moment they will serve that same child a hamburger without telling them how that 'food' came to be. The sin of omission is only part of the story, though, as children are naturally inquisitive and will ask all sorts of questions about anything and everything, including what they are being given to eat. It is at that stage that the lies begin to manifest.

How often do parents shelter their children from the truth about the lives of animals, purposefully redirecting the line of questioning that a child inherently follows? "Lambs are cute, why would anyone want to kill them for food?" a child will ask. "Now dear, never mind and eat your supper", comes the parent's reply. "If mammals produce milk for their offspring, isn't cow's milk meant for baby cows and not humans?", a child will ask. "Don't be silly. It will help you develop strong bones, now drink up" is the response. Such apparently innocent untruths, deflections and dissimulations are seemingly innocuous to an adult inculcated in carnist thought. Yet to a child only beginning to develop a sense of justice in this world they are profoundly damaging lessons in prejudice. They teach children that the lives of those without voice or power are somehow not worth as much and are perhaps even expendable (Olivier and Cordeiro-Rodrigues, 2017). They uproot a child's capacity for empathy and undo the impulse for greater communion with the natural world by sowing the seeds of exceptionalism. Quite literally they compel a child to discriminate, a learned behaviour that will ultimately manifest in other domains. In opposition to a child's inclination to include and share, children learn that those who don't look like them are not only to be excluded but may be subjected to profound forms of violence. These ostensibly harmless and mundane moments of mealtime are in fact the foundations of all forms of othering in our contemporary society. For these, among myriad other reasons, parents have an ethical obligation to raise their children vegan (Alvaro, 2019).

For my own children, they have been appalled by the food choices of their relatives and some of their friends. Rather than redirect, Marni and I have encouraged them to follow their own sense of justice and draw their own conclusions. So, when my youngest son at age six confronted his grandfather about why he continued to eat animals knowing that they suffered and was met with the retort that carrots have feelings too, he was dismayed. At first this deflection ruptured his sense of justice. He became anxious and felt that perhaps he too was contributing to suffering. But of course, a carrot is not sentient, and after debriefing with Marni, he started to recognize that his grandfather was attempting to assuage his own feelings of guilt by deflecting them onto his grandson. This should not be a proud moment for any grandparent, but it has been pivotal in my son's development, and he often refers back to it. It has helped him grow in terms of connecting consciously with his own sense of justice, but also in terms of understanding the shame, guilt and cognitive dissonance that the wider society he lives in maintains with respect to killing and consuming animals. Justice for my son can never be found in the suffering and death of others.

Vegan geographies in the classroom: interspecies care, violence and sense of (in)justice (Richard J. White)

I have been a university lecturer in England now for over 17 years. My intervention draws on some of the regular experiences and encounters I've had over this time, principally when discussing MSJ in lectures or seminars on critical animal geographies and vegan geographies. It's probably worth noting early on that these sessions are not offered within elective modules. Rather, they fly 'under the radar' to a degree, insofar as they are located within broader mandatory first- and second-year undergraduate modules;

modules that have general titles like 'Approaches to Human Geography', or 'Philosophy, Space and Place'. It's an interesting question to consider when reading this reflection: how many students would choose to take an elective module on *Vegan Geographies*?

Given this context, I would estimate that the majority who turn up to these sessions have successfully internalized the dominant speciesist assumptions and practices of the(ir) wider society. In an average year, in a given class of 100 students perhaps only seven or eight might explicitly identify themselves as being vegetarian, and perhaps only one or two (or none at all) as vegan! Unsurprisingly, the typical student cohort are for the most part sceptical, if not hostile, to the very idea that they should engage with, let alone care about, questions of justice in the context of the animal plight (see Wolch and Emel, 1998; White, 2015). In most years this hostility comes to the surface quite early on. One of the most common ways is through a student not checking their anthroprivilege (see Springer, 2022). They appeal confidently – and aggressively – to narrow and problematic anthropocentric readings of justice, as a way of negating the validity of an MSJ framework with which to view the relationships between humans and other animals. Essentially, so the argument goes, we should first focus on addressing the everyday geographies of injustice that concern humans and then – when these problems have been solved – and only then should we spare *any* thought or time to address the violence, suffering and exploitation of other animals.

Taken at face value, the rebuttal is pretty weak. For one thing, the very idea that humans have a limited or finite ability to think and act in ways that are *just*, quite frankly seems to do a great injustice and disservice for the extraordinary capacity most humans believe they – and others – have to empathize and care: an empathy which certainly transgresses species boundaries, as will be illustrated shortly. For another, it deliberately evades, obscures and ignores the extensive *shared* spaces and realities of injustice, violence and misery that makes a mockery of entrenched human–animal binaries (White, 2021). In fact the only positive takeaway is that the argument – which is rehearsed and repeated in many other everyday contexts 'beyond the academy', is that it offers something important to focus on and work with.

One way to respond here is to encourage the students to understand how ridiculous and self-defeating de facto 'humans-first' appeals to justice are. This might be achieved, for example, by inviting them to carefully think about the relationships they have – or have had – with other animals. Asking the class to talk about their experiences here and share examples becomes a 'fun' and wholly disarming exercise, given the assumption that a class on justice and vegan geographies might be altogether challenging, and distressingly 'woke'. Illustrations are given freely and confidently, and are grouped with reference to common 'framing' and spatial proximities.

For example, there's the literal 'shared-spaces' of the home; a place where dogs, cats, rabbits, hamsters, guinea-pigs, mice, fish are included, and treated as 'pets' or companion animals. Here, in keeping with findings elsewhere (for example, Cudworth, 2011), the students talk openly about how these animals are 'a part of the family' and how they miss them, and look forward to seeing them when back home from university. Alternatively, if recalling the death of a 'pet' they'd say how this upset them, and how they grieved deeply for their loss. It isn't difficult to see how the 99 per cent of the class already consciously think and act with care and compassion regarding some other animals.

Having completed this exercise, I've often then moved to focus on a number of 'hypothetical' scenarios; scenarios that highlight acts of abuse that companion animals/'pets' may experience. I've asked the class whether questions of justice applies (or indeed matters) in these contexts? If it does, what should be done to the perpetrators of such abuse? I say hypothetical, because, unfortunately, all the examples used are drawn from all too common real-life scenarios. Over the years these have ranged from examples of children (moral patients) throwing puppies into a bonfire, to adults (moral agents) punching and kicking 'their' dogs to death, to families who abandon 'their' dogs at the side of a motorway. Reassuringly, the students have no trouble in determining that the harmed animal(s) have been treated *unjustly*. Moreover, the students also express a sense of outrage and anger towards those who would abuse and neglect other animals in such a callous way: who could be so *evil*? In the case of adults who abuse animals there's generally a clear consensus from the class that the governing laws ostensibly in place to protect domestic animals from cruelty would not ensure that they would get their just desserts. Indeed a lot of students, to various degrees, have no trouble in promoting an 'an eye-for-an-eye' sense of justice here: those who commit extreme and outrageous violence against innocent/defenceless animals should be met with equally extreme violence.

It is from these emotive and applied discussions that the question of farmed [*sic*] animals is considered. The collective mood continues to be more sober and serious. Justifications for eating the fragments of corpses of other animals, or drinking their fluids, are more carefully constructed. Rarely will a student throw out, 'Cos they taste nice!', 'Cos God made them that way!', 'MMM bacon!!' into the room. Most, however, still believe there isn't a moral equivalence to be drawn between the treatment of companion animals and farmed animals. If pushed, a popular defence is an appeal to a welfarist ethics as a means of justifying the way farmed animals are treated. In short, as long as farmed animals have been well looked after, and they are killed in a 'humane' fashion – according to the laws that govern their lived – and death – experiences – then they have been treated justly. One obvious way to take apart the welfarist appeal to justice is head-on, through exposing the embarrassingly faulty principles and premises it rests on (see Wrenn, 2012). However, what I want to offer here is a MSJ approach that not only refutes the welfarist argument, but also the human supremacist argument highlighted at the start of this illustration: namely that we should focus and solve questions of human injustice first.

With this intention in mind, I focus the class's attention towards the rapidly expanding body/ies of evidence that focus on the lived experiences and realities of the *human animals*; people who are legally employed in the state-sanctioned killing of farmed animals, and desecration of their corpses, for 'meat'. From a geographical perspective, this of course brings sharply into view the everyday violences that takes place within the slaughterhouse. The levels of ignorance that young people have about slaughterhouse workers (SHWs) is considerable, though not unexpected. How many times have they – have we – been encouraged to think about the connections that trace the 'meat' on our plates back to the moments when a living being – a subject of a life – was brutalized in such a serious and violent way that they lost their lives, still less being troubled by thinking about 'who' did the killing? While drawing on a global evidence base my focus – given the geographical context of the students – looks to foreground evidence that speaks to the experiences of UK and European SHWs. I also supplement this with any local relevant articles/events that focus on the city/county in which the university is based: in this case Sheffield, Yorkshire. As an opening exercise, ask your students to map the location of the local slaughterhouses: I would be amazed if any did so successfully!

Such a focus on the slaughterhouse though is not a 'marginal' or niche area for MSJ to address – indeed it serves as an illustration *par excellence* of the (violent) interface between human and non-human animals. As Slade and Alleyne note:

> Slaughterhouse workers (SHWs) are involved in the deaths of more than 70 billion animals each year worldwide (Sanders, 2018). In order to meet market demand, the meat industry employs a workforce of approximately 75,000 people (British Meat Processors Association, 2019) in approximately 250 slaughterhouses in the United Kingdom (Department for Environment Food & Rural Affairs, 2019), with equivalent numbers in the United States (United States Department of Agriculture, 2020). (Slade and Alleyne, 2021: np)

For the sake of brevity, and with the intention of making connections with the extant research here, the takeaway message is that the slaughterhouse is a hellish and unjust place for all those who find themselves there. Without a shadow of a doubt, fundamental human rights – the right to engage in safe working conditions, to engage in meaningful work, to avoid suffering and trauma – are abandoned at the slaughterhouse door. The inescapable truth that we are confronted with is that SHWs suffer terribly, and will continue to do so even in those slaughterhouses that claim to have some of the best industry standards in the world (as the UK claims to have [BBC, 2020]). It is impossible to imagine otherwise, when a cursory understanding of the impacts that SHWs experience when deliberately killing other animals is gained. I emphasize to the students that we are not simply talking about physical injury, though it is true that the slaughterhouse remains one of the most dangerous places of employment (Sundstrup et al, 2017), rather it is the intrinsic, persistent psychological and mental suffering and anguish that takes place and needs acknowledging, and acting upon. Time after time, research shows how SHWs experience far lower levels of physical and psychological wellbeing (Baran et al, 2016; Slade and Alleyne, 2021), exhibit higher rates of depression, trauma, paranoia (Streeter, 2022) and display post-traumatic stress (PTSD) disorders (Newkey-Burden, 2020). In this context perpetration-induced traumatic stress (PTSS) is a particularly common form of PTSD:

> Unlike many forms of traumatic stress disorders in which sufferers have been victims in a traumatic situation, sufferers of PTSS are the 'causal participant' in a traumatic situation. In other words, they are the direct reason for another being's trauma: Living with the knowledge of their actions causes symptoms similar to those of individuals who are recipients of trauma: substance abuse, anxiety issues, depression, and dissociation from reality. (Lebwohl, 2016: np)

At this stage, the students are genuinely shocked: a whole dark underbelly of society: a known-unknown is played out in plain sight. If this wasn't enough, research on SHWs also highlights how such suffering leads to a range of negative coping strategies; strategies that cause further harm for SHWs and across wider relations (particularly family and friends) and local communities. For example, researchers have highlighted increased levels of alcohol consumption (Baran et al, 2016) in SHWs as well as other forms of 'substance abuse' (Victor and Barnard, 2016: 2), 'intimate partner violence, and an increase in crime rates' (Victor and Barnard, 2016: 2).

'Why', some students naively ask, does anybody choose to work there? Why indeed? It is certainly not a career – despite it being officially designated as 'essential' work in the UK during COVID-19 lockdowns – that anyone (in class) openly aspires to, nor does it seem to feature as an option in the careers library and employability talks on Open Day! I imagine a deafening silence in response to this question to echo well beyond the classroom, particularly from the self-titled 'progressive' (meat-eating) critical academics, and general population, who want to be seen to go 'all the way' in expressing their solidarity with marginalized and disenfranchised populations. This silence is obvious because the truth is not surprising: it's these same vulnerable and poorest populations who are forced to sell their labour in this type of work. The data concerning the socio-economic backgrounds of SHWs in Britain is not atypical: '[S]tatistics show that the majority of [Slaughterhouse Workers] employees have limited educational attainment and come from a low socioeconomic background (*Victor & Barnard, 2016*), with migrants making up 70% of the workforce in the United Kingdom (British Meat Processors Association, 2019)' (Slade and Alleyne, 2023: 429).

What I hope to emphasize to the class, and to the reader, is that ethics, and questions of justice focused on the production of 'meat' concern all animals, human included! To try and say otherwise is simply not true, and reflects a genuine ignorance of the facts, or a wilful dismissal of them. For anyone who claims to stand for social justice – yet continues to consume animal bodies – stands to be guilty of rank hypocrisy. Given these realities, we then explore ways in which we can take appropriate courses of action. Arguably, the single most important step to take is to stop paying for animals to be commodified and brutalized in farming systems. Buy plant-based foods and drinks which, while not necessarily 'cruelty-free' (see White, 2018), are certainly far more consistent with the principle of 'doing least harm'.

It is at this junction that an open discussion about what veganism praxis is and stands for in the context of MSJ is made. In many ways the sense of justice and ethics of care that the students already articulated, believe in – sincerely and deeply – and act upon when it comes to companion animals, is just extended to include all other species. That principle of 'least-harm', and the desire to embody and enact worlds rich in social and spatial justice, lies at the heart of vegan geographers and vegan geographies. As I stress to the students, and anyone else who will listen, the eradication of the slaughterhouse from the face of the earth would be a tremendous day for *all* animals, humans included.

As a final note, when the students finish my classes, I do try and encourage them to envisage what a MSJ perspective(s) might look like in their everyday lives. It is so important to connect the classroom to other spaces (and not allow this to be uncoupled)! I'm keen that the students go beyond 'knowledge' (that is, seeing the only value in the sessions as to how they help them respond to the module assessment), and actually *care* about what they've seen and heard. In this context I encourage them to think through what differences they might make – and how small differences can have a big impact. It doesn't have to be attending a 'spectacular' event, an animal liberation march, for example. Rather it could be having conversations with friends and family, getting them to perhaps appreciate some of the 'new' ideas and connections you've made. It could be using your power (as a student) for example in other ways, looking to influence catering options (more plant-based foods). It might also be taking some of the uncomfortable truths that they've been exposed to in 'my' classroom, and asking these questions of other lecturers and instructors, particularly those who profess to be 'critical' in their approach to social, environmental forms of justice and activism. I hope that many have taken up this invitation. As always though, beyond a few that do let me know how they've thought and acted differently thereafter: I just don't know.

Towards multispecies justice? Tensions, dilemmas and critical transformations in militant (auto)ethnography (Ophélie Véron)

As a geographer engaged in issues of social justice, grassroots activism and socio-ecological transformations, I have always conceived my research as a political intervention in the communities I work on and, most importantly, with. Most of this work builds upon militant (auto)ethnography. Militant ethnography is a form of participatory action research that brings together reflexive thought and action to produce a situated knowledge constituted through rather than about social engagement (Russell, 2015). Breaking with the academic/activist dichotomy, my research is therefore characterized by the attempt to blur the traditional lines separating observation, participation and analysis, while contributing to the critical transformation of the groups in which I am involved. This is not a solitary but a collective attempt to identify, understand and overcome potential inconsistencies or paradoxes within and together with these movements. I use the notion of (auto) ethnography to denote my personal experience and engagement with the subjects I study. Autoethnography differs from traditional ethnography in its use of the personal position in data collection and analysis, and its emphasis on the subjective experience of the researcher (Butz and Besio, 2009). I use the term (auto) in brackets to denote that my work is informed by auto-ethnography rather than being entirely auto-ethnographic. In my research, I explore the experiences of individuals and communities without losing sight of my own experiences, practices and observations as a scholar-activist. However, these are never central to my data collection and analysis, they are simply part of it.

This work has led me to explore the issue of MSJ in the context of grassroots food initiatives. From 2015 to 2019, I carried out several research projects on veganism, and conducted fieldwork among vegan groups and individuals. From 2019 onward, veganism has ceased to be the focus of my research, which turned more broadly to community food spaces. This has involved work both on vegan and non-vegan initiatives, for which the question of what it means to advance more just food systems, as well as who should be included in notions of justice, is central. This research has repeatedly confronted me with a major interrogation – how to imagine and invite a multispecies, intersectional reading of justice in these communities? I will illustrate this interrogation, and the ethical dilemmas and practical tensions involved, with two examples from my work and personal experience – the two being intrinsically related in a militant (auto)ethnographic setting.

Adopting a more intersectional reading of justice affects the way I navigate my research and negotiate my participation in non-vegan food communities. These dynamics may at times appear contradictory, even irreconcilable. For the past three years, I have been participating in a small collective against food waste, which collects and cooks with salvaged food. Every week, I am faced with the following question: should I eat the non-vegan products I rescue or let them go to waste? This raises the question of my own priorities – the purity of my vegan practice or the fight against food waste. It also reflects my privileged middle-class positionality as I can choose what I eat or not. While I have so far navigated this dilemma by distributing this food to charities or non-vegan friends, the same question is raised at a broader level when we organize collective cooking sessions and community meals. Should I refuse to cook with non-vegan food and let other participants do the 'dirty work'? Or should I take my politics to a collective level and push fellow activists towards a more inclusive reading of justice, by inviting them to similarly favour vegan preparations and leave non-vegan products for redistribution? The more I have been involved in the project, the easier it has been for me to opt for the latter solution, but it has not always been possible.

Likewise, should I inform the co-operative supermarket I work with about the ethical issues raised by the so-called 'humane' meat they sell, and invite its leading members to instead consider having an exclusively vegan assortment of products on offer? Yet, by reflecting white middle-class economic and cultural capital, such a move could also thwart their ambition to reach out to a diverse audience and lead to other forms of injustices. Such tensions can be difficult to navigate as they also raise questions about my own positionality as a researcher carrying out militant (auto)ethnography. Should I bring up issues that have not yet been identified by the groups I am involved in or wait for them to do so? Should I use (and abuse) my authority as a scholar to advance social justice and take the lead in their critical transformation, thereby risking reproducing uneven power dynamics between academics and community-based activists? What place should veganism have in the way I construct the boundaries around my personal, activist and professional ethics and politics?

Similarly, inviting a more intersectional, multispecies reading of justice within vegan circles raises several tensions and dilemmas. After years of involvement as a scholar-activist, author and speaker, I eventually took my distance with the vegan community while still identifying with veganism and remaining attached to defending animal liberation. Among the various factors that led to this withdrawal were internal differences about what the commitment to live without harming animals entails for both non-human and human animals. Calls for single-issue campaigns and apolitical 'vote with your wallet' forms of mobilization are still predominant within mainstream vegan activism (Wrenn, 2019), thereby obscuring the global geographies of veganism and its intersections with political, economic and ethical dynamics that occur at multiple stages and scales of food production and consumption.

This focus on animal exploitation also reveals a compartmentalization of oppression that indicates unacknowledged privilege and problematic behaviours within the movement. 'Non-human first' campaigns often feature racist tropes, sexist prejudices or ableist stereotypes. PETA's controversial campaigns juxtaposing images of animal cruelty and US Black slavery, claiming that dairy products cause autism, or fat-shaming women into going vegan, are examples of a broader tendency within vegan advocacy to disregard a more intersectional approach to animal liberation. Studies have revealed that violence and injustice connect the exploitation of non-humans to human animals (and vice versa), and that animal-free food systems are not exempt of social and ecological injustices (Serrano and Brooks, 2019; Sexton et al, 2022). Scandals surrounding the supposedly 'cruelty-free' cultivation of vegan products such as avocados, cashew nuts or quinoa have made the headlines in recent years. This shows that the politics and economies of veganism cannot be considered independently but are embedded in multiple networks of spaces, cultures and practices, and that its realization is rooted in practical and ethical tensions. Just as issues of (in)justice are not exclusively about human animals, they cannot be framed exclusively with reference to non-human animals in vegan advocacy. Rather, they should reflect the intersection of veganism, social justice and wider environmental ecosystems.

I have unfortunately no definitive or general answer to the questions and issues I have raised, for it is only in the here and now that I have been able to negotiate the dilemmas I encounter every day as a vegan scholar-activist. While these dilemmas may reveal unattainable ideals for some, they can also be understood as a call for a broader, more inclusive and radical understanding of what 'justice for all' entails. My own answers may be contingent and imperfect, but they also reflect how, as the borders of our ethical concerns shift from the human to the more-than-human, and from the more-than-human to an intersectional reading of justice, such a notion can never be fixed. It is necessarily fluid and situated, and should not be any less considered for that, for it is in these lived spaces that a multispecies praxis can emerge and lay the outlines of a politics of total liberation.

Conclusions

In reflecting on how we use concepts of MSJ in our own work, activism and day-to-day living we hope that the illustrations, reflections and arguments offered up in this chapter have given pause for thought and, perhaps, inspiration. There is without doubt an urgent need to carefully consider what emancipatory grounds imagining, envisioning and enacting 'justice' should emerge from, and the 'just-worlds' we desire to be built upon. The central argument we hope to have impressed upon here is one firmly in keeping with the conclusions of Celermajer et al (2021: 120), that '[a]s humans and other beings surround, infuse, and support each other, justice for any cannot be divorced from MSJ for all' (2021: 120). Certainly, the injustices that are giving rise to the crises that are currently manifesting themselves in ways that threaten the end of the world as we know it are rooted to a greater extent in the arrogance, conceit and hubris of 'the human'.

The interspecies solidarity aspect that runs through these arguments is also something to think through seriously. For example, how can we (scholar-activists) better enable and empower the marginalized, hidden voices of non-humans? How can we 'unsilence' the non-human in our research, our teachings and our writings? This is something that we continuously reflect on. At this moment in time much of our work that animates vegan geographies strives to create a meaningful space – a presence – where non-humans become visible and morally considerable. By creating a presence perhaps they are heard. However, humans have generally been poor listeners when it comes to interspecies communication and, as industrialized animal production systems are evident of, even worse at interspecies empathy and care. We try to elicit interspecies solidarity through drawing attention to photographs, documentaries, and recordings in our own projects. These make the spaces of animal abuse more visible, such as industrial-scale farms and slaughterhouses witnessed and recorded by activists despite the legal threats of ag-gag laws, as well as the more peaceful and positive spaces where humans and other animals interact, such as sanctuaries. In this context we are always keen to emphasize that geographies matter! There is no substitute for making non-humans heard through witnessing and communicating *first-hand*, rather than witnessing through research outputs – whether written and/or visual.

Embracing geographies of MSJ and using this as a lens to evaluate our everyday worlds, should give both inspiration and guidance about how we can (continue to) act 'justly' in future. In many ways embracing a MSJ awareness gives us permission to tap into something that many of us know intuitively and instinctively to be true. However, it is important to also acknowledge the violent ideologies that we have been indoctrinated with from birth – speciesism, anthroparchy and so on – will not fade away willingly. To swim against the tide demands resisting many of the everyday social and spatial tapestries that we live in, and it also means defying the dominant narratives of the institutions and elites that try to govern and dictate the terms of our very existence. As an act of defiance and hope, we have found strength and resolve through researching, teaching and embodying vegan geographies. If this chapter has helped provoke an interest in this radical field, and ways to constructively engage with it, then it will have more than served its purpose.

References
Alvaro, C. (2019) Veganism and children: a response to Marcus William Hunt, *Journal of Agricultural and Environmental Ethics*, 32(4): 647–661.
Alvaro, C. (2020) Vegan parents and children: zero parental compromise, *Ethics and Education*, 15(4): 476–498.
Appleby, M. (2008) *Eating Our Future: The Environmental Impact of Industrial Animal Agriculture*, London: World Society for the Protection of Animals.
Baran, B.E., Rogelberg, S.G. and Clausen, T. (2016) Routinized killing of animals: going beyond dirty work and prestige to understand the well-being of slaughterhouse workers, *Organization*, 23(3): 351–369.
BBC (British Broadcasting Corporation) (2020) *Confessions of a Slaughterhouse Worker*, https://www.bbc.co.uk/news/stories-50986683
Bennett, C.E., Thomas, R., Williams, M., Zalasiewicz, J., Edgeworth, M., Miller, H., et al (2018) The broiler chicken as a signal of a human reconfigured biosphere, *Royal Society Open Science*, 5(12): 180325.
Butz, D. and Besio, K. (2009) Autoethnography, *Geography Compass*, 3(5): 1660–1674.
Celermajer, D., Schlosberg, D., Rickards, L., Stewart-Harawira, M., Thaler, M., Tschakert, P., et al (2021) Multispecies justice: theories, challenges, and a research agenda for environmental politics, *Environmental Politics*, 30(1–2): 119–140.
Cronon, W. (1996) The trouble with wilderness: or, getting back to wrong nature, in Cronon, W. (ed) *Uncommon Ground: Rethinking the Human Place in Nature*, New York: W.W. Norton and Company, pp 23–56.
Cudworth, E. (2011) *Social Lives with Other Animals: Tales of Sex, Death and Love*, New York: Palgrave Macmillan.
Emel, J. and Neo, H. (2015) *Political Ecologies of Meat*, London: Routledge.
FAO (2006) *Livestock's Long Shadow: Environmental Issues and Options*, Rome: Food and Agriculture Organisation of the United Nations.
Gillespie, R. and Collard, K. (2015) *Critical Animal Geographies: Politics, Intersections, and Hierarchies in a Multispecies World*, London: Routledge.
Giraud, E. (2021) *Veganism: Politics, Practices and Theory*, London: Bloomsbury.
Glasser, C. (2015) Beyond intersectionality to total liberation, in Kemmerer, L. (ed) *Animals and the Environment: Advocacy, Activism, and the Quest for Common Ground*, Abingdon: Routledge, pp 41–49.

Hodge, P., McGregor, A., Springer, S., Veron, O. and White, R.J. (2022) *Vegan Geographies, Ethics Beyond Violence, Ethics Beyond Speciesism*, Brooklyn: Lantern Press.

Joy, M. (2020) *Why We Love Dogs, Eat Pigs, and Wear Cows: An Introduction to Carnism*, San Francisco: Red Wheel.

Lebwohl, M. (2016) A call to action: psychological harm in slaughterhouse workers, *The Yale: Global Health Review*, https://yaleglobalhealthreview.com/2016/01/25/a-call-to-action-psychological-harm-in-slaughterhouse-workers/

McGregor, A. (2022) Vegan environmentalism: practicing care for socio-ecological futures, in Hodge, P., McGregor, A., Springer, S., Véron, O. and White, R. (eds) *Vegan Geographies: Spaces beyond Violence, Ethics beyond Speciesism*, Woodstock: Lantern Publishing Media, pp 119–216.

McGregor, A., Rickards, L., Houston, D., Goodman, M. and Bojovic, M. (2021) The biopolitics of cattle methane emissions reduction: governing life in a time of climate change, *Antipode*, 53(4): 1161–1185.

Newkey-Burden, C. (2020) Abbatoir workers are the forgotten frontline victims at the heart of this crisis – and now they're spreading coronavirus, *Independent*, https://www.independent.co.uk/voices/coronavirus-slaughterhouse-abattoir-spread-infection-ptsd-mental-health-a9593511.html

Olivier, A. and Cordeiro-Rodrigues, L. (2017) Racism, speciesism and suffering, in Cordeiro-Rodrigues, L. and Mitchell, L (eds) *Animals, Race, and Multiculturalism*, Cham: Palgrave Macmillan, pp 147–174.

Puig de la Bellacasa, M. (2011) Matters of care in technoscience: assembling neglected things, *Social Studies of Science*, 41: 85–106.

Russell, B. (2015) Beyond activism/academia: militant research and the radical climate and climate justice movement(s), *Area*, 47: 222–229.

Serrano, A. and Brooks, A. (2019) Who is left behind in global food systems? Local farmers failed by Colombia's avocado boom, *Environment and Planning E*, 2(2): 348–367.

Sexton, A.E., Garnett, T. and Lorimer, J. (2022) Vegan food geographies and the rise of Big Veganism, *Progress in Human Geography*, 46(2): 605–628. https://doi.org/10.1177/03091325211051021

Singer, P. (2009) Speciesism and moral status, *Metaphilosophy*, 40(3–4): 567–581.

Slade, J. and Alleyne, E. (2021) The psychological impact of slaughterhouse employment: a systematic literature review, *Trauma, Violence, & Abuse*. 10.1177/15248380211030243

Slade, J., and Alleyne, E. (2023) The psychological impact of slaughterhouse employment: a systematic literature review, *Trauma, Violence, & Abuse*, 24(2): 429–440. https://doi.org/10.1177/15248380211030243

Springer, S. (2016) Learning through the soles of our feet: unschooling, anarchism, and the geography of childhood, in Springer, S., de Souza, M.L. and White, R.J. (eds) *The Radicalization of Pedagogy: Anarchism, Geography, and the Spirit of Revolt*, London: Rowman & Littlefield, pp 247–265.

Springer, S. (2022) Check your anthroprivilege! Situated knowledge and geographical imaginations as an antidote to environmental speciesism, anthroparchy, and human fragility, in Hodge, P., McGregor, A., Springer, S., Véron, O. and White, R. (eds) *Vegan Geographies: Spaces beyond Violence, Ethics beyond Speciesism*, Woodstock: Lantern Publishing Media, pp 129–150.

Streeter, S. (2022) Animals aren't the only victims in slaughterhouses, *Faunalyrics*, https://faunalytics.org/animals-arent-the-only-victims-in-slaughterhouses/

Sundstrup, E., Jakobsen, M.D., Brandt, M., Jay, K. Aagaard, P. and Andersen, L.L. (2016) Associations between biopsychosocial factors and chronic upper limb pain among slaughterhouse workers: cross sectional study, *BMC Musculoskeletal Disorders*, 17: Article 104. https://doi.org/10.1186/s12891-016-0953-7

Swain, M., Blomqvist, L., McNamara, J. and Ripple, W. (2018) Reducing the environmental impact of global diets, *Science of the Total Environment*, 610–611: 1207–1209.

Tschakert, P. (2020) More-than-human solidarity and multispecies justice in the climate crisis, *Environmental Politics*. DOI: 10.1080/09644016.2020.1853448

Victor, K. and Barnard, A. (2016) Slaughtering for a living: a hermeneutic phenomenological perspective on the well-being of slaughterhouse employees, *Qualitative Studies of Health and Well-being*, 11. doi: 10.3402/qhw.v11.30266

White, R.J. (2015) Animal geographies, anarchist praxis and critical animal studies, in Gillespie, K. and Collard, R.-C. (eds) *Critical Animal Geographies: Politics, Intersections, and Hierarchies in a Multispecies World*, London: Routledge, pp 19–35.

White, R.J. (2018) Looking backward/moving forward: articulating a 'yes, BUT…!' response to lifestyle veganism, and outlining post-capitalist futures in critical veganic agriculture, *EuropeNow*, 20. https://www.europenowjournal.org/

White, R.J. (2021) Towards trans-species social and spatial justice through critical animal geographies, anarchist praxis and a total liberation ethic, in Hovorka, A., McCubbin, S. and Van Patter, L. (eds) *A Research Agenda for Animal Geographies*, Cheltenham: Edward Elgar pp 183–198.

Wolch, J. and Emel, J. (1998) *Animal Geographies: Place, Politics and Identity in the Nature-Culture Borderlands*, London: Verso.

Wrenn, C.L. (2012) Abolitionist animal rights: critical comparisons and challenges within the animal rights movement, *Interface*, 4(2): 438–458.

Wrenn, C.L. (2019) *Piecemeal Protest: Animal Rights in the Age of Nonprofits*. Ann Arbor: University of Michigan Press.

10

The Priority of Justice

Don Mitchell

I sometimes wonder if there is any emptier word in the geographer's lexicon than *justice*. Those of us who style ourselves as critical or radical geographers, as I do, use the term all the time. We use it for a lot of reasons. It is a marker of our politics. It is a sign of our solidarity with the marginalized and oppressed. It is an orientation for our research (against the bad, in favour of the good; against the technocratic and the irrelevant, in favour of the social and the pertinent). It is a dog whistle, only to the left rather than the right. It is a noun that just sounds good when modified by geography's key concepts: *spatial, environmental, landscape, climate* .... It is just so bloody obvious: we all know what justice is and we want it now.

But of course, it is not at all obvious, no more obvious than those other famously intuitive and remarkably complex terms so central to the geographer's lexicon, like *nature* and *culture* (Williams, 1976). Yet unlike nature and culture, *justice* has not accreted the same volume of theoretical debate and attention these two have. There is a bit, of course: David Harvey's (1973; 1996) significant explorations of liberal and radical justice theory; David Smith's (1994) spatializations of the (primarily) liberal tradition; Laura Pulido's (1996) exploration of environmental justice movements in New Mexico and California; Clive Barnett's (2017) dismissal of justice *as such* as an organizing principle and his argument instead for prioritizing *injustice* in geographical theorizing; and to a much lesser extent Edward Soja's (2010) promotion of spatial justice.[1] And there is significant work by fellow travellers, such as Susan Fainstein's arguments for a *Just City* (2007). But on the whole, justice theorizing – especially engaging deeply with the extensive literatures on justice in political philosophy and critical theory – is quite thin on the ground within academic geography. There is, I think, a good reason for this. But there is also good reason for why *justice* theorizing ought to become a priority among critical, radical geographers and other theorists interested in space and spatiality.

★★★

The standard story told about the ground-breaking move Harvey (1973) made in *Social Justice and the City* from 'liberal formulations' to 'socialist formulations' of justice, not least by Harvey himself, is that the liberal approaches to justice were simply unable to explain the root causes of the injustice they sought to remedy. They were thus unable to prescribe appropriate interventions. 'Socialist', or more accurately Marxist, approaches did a much better job, especially since they were not vested in upholding the status quo. In Harvey's view, one of the problems with liberal formulations – and here, of course, the central formulation was that of John Rawls, whose foundational *A Theory of Justice* (1971) had been published only two years before – was that they were essentially 'counter-revolutionary' in that they had no mechanisms for (or desire to) change the basic conditions of society. They merely sought to tinker with them, to smooth off the rough edges of liberal (or at that point Keynesian) capitalism. More radical approaches to the fundamental injustices of capitalism were needed.

Yet there is another story lurking in the pages of *Social Justice and the City*, more implicit than overt, and in my view quite decisive. What Harvey discovered about the mainstream of justice theorizing was not only that it could be quite counter-revolutionary, but especially that it was fundamentally, ineluctably *idealist*.[2] And, even in its most conservative guises, geography as a discipline is fundamentally – or at least avowedly – *anti-idealist*,[3] the efforts of Richard Hartshorne (1939) to found geography on a constricted Kantian idealism (cf Smith, 1989) and the work of Leonard Guelke (1974) and a few others notwithstanding.[4] It is anti-idealist in the sense that it is concerned with worldly phenomena – the actually-existing spatial arrangements, social relations, environmental processes and institutions that comprise and have produced the world we live in – and *not*, in the first instance, projecting a vision of a 'good and well-ordered society', to adopt one of Rawls' primary starting points. To the degree that geographers do project such visions it has been (for the most part) from the vantage point of what currently *is*, more so than what hypothetically might have been. Utopic visions in geography, at least ones worth paying attention to, have been hard-won.

Moreover, mainstream normative traditions of justice theorizing (not only that of Rawls, but the whole tradition he was working in, from Kant forward, as well as – perhaps surprisingly – alternative traditions like communitarianism) are fundamentally concerned with the *individual* as the subject of justice. Such individualism is as true of 'capabilities' theorists like Sen (2009), Nussbaum (2000), and to a considerable degree Robeyns (2006), as it is – again perhaps surprisingly – of theorists of both international justice like the John Rawls of *The Law of Peoples* (1999) and (again to a considerable degree) global justice theorists like Thomas Pogge (2001). My argument is not that mainstream justice theorizing pays *no* attention to social groups, social structures (like states) or social relations. Of course it does. In much political philosophy, however, groups are understood to only be congeries of individuals, not social actors, relations or processes in and of themselves that form what individuals are (cf Young, 1990). In turn, this means that social groups, social structures and social relations only matter insofar as they condition the relative freedom, autonomy and rights of the sovereign individual. To use language developed by the feminist philosopher Alison Jaggar (2009), social groups, social structures and social relations figure in mainstream justice theorizing as *objects* rather than *subjects* of justice.

My invocation of feminism at this point is not accidental, for feminist theorizing of justice, in my view, provides the primary, and perhaps most important, exception to the liberal individualism that pervades justice theorizing. To be sure, the liberal individual remains an important figure in some feminist justice theorizing – for example, the remarkably radical arguments of the avowedly liberal feminist Susan Moller Okin (1979; 1989)[5] – but (to state the obvious) one of the primary, crucially political as well as theoretical contributions of feminism since the 1960s has been to force a radical reconsideration of what constitutes the individual. Or rather, it has been to make us fully rethink how individuals are constituted, how individuals cannot be separated out from the social groups and social forces that shape them. Iris Marion Young's (1990: 43–44) clear-eyed discussion of just these matters has been particularly influential in geography and other spatial disciplines, but just as important has been the concerted effort over the last 30 years by feminists, especially radical Black feminists, to theorize *intersectionality* not only as a methodological priority, but especially as an ontological fact: that our ability to *be* as individuals is fully determined by how myriad social forces combine and intersect so as to structure *group differentiations* (cf Gilmore, 2007; 2022).[6]

The turn to group differentiality – to intersectionality – has its antecedents, of course. Marx's critique of capitalist production is one. *Capital* and his other works were written from the perspective of the working *class* (not the individual worker) as a critique of *capitalist social relations* (not the individual capitalist), and operated through a complex dialectical account requiring that analysis proceed through several levels of generality (in which the individual is always formed through the simultaneous operations of nature, class and more immediate social processes [Ollman, 1991]), with the ultimate aim of understanding the actually-existing processes (for example, capitalism's need always to push towards the creation of a 'purely atomic' individual, stripped of its entanglements in social life) that shaped not only what individuals could be but also whether and how humanity could achieve its 'species-being'. Another, more immediate antecedent was socialist-feminist standpoint theory (Harding, 1988; Harstock, 1998), which readily acknowledged its debt to Marx and Marxism but pushed the argument further by showing how 'thinking from women's lives' (to use Sandra Harding's phrase) not only better revealed the dialectically entwined socio-natural forces that shaped those lives (and therefore what gender *is*), but better, more fully revealed the *truth* than could an unlocalized 'view from nowhere'.

The crucial point, of course, is that the focus on group differentiation, whether in its Marxist, feminist standpoint, or intersectional guises turns attention towards the social forces that produce such differentiation. They turn our attention towards questions of *injustice*. Within geography, the work of Iris Marion Young has been especially influential, especially her 1990 book, *Justice and the Politics of Difference*, perhaps in part because its title was reflected in Harvey's return to questions of justice in *Justice, Nature, and the Geography of Difference* (1996), but surely primarily because Young consistently concerned herself with spatial questions, including the question of how city space and 'city life' formed the 'actual experience' of oppression which could animate the 'ideals' that might 'inspire action for social change' (Young, 1990: 241). In later work – which unfortunately has received comparably less attention in geography – Young (2011) likewise sought to understand how responsibility for producing injustice was distributed across complex global networks of causality, arguing that oppression and domination in a globalized world was always a question of the complexity of geographical scale (though she did not use exactly this language).

For Young, of course, oppression has 'five faces' – exploitation, marginalization, powerlessness, cultural imperialism and violence (Young, 1990: 40) – and it was the ways in which these intersected that produced actually-existing conditions of oppression. Oppression was thus a 'structural concept': the 'systemic constraints on groups that are not necessarily the result of the intentions of a tyrant', and constraints whose 'causes are embedded in unquestioned norms, habits, and symbols, in the assumptions underlying institutional rules and the collective consequences of following those rules' (Young, 1990: 41). Thus: 'Oppression refers to the vast and deep injustice that some groups suffer as consequence of often unconscious assumptions and reactions of well-meaning people in ordinary interactions, media and cultural stereotypes, and structural features of bureaucratic hierarchies and market mechanisms – in short, the normal processes of everyday life' (Young, 1990: 41). For Young, then, the first step towards developing a full theory of justice that transcended liberalism's methodological – and ontological – individualism was to reveal the ordinary and systemic processes and practices that produced oppression in any or all of it guises.

Yet despite Young's clear focus on ordinary and systemic practices, Harvey (1996: 350, 349) found lurking in her arguments a remnant idealism. In particular he accused her of failing to inquire deeply enough into 'how and why these different dimensions of injustice intersect in the ways they do in particular places and times', how 'multiple forms of oppression coalesce'. By contrast, other geographers – myself included (Mitchell, 2003c; 2007; 2008) – took Young's arguments as inspiration to dig more deeply into the social, material and spatial processes that produce oppression and injustice. I have argued on more than one occasion (for example, Mitchell, 2003a; 2008; 2012) that the very shape and structure of public space and landscape concretize 'justice' as it actually exists, by which, more accurately, I mean that public spaces and landscapes are the 'hard surfaces of life' that reflect – and that in part cause – oppression and injustice. The image of 'hard surfaces of life' comes from Paul Farmer's (2003) theorization of structural violence, a theorization that I find to be fully compatible with Young's overall account of oppression, not merely its face of 'violence'. Inspired by Gilmore (2007), Loyd (2014) and others, I have argued that geographical landscapes are concretizations of, express and promote structural violence which itself is always group-differentiated. I have been interested, in other words, precisely in 'how and why ... different dimensions of injustice intersect ... in particular places and times' *but also* in how through these intersections, different kinds of places (landscapes, public spaces) are produced in ways that tend to *reproduce* these different dimensions of injustice *as part* of 'the normal process of everyday life'. If any idealism lingers in Young's work (and I am not sure it does), it is not hard to move beyond it to develop a more fully historical-materialist account of the spatial processes of domination, oppression and injustice.

Undertaking such a historical-materialist analysis is, in fact, to accomplish a great deal, analytically as well as politically, and it is precisely in undertaking such analytical work that geography is at its best as a critical social science. This is to say that geography's primary contribution to social justice scholarship since the field's radicalization in the 1960s–1970s, has not been in theorizing justice, but in theorizing and showing the forces that produce injustice.

★★★

But is that enough? Can we really do a good job of theorizing and showing injustice if we do not have a more fully elaborated conception – or theorization – of justice? The late Clive Barnett (2017) thought so. Barnett's avowed object of concern in *The Priority of Injustice* is theories of radical democracy, but the last third of the book was given over to airing out theories of justice, or rather what he usually (though not consistently) called 'democratic justice'. Precisely what 'democratic justice' denotes is never clear; what is clearer is that Barnett found 'justice' to be an untenable ideal, an inappropriate starting point for either political theory or for the analysis of actually-existing democratic practice. His concern was not that 'justice' is an empty concept, but that it is not empty enough.

Barnett's favoured theorists – Axel Honneth, Iris Marion Young, Amartya Sen, Judith Shklar, Rainer Forst, Miranda Fricker, and to a lesser extent Nancy Fraser – all argue, he averred, for a turn towards the analysis of domination, and 'what is most distinctive' about this move 'in favor of non-domination is that it involves a shift away from developing and applying egalitarian ideals of justice and toward theorizing about injustice' (Barnett, 2017: 210). In turn, 'the reorientation of democratic theory around concepts of domination ... alters the way in which the vocation of critical theory is viewed' (Barnett, 2017: 237). And 'in a more pragmatist spirit, the concern with the value of non-denomination focuses attention instead on developing a more reflexive critical theory, understood as informing inquiry into the dynamics of domination and the felt experiences of injustice' (Barnett, 2017: 237). From what I have already written, it will come as no surprise that I find this a fairly attractive proposition. It accords well with what I have said about geography's 'vocation' as a materialist and non-individualist discipline and it aligns nicely with my own interest in the 'hard surfaces of life' as they appear in and are reproduced through landscapes and public spaces. But now I also find it a deeply unsatisfying proposition. It is not that Barnett pushed the stick too far in the other direction – away from justice theorizing and towards injustice theorizing – but that he ignored the stick altogether: the content of justice.

'What', Engels once asked 'is it [justice] if not the stick with which to measure all human affairs, if not the final arbitrator to be appealed to in all conflicts?' For Engels, the stick of justice had 'been nothing up to the present, but ... ought to be everything' given that it was 'the organic, regulating, sovereign basic principle of societies' (quoted in Merrifield and Swyngedouw, 1995: 1). There is a great danger, in other words, in allowing the concept of justice to remain empty. Engels was no idealist, of course. But, like Marx, he was something of a teleologist (if that is a word). There was indeed an end towards which humans struggled: our 'species-being', our full, collective, solidaristic, humanity, our unalienated selves. *Exactly* what that meant may not have been fully clear – indeed it was something that would be invented and realized in the course of struggle itself – but it was a normative ideal nonetheless. At the same time, Engels, also like Marx, understood, on the one hand, that the relations of class society, especially capitalist class society, with its specific forms of oppression, domination and alienation prevented humans from achieving that species-being. On the other hand, *within the norms of capitalism itself* these forms of oppression, domination and alienation were not necessarily unjust. In fact, they could be perfectly just, as with the relations of exploitation that allow for the production and ownership (by the capitalist class) of surplus value. As Marx so clearly showed in the first volume of *Capital*, in both juridical and normative terms the selling and buying of labour power was an equal and just exchange. No doubt the exchange of labour power for wages sometimes veered into the territory of injustice – when capitalists could get away with paying less than full value for the labour power they purchased, for example, or when because of social circumstances (produced within the relations of production and reproduction themselves) parents were forced to sell the labour power of their children who were then hyper-exploited – but there was nothing unjust about the exchange relationship that allowed for exploitation *as such*. The Marxist historical-materialist project, in other words, has always been one of working dialectically between the actually-existing conditions of justice in the world as it is (just relations of exploitation and domination), and a normative vision of what it could be (species-being achieved).

In this sense, injustice *alone* is not, in my view, a historical-materialist priority, even if seeking to theorize, understand and explain it is of the highest historical-materialist urgency. Such theorizing and explanation are not, and cannot be, *prior* to normative theorizing about justice. And, in my reading at least, it is not a priority before – prior to – such normative theorizing for exactly those theorists Barnett leaned on in this last third of his book. Whatever their other differences, for them, theorizing injustice always develops in a tight dialectical dance with the development of normative theories of justice.

This is certainly the case with Iris Marion Young, no matter how much geographers, myself very much included, have prioritized her theories of oppression over her normative arguments about justice as such. The normative arguments are hard to miss (Harvey didn't: it might be why he accused her of a residual idealism). To take only one example from *Justice and the Politics of Difference*:

> A goal of social justice, I will assume, is social equality. Equality refers not to the distribution of social goods, though distributions are certainly entailed by social equality. It refers primarily to the full participation and inclusion of everyone in a society's major institutions, and the socially supported substantive opportunity for all to develop and exercise their capacities and realize their choices. (Young, 1990: 173)

Such a normative focus on justice hardly faded over Young's career. Rather, it grew in strength. The whole premise of *Inclusion and Democracy*, for example, is that the connection between democracy and justice is '*normative*'

(Young, 2000: 17, emphasis added) and that 'democratic practice is a means of promoting justice' (Young, 2000: 5). To be sure, Young holds that:

> [A] critical theory does not derive [its] principles and ideals from philosophical premises about morality, human nature, or the good life. Rather the method of critical theory ... reflects on existing social relations and processes to identify what we experience as valuable in them, but as present only intermittently, partially, or potentially. (Young, 2000: 10)

But to argue thus is precisely to centre an argument in the space between reality and potential, the world as it is and the world as it could be.

Young's normative bent – perhaps best described as a materialist-normative orientation – in fact becomes clearest in her last works collected together as *Responsibility for Justice*. Here Young's (2011) concern is primarily how we can apportion responsibility within geographically complex systems that produce harms. What responsibility should an American consumer have for the oppressions and exploitations entailed in the production of the apparel in sweatshops halfway around the world (oppressions and exploitations that, within the norms of capitalist society, might very well be *just*)? Young develops what she calls a 'forward-looking' model. As agents in the world, our responsibility is not to address past harms, though she does not at all deny the juridical and social importance of assigning liability, but to intervene to prevent the perpetuation of those harms. Any such intervention must be collective, not just individual, not only for reasons of effectiveness, but especially because intervening in processes of domination and exploitation must be solidaristic. Young calls this a 'social connection model' of responsibility for justice.

This is a highly normative argument in that it names a set of ideals to be striven for (solidaristic action, remade relations of production, reformed chains of causality after a very different image of what a globalized world could be) and it is one not without its shortcomings. In her Foreword in *Responsibility for Justice*, Martha Nussbaum (2011) names the primary shortcoming succinctly: the forward-looking model of responsibility suffers from infinite regress. In Young's argument, our primary responsibility is not to assume liability for past wrongs, within which we may have been implicated in however a distended and attenuated form (for example, as consumers), but to act now. Today. The problem with this, as Nussbaum explains, is that each day we are absolved of yesterday's sins. We're given a perpetual get-out-of-jail-free card. Young recognized this problem, as her frequent reference to the remaining importance of the 'liability model' of apportioning blame attests. But she did not really integrate a solution to the problem into her theory.

Her final essay in *Responsibility for Justice*, unfinished at the time of her death, however, was a start on just this task. This last chapter, 'Responsibility and historic injustice', starts by engaging with Franz Fanon's (1967: 229, 231) refusal to be 'a prisoner of history' and his claim that 'I as a man of color, to the extent that it becomes possible for me to exist absolutely do not have the right to lock myself into a world of retroactive reparations'. Instead, his responsibility, and his right, is to create a future. Young (2008: 172) finds this a 'compelling vision, but ultimately flawed', not, obviously, for its refusal to assign liability (especially to present generations for past crimes), but 'because it is too radically individualist and dehistoricized'. Yet she accepts the general thrust: 'We should neither seek guilt for the past in the present nor try to forget it.' Her hope was thus to develop her social connection model such that it could 'focus on the problem of present injustice and on a forward-looking responsibility to remedy this justice' (Young, 2008: 181). That this *present* injustice was forged in the *past*, made it 'not plausible to argue, however, that a relationship to the past is irrelevant to this project'. It was not only that 'collective discussion and the retelling of historical injustice' is a way of nurturing 'respectful relations with one another now', but also that such historical analysis allows for understanding the *structures* in structural injustice and thus 'where intervention in them may be most effective' (Young, 2008: 181–182). This too is a normative argument. It is an argument about how past injustices *continue* within present structures and thus how the struggle for justice – for a world without domination, a world of 'social equality' – must concern itself with structural transformation that accounts for the past while envisioning a very different future.

The problem with Barnett's (2017) text is that he did not understand how any focus on *injustice* has to be understood through normative principles of *justice* no matter how dimly or intuitively felt. This problem came to a head in his analysis of the work of Rainer Forst, in whom Barnett (2017: 264) found 'the clearest articulation of the priority of injustice as an account of the dynamics of democratic public life'. Barnett (2017: 264) admitted that there is a normative, core notion of justice in Forst's work: for Forst justice is 'the right to justification' and as such 'justifiability of social relations [is] the core problem for a theory of justice'. Moreover, as Barnett (2017: 264) noted, 'the meaning of justice for Forst is primarily defined in terms of opposition to arbitrary rule'. But Barnett (2017: 264–265) erred – or rather over-simplified – when he suggests that Forst equated 'demands for justice' with 'demands to eliminate domination'.

To be sure, across his work, Forst (2011; 2014; 2017) makes it clear that the elimination of domination is a necessary condition of justice. But he makes it equally clear that it is not sufficient. Sufficiency consists in the fulfilment of what Forst calls the two principles (or sometimes 'decisive criteria') of justice: reciprocity and generality.[7] Reciprocity means that one cannot make a claim that she or he denies to another, nor can he or she assume the other shares 'his or her perspective, evaluations, convictions, interests or needs' (Forst, 2014: 101). Generality means that all affected persons have an unconditional right to raise objections to a norm, and that any justification used to legitimize the norm must ultimately be seen as legitimate by all those affected. While Barnett (2017: 265) recognized that reciprocity and generality are integral to Forst's theorizations, he underplayed their importance as normative guideposts. And this is primarily because Barnett did not follow Forst all the way to where the logic of these principles leads to an argument for what Forst calls conditions of *minimal justice* and *maximal justice*. Let's follow Forst the whole way, and see what these might mean.

As Barnett discusses, the question of *power* is central in Forst's work. Indeed, Forst calls power 'the first question' or 'the primary question' of justice. Barnett (2017: 265) quotes Forst's (2014: 103) definition of power: it is 'the ability to order and influence, to occupy, and, in extreme cases, to dominate the space of reasons for others, that is, to determine the limits of what can be said and thought and, above all, of what is accepted and acceptable, of what is justified'. Or rather, Barnett cites *one* of Forst's definitions of power, because he also argues that 'power is the art of binding others through reasons; it is a core phenomenon of normativity' and while it can be imposed, it can also be shared (Forst, 2014: 11). When power fails, it is replaced by 'violence', which for Forst is the opposite of power. In this sense, power can reside not just in those 'occupying' or 'dominating' the 'space of reasons', but also those demanding – perhaps from outside the space itself – justification. Power is the first question of justice, in Forst's (2014: 120) theory, because 'in matters of justice *power* is most important of all goods, a true "hyper-good"' (original emphasis) and thus the first question of justice is power because everything hinges on how power is distributed. In turn, this distribution shapes the conditions of possibility for justification (which in Forst's view is a discursive practice), that is, for exercising the right to justification.

The distribution of power may be the first question of justice, but, however, it is not the last. Or rather, it is not the *only* 'first question of justice'. Another one is the question of production. In an essay entitled 'Justice after Marx', Forst (2017: 121) criticizes 'restrictive and misleading theories of justice', which in fact are the predominant mainstream theories of justice like Rawls', but also Sen's and Nussbaum's capabilities approaches, which are, he argues, 'held captive' by the principle of *suum cuique* ('To each his/her own').[8] In its various guises, justice theory based in *suum cuique* leads either to comparative approaches that assess whether the distribution of goods is basically equal or justifiably unequal (as with Rawls' 'difference principle') or whether each 'gets enough' (as with the capabilities approaches). The problem with both, Forst argues (while acknowledging his debt to Iris Marion Young), is that they reduce justice to a question of goods allocation and thus are deficient on four grounds. They ignore the organization of the production of goods; ignore the '*political* question of who determines the structures of production and distribution and in what ways'; disregard the fact 'that *justified claims* to goods do not simply "exist" but can only be ascertained discursively' and must be defined 'in normative terms as a matter of justice'; and finally set aside 'the question of *injustice*' (original emphasis, Forst, 2017: 122). In these theories, *justice* disappears, only to be replaced by 'a giant distribution machine that only needed to be programmed correctly', with the result being, first, that those who should be subjects of justice (you, me and everyone else) are turned into 'passive recipients' of goods, and, second, that there is no way to determine those who are lacking goods because of a basic injustice – like exploitation or oppression – and those who are lacking perhaps because of some calamity (like a natural disaster or a failed harvest). A better approach, following Marx, is to 'focus on the real question, that of the organization and distribution of the means of production, which is, as I would say, the first question of justice' (Forst, 2017: 126).

So now we have two 'first questions of justice': the distribution and deployment of power, and the distribution and organization of the means of production. Together these create the conditions of possibility for justice both in its local and contingent sense (this is what justice *is*, here and now: what you call exploitation is fully justified within the context of the system) and its transcendent sense (what you seek to justify as justifiable exploitation is nothing of the sort, given how it thwarts the achievement of our species-being). And together they point to Forst's foundational, normative conception of justice. This conception has two forms: minimal justice and maximal justice. Forst defines minimal justice as '*a basic structure of justification*' and maximal justice as '*a fully justified basic structure*' (original emphasis). A society would be minimally just if it possessed the first of these and maximally just if it possessed both. A basic structure of justification means the structures and relations of power that make it truly possible for all those affected to exercise their right to justification. In normative terms it would be something like Habermas' ideal speech situation. It would be the basic conditions that assure that '*intersubjective relations and structures*' (original emphasis, Forst 2017: 122) allow for the basic claim of injustice to be heard, understood and responded to.[9] The basic claim of injustice is not lacking goods, though the allocations of goods can be important, as Forst avers, but rather to 'not *count* when it comes to producing and allocating goods' (original emphasis, Forst, 2017: 122).

The notion of a fully justified basic structure is rooted in Rawls' theory of justice, in which the 'basic structure' (institutions, social relations, distribution of offices, and so on) is the central object of normative justice theory. The basic structure is what people in the original position, shrouded in their veil of ignorance, seek to determine the distribution of. For feminists like Susan Moller Okin (1989) one of the shortcomings of Rawls' argument was his highly constricted definition of the basic structure. In his original formulation, for example, he did not include the family as part of the basic structure of society, and Okin thought this was a near-fatal oversight, given how important within-family relations of production, distribution, domination and oppression are in actually-existing society. For Forst, this issue is somewhat moot. The precise content of the basic structure could very well be local and contingent – historically specific – but what was necessary and transcendent was that the structure, *whatever it is*, had to be fully justified under the principles of reciprocity and generality, which also means that the question of power remains a first question of justice just so long as it is possible that some people may be forced, coerced or even tricked into accepting a 'false' or 'misleading' justification.

And this is one place where Forst's arguments, which I find immensely attractive precisely because of their normative focus on *justice* and not only on *injustice* (as important as the analysis of injustice is in his framework), come up short. His imaginary of the processes and practices of justification strike me as too limited. On the one hand, and especially in his earlier works, he stands too firmly on a Rawlsian-Habermasian foundation of *intersubjective* justification. Too often his subject of justice is the individual; his sense of collective identity, that is of race, class and gendered identities and thus shared oppressions and interests, is weak (though perhaps stronger on the class front in 'Justice after Marx'); his sense that claiming the *right to justification* might be a collective struggle is almost non-existent. On the other hand, he lacks a fully-enough worked-out theory of hegemony and thus of how 'the question of power' also shapes the facts of consent. Something like a theory of coerced consent does appear in the pages of his collected works, but it is never fully articulated. We get a sense of how violence is the failure of power, but not enough of a sense of how power produces consent. Without such a worked-out theory Forst's theory of justice as the right to justification comes up short: we have no way of judging – of *justifying* – when and how an accepted justification has been justly accepted, when and how a claim really *is* reciprocal and general, when and how a basic structure of justification is just and a fully justified basic structure has indeed been fully justified.

One solution to this problem might be to admit that that is exactly the point: no structure of justification or basic structure will or can ever be fully justified. This is a position I am fully prepared to accept, but accepting it returns us right back to Engels' question: what is justice, but the stick which is everything but heretofore has been nothing? But now we have a quite different answer to the question than one that can be derived from Barnett's *Priority of Injustice*. First (and with my own acknowledgement to

Iris Marion Young), we have a responsibility – working collectively and working solidaristically – to determine what constitutes and *what ought to constitute* these basic structures, not only to focus on injustice. Second, we have a responsibility to finish Young's project of understanding how to orient ourselves towards a just future while accounting for and mending an unjust past. Third, we have a responsibility to understand how power works hegemonically in processes of justification. And fourth, we – at least those of us who are geographers – have a responsibility to work out the role that geography – space, spatiality, landscape – plays in structuring what constitutes and ought to constitute both the basic structure of justification and a (potentially) fully justified basic structure. All of these require not an empty concept of justice, but one that is constantly being refilled.

★★★

I have not always thought this way. Though I have called for an engagement with theories of justice in landscape research and developed some arguments in relation to a positive theory of social justice in research on homelessness and public space (Mitchell, 2003a; 2003c), I have not fulfilled my responsibility for justice theorizing as I just outlined it. In fact, I pretty much thoroughly agreed with Clive Barnett: the study of *injustice* ought to be the priority, politically as well as theoretically. But recently I have been on a crash-course in justice theorizing. The impetus was involvement in a big interdisciplinary research project (though the less said about that the better, given how unjustified and unjust the behaviour of some of those involved with it was). In the project, I had the opportunity to work with a half dozen other scholars (from a range of fields), and together we read widely, and sometimes deeply, in the literatures on cosmopolitan, feminist, Marxist, postcolonial and liberal justice, as well as on matters of spatial, landscape, environmental, climate, Indigenous and energy justice. I focused my own energies on coming to grips with literatures on justice in feminism and Marxism (as well as anarchism) and on rereading and thinking again about landscape and environmental justice. In revisiting the landscape justice literature, which I have contributed to, I became quite frustrated in our collective inability to theorize justice, instead of just pointing at it as a self-evident concept. And I have come to realize that our deficiency on this front is just like the fault Kafui Attoh (2011) rightly accused me and other contributors to the literature on the right to the city of perpetuating. By failing to adequately theorize *rights* when discussing the right to the city, we evacuated the concept of its true political importance while merely postponing inevitable fights over just what the right to the city is, and especially who should benefit from it, how and why. The emptiness (or what I have called 'capaciousness') of the right to the city slogan might offer some political openings – creating a rallying cry around which disparate collectivities can rally – but it also fails to allow for a deep enunciation – a justification, if you will – of the bases upon which those collectivities can (and perhaps cannot) work solidaristically. Invoking 'justice' in critical/radical geographical research might indeed plant a flag or signal an allegiance, but it does little to help us understand just what the justice we want should be.

Through rereading the work of Iris Marion Young, Nancy Fraser and, yes, David Harvey, being turned on to the work of Susan Moller Okin, Rainer Forst and many others, fighting with the emptiness of my own earlier work, listening to and learning from some of my colleagues in the project, I came to see that, while I still think that 'justice' is one of the emptiest of terms in the geographical lexicon, it is high time we started to fill it up, to ensure that the stick really is something we can (and should) measure reality against, while always paying close, dialectical attention to that material reality – those 'hard surfaces of life' themselves. In no other way can our vocational priority become as it should be: the priority of justice.

Notes

1. To a lesser extent because Soja never really theorizes *justice* in *Seeking Social Justice* (2010), preferring instead to (a) excoriate geographers for subsuming the spatial within the social, and (b) describe various social movements he had connections with that he argued were fighting for spatial justice. For a fuller, early elaboration of the potential for a theory of spatial justice, see Dikeç (2001).
2. Harvey is not wrong about the idealism of justice theorizing, but at the same time he also missed that this idealism sits uncomfortably alongside a more materialist foundation for thinking about what the fundamental core of justice is, for example in Rawls' concept of the 'basic structure', which I will come back to, and which I explore more fully in Mitchell (forthcoming).
3. Avowedly because, in my view, much contemporary theorizing in geography is, despite its claims to the contrary, ineluctably idealist, preferring to trade solely within the universe of ideas – usually signified with the unexamined codeword, 'discourse' – that is, it tends to be ungrounded in *historical* materialism. For a fuller take on my views in this matter, and especially why 'historical' is the more important term in the phrase 'historical materialism', see Mitchell (2003b; 2013).
4. The ripostes to Hartshorne by the hardly revolutionary Carl Sauer in 'Foreword to historical geography' (1941) and 'The education of a geographer' (1956) remain valuable reading on this front, though perhaps the best riposte to Hartshorne's Kantian idealism came in the form of the monumental *Man's Role in Changing the Face of the Earth* (Thomas, 1956).
5. On Okin's radicalism, see Rosenblum (2009).
6. The *language* of intersectionality is not without its problems. As a metaphor it rests on a rather untenable assumption of absolute space (Smith and Katz, 1993; Mitchell, 2021). But what it seeks to describe – a dialectical process of subject formation shot through with relations of power, domination, oppression and resistance – is of utmost centrality to any account of justice.

7   Forst's major works in English are collections of essays. These essays add up to a remarkably single-minded and consistent normative-philosophical project: (1) to promote justice as the right to justification; (2) to insist on the necessity and sufficiency of reciprocity and generality as normative principles of justice; (3) to insert the question of *power* and the centrality of *relations of production* at the heart of normative analyses of claims of justice and injustice; and, based on these (4) to work out what both 'minimal' and 'maximal' social justice would be. The first three points appear in almost every one of his essays; the fourth in many. Hence the lack of direct citations in the discussion that follows, except when very specific points are being made.

8   Forst makes similar critiques of distributional justice and promotes the priority – if you will – of production throughout his work and so even if the essay I am citing was published in English around the same time as Barnett's work, he would have had access to very similar arguments.

9   The similarities here with Fricker's (2007; 2013) theories of epistemic (in)justice should be clear.

References

Attoh, K. (2011) What kind of right is the right to the city? *Progress in Human Geography*, 35(5): 669–685.

Barnett, C. (2017) *The Priority of Injustice: Locating Democracy in Critical Theory*, Athens, GA: University of Georgia Press.

Dikeç, M. (2001) Justice and the spatial imagination, *Environment and Planning A*, 33(10): 1785–1805.

Fainstein, S. (2007) *The Just City*, Ithaca: Cornell University Press.

Fanon, F. (1967) *Black Skin, White Masks*, New York: Grove Press.

Farmer, P. (2003) *Pathologies of Power: Health, Human Rights, and the New War on the Poor*, Berkeley: University of California Press.

Forst, R. (2011) *The Right to Justification: Elements of a Constructivist Theory of Justice*, New York: Columbia University Press.

Forst, R. (2014) *Justification and Critique*, Cambridge: Polity.

Forst, R. (2017) *Normativity and Power: Analyzing Social Orders of Justification*, Oxford: Oxford University Press.

Fricker, M. (2007) *Epistemic Injustice: Power and the Ethics of Knowing*, Oxford: Oxford University Press.

Fricker, M. (2013) Epistemic justice as a condition of political freedom, *Synthese*, 190: 1317–1332.

Gilmore, R.W. (2007) *Golden Gulag*, Berkeley: University of California Press.

Gilmore, R.W. (2022) *Abolition Geographies: Essays Towards Liberation*, New York: Verso.

Guelke, L. (1974) An idealist alternative in geography, *Annals of the Association of American Geographers*, 64(2): 193–202.

Harding, S. (1988) *Whose Science? Whose Knowledge? Thinking from Women's Lives*, Ithaca, NY: Cornell University Press.

Harstock, N. (1998) *The Feminist Standpoint Revisited and Other Essays*, Boulder: Westview Press.

Hartshorne, R. (1939) *The Nature of Geography*, Washington, DC: Association of American Geographers.

Harvey, D. (1973) *Social Justice and the City*, London: Edward Arnold.

Harvey, D. (1996) *Justice, Nature and the Geography of Difference*, Oxford: Blackwell.

Jaggar, A. (2009) The philosophical challenges of global gender justice, *Philosophical Topics*, 37(2): 1–15.

Loyd, J. (2014) *Health Rights are Civil Rights: Peace and Justice Activism in Los Angeles, 1963–1978*, Minneapolis: University of Minnesota Press.

Merrifield, A. and Swyngedouw, E. (eds) (1995) *The Urbanization of Injustice*, New York: New York University Press.

Mitchell, D. (2003a) Cultural landscapes: just landscapes or landscapes of justice?, *Progress in Human Geography*, 27(6): 787–796.

Mitchell, D. (2003b) Historical materialism and Marxism, in Duncan, J., Johnson, N. and Schein, R. (eds) *The Blackwell Companion to Cultural Geography*, Oxford: Blackwell, pp 51–65.

Mitchell, D. (2003c) *The Right to the City: Social Justice and the Fight for Public Space*, New York: Guilford.

Mitchell, D. (2007) Work, struggle, death, and the geographies of justice: the transformation of landscape in and beyond California's Imperial Valley, *Landscape Research*, 32(5): 539–577.

Mitchell, D. (2008) New axioms for reading the landscape: paying attention to political economy and social justice, in Wescoat, J. and Johnston, D. (eds) *Political Economies of Landscape Change*, Dordrecht: Springer, pp 29–50.

Mitchell, D. (2012) *The Saved the Crops: Labor, Landscape and the Struggle over Industrial Farming in Bracero-Era California*, Athens, GA: University of Georgia Press.

Mitchell, D. (2013) Historical materialism, in Schein, R., Johnson, N. and Winders, J. (eds) *The Blackwell Companion to Cultural Geography*, Oxford: Wiley Blackwell, pp 39–41.

Mitchell, D. (2021) Geography sculpts the future: or, escaping – and falling back into – the tyranny of absolute space, *Studia Neophilogica*. https://doi.org/10.1080/00393274.2021.1916990

Mitchell, D. (Forthcoming) Landscape as basic structure: towards a 'concept of landscape that will assist in the development of the very idea of social justice', in Jones, M., Setten, G., Strecker, A. and Mitchell, D. (eds) *Landscape, Law and Justice*, Stockholm: Vittterhetsakademien.

Nussbaum, M. (2000) *Women and Human Development: The Capabilities Approach*, Cambridge: Cambridge University Press.

Nussbaum, M. (2008) Foreword, in Young, I.M., *Responsibility for Justice*, Oxford: Oxford University Press, pp ix–xxv.

Okin, S.M. (1979) *Women in Western Political Thought*, London: Virago.

Okin, S.M. (1989) *Justice, Gender, and the Family*, New York: Basic Books.

Ollman, B. (1991) *Dialectical Investigations*, New York: Routledge.
Pogge, T. (2001) Priorities of global justice, *Metaphilosophy*, 32(1/2): 6–24.
Pulido, L. (1996) *Environmentalism and Economic Justice: Two Chicano Struggles in the Southwest*, Tucson: University of Arizona Press.
Rawls, J. (1971) *A Theory of Justice*, Cambridge, MA: Harvard University Press.
Rawls, J. (1999) *The Law of Peoples*, Cambridge, MA: Harvard University Press.
Robeyns, I. (2006) The capability approach in practice, *Journal of Political Philosophy*, 14(3): 351–376.
Rosenblum, N. (2009) Okin's liberal feminism as a radical political theory, in Satz, D. and Reich, R. (eds) *Toward a Humanistic Justice: The Political Philosophy of Susan Moller Okin*, Oxford: Oxford University Press, pp 15–48.
Sauer, C. (1956) The education of a geographer, *Annals of the Association of American Geographers*, 46(3): 287–299.
Sauer, D. (1941) Foreword to historical geography, *Annals of the Association of American Geographers*, 31(1): 1–24.
Sen, A. (2009) *The Idea of Justice*, Cambridge, MA: Harvard University Press.
Smith, D. (1994) *Geography and Social Justice*, Oxford: Blackwell.
Smith, N. (1989) Geography as museum: private history and conservative idealism in the nature of geography, in Entrikin, J.N. and Brunn, S.D. (eds) *Reflections on Richard Hartshorne's 'The Nature of Geography'*, Occasional Publication of the Association of American Geographers, Washington, DC: Association of American Geographers, pp 90–121.
Smith, N. and Katz, C. (1993) Grounding metaphor, in Keith, M. (ed) *Place and the Politics of Identity*, London: Routledge, pp 66–81.
Soja, E. (2010) *Seeking Spatial Justice*, Minneapolis: University of Minnesota Press.
Thomas, W.J. (ed) (1956) *Man's Role in Changing the Face of the Earth*, Chicago: University of Chicago Press.
Williams, R. (1976) *Keywords: A Vocabulary of Culture and Society*, London: Fontana.
Young, I.M. (1990) *Justice and the Politics of Justice*, Princeton: Princeton University Press.
Young, I.M. (2000) *Inclusion and Democracy*, Oxford: Oxford University Press.
Young, I.M. (2008) *Responsibility for Justice*, Oxford: Oxford University Press.

11

Concluding Thoughts: What Does It Mean to Do 'Just' Research?

Agatha Herman and Joshua Inwood

This book comes together at a moment of deep crisis. As we write the sky in State College, Pennsylvania is an eerie colour, and the sun has taken on an otherworldly hue driven by climate change induced wildfires thousands of miles away rendering the air quality dangerous. In many Western nations nationalism and white supremacy are resurgent and threaten fragile political coalitions and, in the case of the United States, democratic governance at various political scales. More broadly, anthropogenic climate change and increased global competition sharpens already uneven distributions of resource scarcity, and reliance on militarism and neocolonialist processes of structural abandonment make vulnerable lives more precarious. These challenges render hope in the context of the present political realities difficult and hard to sustain. The reality is, the world and its places and peoples are being made more vulnerable by the day, and as a result the struggle to imagine alternatives has never been more important.

Within this context it is necessary to engage in broad conversations around justice and, more specifically, how and in what ways we practice justice in our work and through our lives. This edited book is meant to challenge existing paradigms that render researchers and our practices somehow separate from the work we do and the communities we engage with. Through these interventions we have perspectives that are grounded in a range of paradigms, which push the discussion of practising justice in new directions and challenge all of us to render justice more visible in both our work and our everyday lives. The concept of justice itself is slippery, it is often much easier to name *injustices* and human wrongs than it is to define what justice is and how it looks in operation. On the one hand, we often define justice geographically and the idea is mediated through the kinds of societies in which the concept emerges. Lisa Lowe (2015), for example, in her book *The Intimacies of Four Continents* describes the ways Western notions of freedom, democracy and justice, among other examples, emerged through the subordination of Black and Brown labour through enslavement and colonization as well as Indigenous genocides. The recognition that foundational concepts in Western understandings of justice dialectically relate to broader systematic oppressions is one example of how contested notions of justice are. We, as critical social researchers, need to be cognisant of the ways justice emerges through the making of space and place and a set of economic, political and cultural realities that render certain understandings of justice visible while simultaneously erasing the harm done through some of these very concepts. This contradiction lies at the heart of debates around justice and, when placed within the context of the multifaceted crises that challenge long-term human survivability, the chapters included in this book speak to the varied and contested ways we enact justices and build solidarities within our work and lives.

Perhaps more than these contested realities and the articulations of justice outlined in this collection, these chapters – in their various ways – also contain hope. The idea of hope is a precious commodity in the face of such widespread challenges. Laura Pulido in her book *Black, Brown, Yellow and Left: Radical Activism in Los Angeles* writes that in order to create, we must first 'develop a vision of the kind of world [we] would like to live in' (2006: 238). She goes on to note that the vision of the world has to be 'compassionate and humane and must reach people's hearts and souls as well as their minds' (Pulido, 2006: 238). What Pulido means, we think, is that in order to create the kind of world that recognizes the broad contours of justice articulated in this book, the work we do must necessarily connect with the visions of justice that are operationalized in the communities we work in and with. These visions must be collaborative and reflect what Pulido describes as a 'willingness to open our hearts and minds to something entirely new and different' (2006: 238). That vision can only be accomplished by delving deeply into communities and enacting visions of justice within contexts that build on and *with* communities most affected by the struggles over justice. This is the kind of vison outlined in this book and, for researchers, the melding of these various intellectual and emotional strands is something that powerfully stands against hopelessness.

Emerging common narratives

While the bibliographic accounts and strategies of engaging with the brief were unique across our contributors, a series of common themes emerged across the nine chapters: a questioning of the purpose of the university and, following that, the role of the academic within and beyond these institutions;

an emergent sense of how the spaces, practices and ideologies of our contexts shape our capabilities to *do* just research; and reflections on the often little-discussed emotional labour, particularly feelings of discomfort.

Debates around the nature, purpose, management and future of universities have been long-standing (McCann et al, 2020) but there is largely agreement among academics that the questions now being asked about knowledge production – fundamentally about the purpose of research and education – are largely determined by market forces (Giroux, 2014). The pervasive logic of the 'neoliberal university' is centred on measurable targets, monitoring and the fear of not meeting expectations (Coster and Zanoni, 2019; McCann et al, 2020). The rise of the impact agenda as a governance tool, particularly in British and Australian universities, arguably polices academic work along market-based criteria, stripping the recognition of research's social and political value(s) from funding assessment criteria (Rhodes et al, 2018). Coster and Zanoni (2019: 412) further argue that such neoliberal practices are promoting 'a new ideal academic subject profoundly imbued with masculinity ... centred on individualism, entrepreneurship, competition and performance'. As we raised in the Introduction, how do the needs and drivers of just research – which our contributors have grounded in practices and relations of collaboration, collegiality and care – interact with or, rather, fare against the measurable deliverables demanded by the contemporary neoliberal university?

Adlerova and Moragues Faus (Chapter 4) reflect on this through highlighting the unsustainability of this model in terms of researcher experiences, drawing out the ongoing health crisis – 'the fantasy of achieving work-life balance' (Coster and Zanoni, 2019: 412) – and the raced/gendered inequalities within academia's structures and operations. Coster and Zanoni (2019: 412) reflect on ongoing gendered patterns in faculty practices with male academics more likely to be institutionally accountable (meeting the expectations of the university) while female academics are more likely to be relationally accountable (seeking to be responsive to diverse and multiple fora). They note that this leads to greater potential for failure by women who do not 'make the right choices'. Arguably, we can see this gendered approach in Adlerova and Moragues Faus wondering whether they have jeopardized future success by prioritizing co-design and care for research participants over individual progress in the use of their personal research funds.

To what extent then is this a supportive environment in which to think, say and do just research if we, the researchers, are stressed, anxious, uncertain, stretched, vulnerable, low and exploited? This connects into the experiences documented by McCann et al (2020) of university restructuring, which emphasizes the emotional affects of neoliberal governance strategies and the personal impacts of working within an institution seemingly actively hostile to the idea of a university for the public good. While this is, as Weiner (2020) puts it, set against a wider backdrop of anti-intellectualism and 'wilful ignorance', there remain loud calls and strong adherence among many academics to Chomsky's ideal of intellectuals speaking truth and exposing lies, of having 'a responsibility to unsettle power, trouble consensus and challenge common sense' (Giroux, 2014: 52). To paraphrase Giroux (2014), what happens to a university when it is treated like a corporation? He argues that we need to push back against academics' reduction to 'technicians and grant writers' (2014: 39) to reclaim the rigour, clarity, courage and political commitment of *being* intellectuals. For Derickson (Chapter 2), the intellectual enterprise is a fundamental site for the realization of justice while Chatti (Chapter 7) positively embraces the language of 'intellectual projects' in her framing of her academic journey. There is a role for such intellectuals inside as well as outside the academy with calls for academic activists to: challenge the neoliberal consensus within the university and in relations between university and society (Rhodes et al, 2018); reshape subverted and debased governance structures (McCann et al, 2020); question governance through accountability (Coster and Zanoni, 2019); and confront the normalization of self-exploitation and success as an individual endeavour (Adlerova and Moragues Faus, Chapter 4).

Broeckerhoff and Magalhaes Lopes (2020) extend this idea of individual success through their reflections on key moments of 'failure' as PhD and early-career researchers, which shows that failure to meet the normative expectations of being an academic can be both constant and potentially transformative. They call for more, 'better' failure through failing together with others, sharing open and honest accounts to establish a sense of solidarity in vulnerability with fellow academics and reject existing scripts of 'correct' research practice and identities. McGarrol (2017) and Maguire et al (2019) note the latter is often lacking acknowledgement of the emotional labour involved in doing research, with formal research training or ethics application procedures offering little or no consideration for the wellbeing of the researchers. Despite the robust body of literatures on the role of emotions in doing fieldwork (as referenced in Maguire et al, 2019), alongside widespread recognition of the innate uncertainties to research, the 'emotional risks to the researcher are often hidden, omitted or undervalued' (McGarrol, 2017: 440). Mavroudi (Chapter 3) draws on a series of 'jarring encounters' to highlight the discomforts of barriers experienced; of events not going as planned; and questions over self-positioning during interviews. For Koefoed and Simonsen (2022), researchers are expected to be able to move between passionate immersion and cool contemplation but this fails to recognize that research can never be disconnected from other aspects of a researcher's life (McGarrol, 2017). The 'baggage' Mavroudi (Chapter 3) reflects on emphasizes that 'emotions do not begin in the field, they are part of the preparation' (Maguire et al, 2019: 302) but may also follow you back into your home life and accompany you across the years.

For the Vegan Geography Collective, the explicitly lived nature of their values blurs any attempt at a distinction between home and research even further, and their accounts highlight the potential emotional discomforts or disjunctures in researching and teaching in contexts that may be sceptical or hostile to vegan discourses, practices and relations. Ophélie Véron considers her role as a militant scholar-activist within grassroots food initiatives, presenting some insights into the dilemmas she faces in terms of if, how and when to push debates in which she believes passionately. Richard J. White reflects on the necessarily uncomfortable classroom discussions that serve to open up different points of view among students. Working in the hostile environment of anti-LGBTQIA+ movements as lesbian, gay or ally researchers placed a 'tremendous emotional strain' on Maguire et al (2019) while Namatende-Sakwa's (2018) research into the 'illicit' subject of homosexuality in her native Uganda provoked feelings of shame, guilt, fear, anxiety and paranoia that affected relationships beyond the research space. No matter how much you intellectually prepare, there is no way you can ever fully anticipate the emotional work a research project might entail (Maguire et al, 2019) or how you will manage the constant, demanding and complex relational skills required for qualitative studies (McGarrol, 2017; Morillon et al, 2021). For Adlerova and Moragues Faus (Chapter 4), this forms part of acknowledging the messy more-than-research nature of their work, recognizing the iterative, flowing and interconnected nature of work as always set within a broader life. Chatti (Chapter 7) also uses the idea of *messiness* to describe and reflect on her research experiences and this descriptor offers, for us, a comforting reminder of the complexities and contingencies that we all face as researchers.

We have to be prepared to accept too that the emotional labour we put in to a project is grounded in 'the effort, the act of trying and not the result, which may or may not be successful' (Morillon et al, 2021: 744). However, this is not about avoiding difficult, painful or what may seem to be fruitless situations but learning how to manage those emotions (Maguire et al, 2019). While the defects of reflexivity have been widely acknowledged, Koefoed and Simonsen (2022) argue that this still offers a useful tool in opening up the messy, uncomfortable realities of doing research. Following Pillow, Namatende-Sakwa (2018) calls for more uncomfortable reflexive practices that are not about gaining clarity or finding solutions but laying bare anxieties and ambivalences. Within these, self-indulgence must be resisted but by creating a space for diligent and purposeful self-care, such reflections can be therapeutic (Maguire et al, 2019). Indeed, a key motivation for this volume was to open up some of the dilemmas, emotions and lived experiences of *doing* research and Adlerova and Moragues Faus (Chapter 4) call for further openness, for us to be prepared to get into the 'uncomfortable spotlight' in order to do justice to ourselves as more-than-researchers.

It is clear from this discussion that the hegemonic ideologies and practices shaping contemporary academic spaces impact on our capabilities to do just research. Dickinson and Uwimanzi (Chapter 5) express frustration with how the nature of their funding governed how they could do their research. Combined with the context of employment within a teaching-intensive neoliberal Northern university, this established tensions between how they were able, and how they would have chosen, to practice their project. Furthermore, the funding timescales precluded the transformative potential of their interventions. For Mavroudi (Chapter 3), pervasive ideals of what it means to 'do' academia impacted more broadly through the assumptions made around her part-time working – the support but also exclusion. She draws out the very real effects this has on her capability to meet 'deliverables' while also being responsive and available to research participants. Nonetheless, the ongoing belief in 'the mandate of the public university' (Balint, Chapter 6) means that many of us are already working actively as intellectuals, as defined earlier. While this may often be within the confines of our neoliberal institutions, creatively mining the cracks of life allows us to seek ways to build, maintain and support collaborations as well as manage and promote care-full and dialogical relations and spaces for everyone, from students and early-career researchers to tenured full professors, to do research that both engages with questions, spaces and relations of justice and internalizes justice within its practices.

Taking things forward

Our nine chapters have engaged with the initial premise and questions in pleasingly diverse and different ways but all share a sense of critical reflection in looking back over work completed as well as considering ongoing and future research practices and relations. From these accounts, the complexity of research is emphasized, all the encounters, emotions, discourses, behaviours, skills, materialities, beliefs and relations that flux and flex. These are often bundled together as 'research' in a way that we just take for granted, being such normalized elements of how we *do* what we do that we don't pause to step back and unpack exactly what they mean for us, our colleagues, participants and communities or consider whether they are done with/through justice. What then can you, the reader, take forward from this?

The questions that Chatti (Chapter 7) poses herself offer an initial framework for critically reflecting on your research practices, acknowledging

Figure 11.1: What should we be asking ourselves?

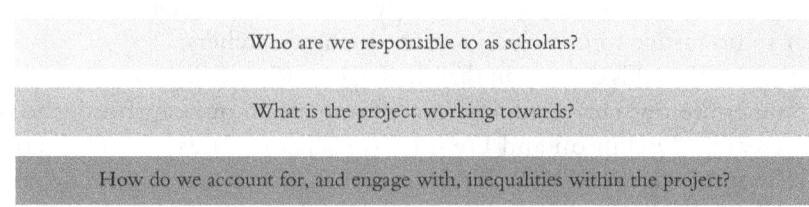

that these are not a set of prescribed and linear steps but part of an iterative analytical spectrum, a dialogical process of constant 'learning, unlearning and relearning' (Datta, 2017 in Held, 2020: 5). Doing *just* research is not an easy tick-box exercise but a messy and constant work-in-progress *and that's OK*. Your answers to the following starter questions (Figure 11.1) may take time to form, change and adapt with your evolving experiences; while it can be frustrating to not have a definitive 'how to' (as you may have hoped by this point in the volume), playing with both the freedoms and fears presented by emergent justice in, with and through our everyday and spectacular practices can enable more responsive, active and care-full research.

Recognizing the sudden shifts and unexpected twists that can happen in any project, these are questions that we suggest are helpful to keep returning to. Your answers at the start of your project when you are feeling excited, hopeful and collegiate may be very different to when a key stakeholder pulls out, a collaborator has a 'Hyde' moment, a disaster strikes the region you are in/focusing on or your funder changes their requirements. What looks like 'best practice' is also, therefore, something that is contextual, dynamic and contingent although we argue that the following elements remain core:

1. *Placed*: engaging with the placed nature of research through acknowledging the impacts of being grounded in specific contexts. This may be through responsive and dialogical understandings of field sites but also in terms of recognizing where your practices come from. This may require the decolonizing of your praxis through efforts to rebalance the formulation and valuation of topics, research questions, knowledges and methodologies by decentring Western ideologies.
2. *Learning*: accepting the emergent process of doing just research requires an openness and willingness to be shaped by the unknown. Research is about discovery and through (re)engaging with old or new stakeholders, ways of thinking, value and knowledge systems, methods or relations, you should be open to your perspectives on the questions posed in Figure 11.1 and/or how you want to approach your project shifting. This may entail a return to the ethics committee to update approvals but ethics, like other

aspects of your research, should be lived and under constant reflection (Cannella and Lincoln, 2007). Recognizing the gaps in your knowledges is healthy and promotes a mindset that will more easily embrace learning opportunities wherever they may appear.

3. *Action*: throughout, our contributors have highlighted their efforts at *making* space (Balint, Chapter 6), *unsettling* asymmetries (Derickson, Chapter 2), *exposing* epistemic silencing (Dickinson and Uwimanzi, Chapter 5), *challenging* disciplinary norms (Wood-Donnelly, Chapter 8) and *negotiating* tensions (Mavroudi, Chapter 3), to note just a few. This emphasizes the constant work and material engagement, which Mitchell (Chapter 10) argues is needed for justice. Just research therefore cannot be a purely theoretical endeavour but must always *do* something.

4. *Working with and through 'more-than-research'*: all of our contributors highlight the essential need to think through the relationships that perform and govern the project in order to enact care-full relations with our participants and colleagues. This may manifest in different ways, for example, through Dickinson and Uwimanzi (Chapter 5) enabling situated experiences, the Vegan Geography Collective (Chapter 9) embodying multispecies justice through everyday and pedagogical practices or Adlerova and Moragues Faus (Chapter 4) building trust and opportunities for learning in and beyond the academy. Whatever its form, this entails ongoing and critical reflection on how the needs, interests and ideals of more-than-human stakeholders are negotiated in and beyond the project, acknowledging that 'our research activities are always already "more than research"' (Adlerova and Moragues Faus, Chapter 4).

5. *Care for the self*: it is easy to forget that a key component in doing just research is you. Even for those comfortable with autoethnographic techniques or critical self-reflection, caring for the self is a different skill. Caring through the messy, contradictory and sometimes frankly uncomfortable encounters that constitute research can be too readily pushed aside to be dealt with in a never-ending 'later'. While discussions around mental health have become more open in academia, the labour involved in managing research can mean that you keep going despite the emotional and psychological exertions and impacts. All of the statements in Figure 11.2 are possibly true, but are ones that ignore or downplay the essential need to recognize when things have become too much, when you need to walk away whether just for a moment or longer term. You have the best understanding of how to manage your own equilibrium and being kind to yourself will enable you to engage with the 'moral considerations and ethical choices that arise as part of a researcher's daily practice' (Rossman and Rallis, 2010: 379) with greater clarity, integrity and focus.

Figure 11.2: The emotional labour of managing research

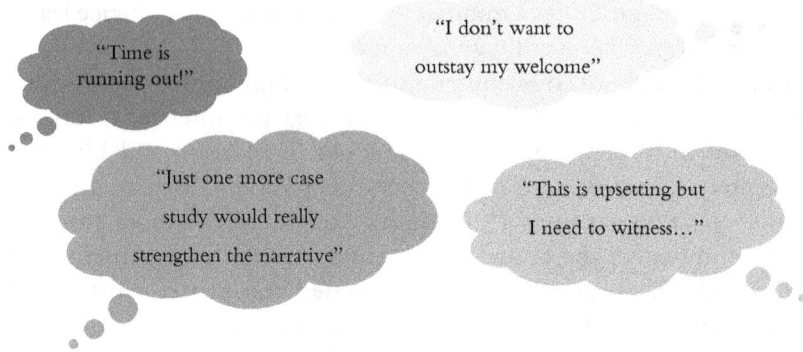

Final thoughts: 'filling up justice'?

Admittedly I (Agatha) am somewhat sleep deprived as I try to write these final words, thanks to the exigencies of industrial action, research project logistics and a teething/vomiting toddler, which further emphasize the 'more-than-research' nature of everything we do, but when I started trying to think through Mitchell's very pertinent and provoking question, my mind went blank. How do we understand just what the justice we want should be? How do we go about filling up justice? Where does one even begin? My starting point was to emulate Brian Bilston ('Twitter's unofficial Poet Laureate') and see if some creative writing with the help of the Google search box would provide inspiration:

Justice is …	blind
Justice is …	gray
Justice is a …	virtue
Justice is a …	weapon
Justice can be defined as a …	paradigm
Justice can be defined as a …	single word
Justice needs …	to be seen to be done
Justice should be …	tempered with mercy
Justice should be …	even-handed
Justice has …	been served
Justice has a …	long arm
Justice has a …	price

Justice requires …	open borders
Justice requires …	the recognition of animal rights
Justice needs …	24 feet of fencing
Justice must …	prevail

What we take from this is the prevalence of common tropes around justice, the ambivalence or fear it can inspire as well as feelings of hope and security, even if these are exclusionary or exclusive. It highlights the necessity of 'filling up justice', in Mitchell's words, in order to move it beyond just being another taken-for-granted concept that is neither unpicked nor unpacked but just left to speak for itself. Considering this poem through Fraser's framework of social justice reminds us of the need to question the process of frame-setting as it highlights the lack of consensus and, in fact, the extraordinary multiplicity of 'whos', 'hows' and 'whats' of justice. Through the endings Google offered for the starter phrases, we have conflicting, tangential, specific, diffuse, concrete and metaphorical responses that continue to militate against any one-size-fits-all framing of justice (Fraser, 2008).

Yes, we have noticed that we're still not providing a definitive response to Mitchell but, for us, any effort to 'fill up' justice must always be reflexive and dialogical, it cannot be lifted off the shelf (even if some of the ingredients can be found there) since it must always be responsive to the dynamic, multidimensional and intersectional contextuality through which all of our research endeavours flow. We, as the researchers, play a critical – if tiring – role in constantly questioning and responding to the ongoing dance, which is sometimes a solo, sometimes a duet and sometimes a group number, of doing *just* research.

References

Broeckerhoff, A. and Magalhaes Lopes, M. (2020) Finding comfort in discomfort: how two cross-disciplinary early-career researchers are learning the embrace 'failure', *Emotion, Space and Society*, 35: 1–4.

Cannella, G.S. and Lincoln, Y.S. (2007) Predatory vs dialogic ethics: constructing an illusion or ethical practice as the core of research methods, *Qualitative Inquiry*, 13(3): 315–335.

Coster, M.D. and Zanoni, P. (2019) Governing through accountability: gendered moral serlves and the (im)possibilities of resistance in the neoliberal university, *Gender Work and Organisation*, 26(4): 411–429.

Fraser, N. (2008) *Scales of Justice: Reimagining Political Space in a Globalizing World*, Cambridge: Polity Press.

Giroux, H.A. (2014) Public intellectuals against the neoliberal university, in Denzin, N.K. and Giardina, M.D. (eds) *Qualitative Inquiry Outside the Academy*, New York: Routledge, pp 35–60.

Held, M.B.E. (2020) Research ethics in decolonizing research with Inuit communities in Nunavut: the challenge of translating knowledge into action, *International Journal of Qualitative Methods*, 19: 1–7.

Koefoed, L. and Simonsen, K. (2022) Emotions and positionalities: experiences from fieldwork among Danish Muslims, *Area*, 54(1): 118–125.

Lowe, L. (2015) *The Intimacies of Four Continents*, Durham, NC and London: Duke University Press.

Maguire, H., McCartan, A., Nash, C.J. and Browne, K. (2019) The enduring field: exploring researcher emotions in covert research with antagonistic organisations, *Area*, 51(2): 299–306.

McCann, L., Granter, E., Hyde, P. and Aroles, J. (2020) 'Upon the gears and upon the wheels': terror convergence and total administration in the neoliberal university, *Management Learning*, 51(4): 431–451.

McGarrol, S. (2017) The emotional challenges of conducting in-depth research into significant health issues in health geography: reflections on emotional labour, fieldwork and life course, *Area*, 49(4): 436–442.

Morillon, A., Kassabian, A. and Heas, S. (2021) Promotion of physical activities among underprivileged populations: researcher's discomforts during the fieldwork, *Italian Sociological Review*, 11(5S): 737–760.

Namatende-Sakwa, L. (2018) 'Madam, are you one of them?' 'Reflexivities of discomfort' in researching an 'illicit' subject, *International Journal of Qualitative Studies in Education*, 31(4): 328–340.

Pulido, L. (2006) *Black, Brown, Yellow and Left: Radical Activism*, Los Angeles: University of California Press.

Rhodes, C., Wright, C. and Pullen, A. (2018) Changing the world? The politics of activism and impact in the neoliberal university, *Organization*, 25(1): 139–147.

Rossman, G.B. and Rallis, S.F. (2010) Everyday ethics: reflections on practice, *International Journal of Qualitative Studies in Education*, 23(4): 379–391.

Weiner, E.J. (2020) Sequestered spaces, public places: the responsibility of intellectuals who teach within the 'safe zones' of the neoliberal university, *Taboo*, 19(2): 133–151.

Index

References to figures are in *italic* type. References to endnotes show both the page number and the note number (84n1).

'5 Rs' (respect, relevance, reciprocity, responsibility and relationality) 6, 7
1965 genocide, Indonesia 94–96
1994 Genocide against the Tutsi, Rwanda 68, 71, 73, 75, 76, 77, 78, 79
see also RDYPP (Rwanda Diaspora Youth Partnership Programme)

A

Aboriginal communities, Australia 88–89
　Aboriginal Tent Embassy, Canberra 92–93
　Minutes of Evidence Project, 1881 Parliamentary Coranderrk Inquiry, Australia 96–97
academia
　academic structures and epistemicide 79–80
　just spaces for staff and students 89, 99
　justice approach in 52
　part-time working 42, 181
　raced/gendered inequalities in 42, 51, 52, 54, 57, 178
　see also universities
academic publishing 51, 52, 112
　see also dissemination
accountability 50, 89, 90
　justice as 90, 98–99, 100
action 183
Adivisi (Tribal) communities, India 106
Aegis Trust 74, 77–78, 81, 82
　Champion Humanity team 72, 75–76, 77
Africa 67, 69
animal agriculture 141–144, 148–151
Anthropocene, the 143
anthroprivilege 141, 147
anti-idealism 160
Arctic 14, 121–123, 124
　dissemination strategies 122, 127, 129–130
　economic development 135–136
　governance 123, 125, 133, 135
　imperialism 124–125, 130–132, 133, 134, 135
　Indigenous peoples 124, 125, 127, 130, 131, 132, 135, 136
　International Relations social constructivism 124, 130, 133–135
　justice perspective 122, 125–126, 134–137
　research methods 122, 127–128, 129
　resource exploitation 131–132, 134–135
　role of justice in research 123–126
　search and rescue operations 125–126
　sovereignty 123, 124, 130, 132–133, 134, 135
　stakeholder engagement 122, 126–127, 129, 135
Arctic Council 125, 132, 134, 135
Arctic Treaty 135
Argentina 58
Athens, Greece 32
Attoh, Kafui 171
Australia 32, 92
　see also Aboriginal communities, Australia
autism 41–42
autoethnography 152
　community food spaces, militant (auto) ethnography 141, 152–154, 180

B

BAME (Black, Asian and Minority Ethnic) communities
　disproportionate impact of COVID-19 pandemic on 51
Barnett, Clive 159, 163–164, 165, 167, 170, 171
basic structures 169–170, 171
BEE (Black Economic Empowerment), wine industry, Western Cape, South Africa 10, 11–13
Black Americans, environmental justice 106
black box of doing research 8, *8*, 9
Black feminism 22, 23, 29, 161
Black Lives Matter movement 98
British Empire, and the Mau Mau 93, 94

C

Canada 124
capabilities approach 126, 160, 168
capitalism 161–162, 164–165
care
  care receiving 52, 55
  caring practices 43
  caring with 52, 55
  self-care of researchers 52, 54, 180, 183, *184*
cattle farming 142, 143
  see also animal agriculture
chicken farming 142, 143
  see also animal agriculture
children, vegan 140, 144–146
China 14
climate change 14, 102, 103–104, 105, 109, 124, 136, 140, 141, 142, 176
climate justice 102–103, 114–116
  animal agriculture 142
  critical research 113–114
  literature review 103–106
  positionality of researchers 111–112
  reciprocity and just relations 112–113
  reflections on research projects 106–109
  scholars' responsibilities 110–111
collaboration 67–68
  developing healthy collaborations 26–28
  justice as 90–93, 99–100
  university-based researchers as a resource in 24–25
  see also research relationships
coloniality
  in African studies 69
  of overseas development aid 80
community-centric methodologies 69–70
community-engaged research 91
companion animals 141, 148, 151
consent 170
co-production 49–50, 91
COVID-19 pandemic 51, 54, 82, 92, 150
CREATE Initiative 28–29
critical animal geographies 139
  see also multispecies justice (MSJ)
Critical Race Theory 3, 91
cultural recognition dimension of justice 47

D

Dakota people 28
Dalit communities, India 106
decarbonization 102, 115
decolonization 7, 67, 69, 84, 128
democratic justice 164
dependency, in researcher-community collaborations 27
diaspora studies 32
  see also RDYPP (Rwanda Diaspora Youth Partnership Programme)
directive model of community-based research 19, 26, 28

dissemination
  accessible 50
  Arctic research 122, 127, 129–130
  see also academic publishing
distribution dimension of justice 47, 52, 126
  energy justice 104
  food justice 59
  research processes 59
distribution of material resources 23–24, 24–26
domination, analysis of 164

E

early-career researchers 13, 14, 51, 58, 59–60, 99, 179
'ecologies of knowledges' 70–71
economic dimensions of justice 46, 47
  food justice 52, 56–58, 58–59
electricity, access to 102, 108–109
  see also energy justice
emotions, and research 35–36, 179–180
energy justice 102–103, 114–116
  critical research 113–114
  literature review 103–106
  positionality of researchers 111–112
  reciprocity and just relations 112–113
  reflections on research projects 106–109
  scholars' responsibilities 110–111
energy sector, decarbonization of 102, 115
environmental justice 106, 122, 135, 142, 159, 171
environmentalism, and animal agriculture 141–142
'epistemic backgrounding' 25–26
epistemic justice 4, 70, 71
  RDYPP (Rwanda Diaspora Youth Partnership Programme) 67–68, 75–84
epistemicide 67, 79
ethics 6, 7–8, 123, 182
  welfarist 148–149
ethics of care 43
  food justice 46, 47, 49, 50, 52, 61
EU (European Union), JUSTNORTH project 129, 135, 136
European imperialism 128–129
extractive model of community-based research 19, 26, 28, 59, 61, 111

F

Fairtrade, wine industry, Western Cape, South Africa 10, 11–13
farmed animals 141–144, 148–151
feminism/feminist theory 13, 22, 30, 111, 161, 162, 170, 171
  Black feminism 22, 23, 29, 161
  feminist and participatory methodologies of food justice 49–52
'field, the,' disruption of 67, 69
'filling up justice' 184–185

INDEX

fish farming 142
see also animal agriculture
food justice 46–47, 61
 care-full participatory justice framework 46, 47, 52, *53*, 54, 60, 61
 experiential knowledge of food insecurity 54, 55–56, 57
 feminist and participatory methodologies 49–52
 social justice lens 47–49
Foodlinks project 51, 59
Forst, Rainer 164, 167–169, 170, 172, 173
forward-looking model of responsibility 166
Fraser, Nancy 23, 24, 25, 46, 47, 61, 164, 172, 185

G

gatekeepers 81
gender
 and care 54
 inequalities in research 42, 51, 52, 178
generality 167, 168
genocide
 1965 genocide, Indonesia 94–96
 1994 Genocide against the Tutsi, Rwanda 68, 71, 73, 75, 76, 77, 78, 79
 Aboriginal communities, Australia 92–93
 and accountability 89
 genocide prevention 98
Global Challenges Research Fund (GCRF) 73, 75, 76, 80, 81
 Quality Related (QR) funding 68, 80, 84n1
global financial crisis 2007 4
Global War on Terror 4
governance
 Arctic 123, 125, 133, 135
Greece 32
Greek diasporic identity 32, 39, 40–41
Gullah/Geechee Sustainability Think Tank 29

H

Harvey, David 159, 160, 162, 163, 165, 172
Holocaust, the 88, 95
homosexuality, Uganda 180
hope 177
human exceptionalism 139–140
 see also multispecies justice (MSJ)
humanization of knowledge 77–78

I

idealism, in justice theorizing 160, 163, 165
identities
 performative 40–42
 social construction of 22
imperialism, and the Arctic 124–125, 130–132, 133, 134, 135
imposition, in researcher-community collaborations 27
India 106
 energy and climate justice 103, 107–108, 111
Indigenous peoples 111
 Arctic 124, 125, 127, 130, 131, 132, 135, 136
 see also Aboriginal communities, Australia
individualism
 in academia 51, 59, 179
 in justice theorizing 160–161, 162
Indonesia, 1965 genocide 94–96
injustice
 geographical theorizing 159
 responsibility for 166–167
 theorization of 162–163
 visibility and accountability of 90, 99, 100
insider/outsider relations 40–41
International Arctic Social Sciences Association 129
International Relations 126, 133, 134, 136
 International Relations social constructivism 124, 130, 133–135
 and justice 121–122, 123
intersectionality 22, 52, 161, 172
 of justice 47–48
interviews 33–34
 silences in 37, 38–39
Israel-Palestine 98

J

Jewish communities 88
 diasporic identity 32, 38
just transitions 105–106
 and the Arctic 136
 just food transition 141–142
 see also climate justice; energy justice
justice
 concepts of 126–127, 176–177
 creating spaces for justice conversations 93–98
 'filling up justice' 184–185
 and International Relations theory 121–122
 intersectionality of 47–48
 liberal formulations of 160
 meanings of 3–4
 multidimensionality of 47
 relationality of 92
 socialist formulations of 160
 'justice for all' 140, 154
 see also multispecies justice (MSJ)
JUSTNORTH project 129, 135, 136

K

Karuk Tribe and Blue Lake Rancheria, California 108–109
knowledge production 23–24, 25–26, 34, 51, 61, 69, 71, 79, 82, 83, 178
 extractive practices 111

L

labour power 165
landscape, and injustice 163, 171–172
learning 182–183
'least harm' principle 151
LGBTQIA+ people 180
liberal justice theory 159, 160, 161

M

Marx, Karl 160, 161–162, 164, 165, 169, 171
material resources, distribution of 23–24, 24–26
Mau Mau, Kenya 93–94
maximal justice 168, 169
meat industry 140
  slaughterhouse workers (SHWs) 149–151
  see also animal agriculture
'meeting points' 97–98
MeToo movement 98
migration studies 32–33
minimal justice 168, 169
Minutes of Evidence Project, 1881 Parliamentary Coranderrk Inquiry, Australia 96–97
more-than-research work 46–47, 50, 52, 54, 180, 183, 184
multidimensionality, of justice 47
multispecies justice (MSJ) 139–141, 155–156, 180, 183
  community food spaces, militant (auto) ethnography 141, 152–154, 180
  food systems transition 140, 141–144
  'non-human first' campaigns 154
  vegan children 140, 144–146
  vegan geographies in the classroom 140–141, 146–152, 180

N

National Association of Rwandese Communities in the UK (NARC-UK) 73, 75, 76, 82
neoliberal universities 7, 178–179, 181
non-extractive research 6, 7

O

online exclusion 81–82
oppression 162, 163, 165
  see also injustice
Othering, of researchers 41–42
Overseas Development Assistance (ODA), UK 73, 80, 84n1

P

Palestinian diasporic identity 32, 36–38, 39, 41–42
participatory action research 28, 43, 79, 91
participatory research 67–68, 70, 71, 84
  care-full, slow scholarship 49–52, 54
part-time working in academia 42, 181
performative identities 40–42
performative storytelling 31, 32–35
perpetration-induced traumatic stress (PTSS), slaughterhouse workers (SHWs) 150
'perspectives from the top' 121, 136
  see also Arctic
PETA 154
pig farming 142
  see also animal agriculture
placed nature of research 182
political dimension of justice 46, 47, 48
  food justice 52, 55–58, 59–60
political geography 122, 123, 126, 136
positionality of researchers 31–32, 35, 41
  climate and energy justice 111–112
postcolonial scholarship 91
post-genocide reconstruction see RDYPP (Rwanda Diaspora Youth Partnership Programme)
post-traumatic stress disorder (PTSD), slaughterhouse workers (SHWs) 150
power
  in academia 44
  distribution of 168–169, 171
  and positionality 31–32
  in research relationships 7, 10, 13, 19
  and women's voices 37
praxis, justice as 5–8
privilege, of academic researchers 35
procedural dimension of justice 127
  energy justice 104
proximity, in researcher-community collaborations 27
public space, and injustice 163

R

radical justice theory 159
Rawls, John 121, 126–127, 160, 161, 168, 169–170
RDYPP (Rwanda Diaspora Youth Partnership Programme) 67–68, 79–84
  background and context 71–74
  creating spaces for action 78–79
  humanizing knowledge 77–78
  multi-sited enquiry 75–77
  Rwanda's political economy of development 68–71
reciprocity 167–168
recognition
  and knowledge production 25–26
  recognition dimension of justice 104, 127
  see also representation
redistribution, as a dimension of justice 23–24
reflection 181–182
  and positionality 31–32
reflexivity 2, 9, 11, 13, 24, 33–34, 84, 106, 111, 119, 133, 180, 185
renewable energy projects 105
  see also energy justice

INDEX

representation 31, 34–35
   as a dimension of justice 23–24
   see also recognition
research 1–2, 14
   common themes 177–181
   encounters with others in 33–34
   placed nature of 182
   praxis 5–8
research methods 2–3
   Arctic research 122, 127–128, 129
research practices
   honesty in 9–13
   see also praxis, justice as
research relationships 6–7, 46
   see also collaborations
researchers
   Othering of 41–42
   positionality of 31–32, 35, 41, 111–112
   privilege of 35
   self-care of 52, 54, 180, 183, *184*
   sharing and self-disclosure, in the research process 41–42
   'unconscious bias' of 36
resource exploitation, Arctic 131–132, 134–135
'resourcefulness,' and knowledge production 24–26
responsibility, for injustices 166–167
right to the city 3, 171–172
Russia 14, 124
Rwanda see RDYPP (Rwanda Diaspora Youth Partnership Programme)

S

Sámi people, Arctic 130
Sápmi people, Arctic 130
search and rescue operations, Arctic 125–126
Sen, Amartya 122, 127, 160, 164, 168
sharing, in the research process 41–42
silences 37, 38–39
slaughterhouse workers (SHWs) 149–151
social connection model of responsibility 166
social constructivism, International Relations 124, 130, 133–135
social contract 123, 124, 125, 126, 127, 128, 131, 132, 134
social justice 185
   food justice 47–49
socialist formulations of justice 160
socio-cultural dimensions of justice 46, 47
   food justice 52, 59
sovereignty, Arctic 123, 124, 130, 132–133, 134, 135
Spain 54, 58
spatial justice 159
speciesism 140, 147, 155
   see also multispecies justice (MSJ)
stakeholder engagement, Arctic 122, 126–127, 129, 135

standpoint theory 162
state, the
   in International relations 123–124, 125, 128
   visibility and accountability of state crime 89
stories, sharing of 31–44
structural injustice 71
   Arctic 125–126, 127, 135
   visibility and accountability of 89, 90, 99, 100
structural violence 163
Sustainable Development Goals 2015 84n1
suum cuique ('to each his/her own') principle 168
Syria 14

T

testimonies 91
timespaces 31, 32–36, 39, 40, 43–44
total liberation 141, 143
   see also multispecies justice (MSJ)
transparency, in research practices 9–13
trust 39, 60
Turkey 14
Tutsi people, Rwanda, 1994 Genocide against 68, 71, 73, 75, 76, 77, 78, 79
   see also RDYPP (Rwanda Diaspora Youth Partnership Programme)

U

Uganda 180
UK
   food security 48
   immigration changes 32
Ukraine 14
UKRI (UK Research and Innovation) 51
'unconscious bias' 36
United Nations Law of the Sea Convention 124
United States 14
   energy and climate justice 103, 108–109, 111
   environmental justice 106
universities
   governance structures 178–179
   inclusivity 43–44
   neoliberal 7, 178–179, 181
   purpose and future of 9, 177, 178–179
   resourcing social justice struggles 21–30
   see also academia

V

vegan geographies 139
   see also multispecies justice (MSJ)
violence 170
   structural violence 163
visibility, justice as 90
voices
   sharing of 31–44
   women's 37

W

welfarist ethics 148–149
WhatsApp, RDYPP (Rwanda Diaspora Youth Partnership Programme) 79, 80, 81
'wicked problems' 115
wine industry, Western Cape, South Africa 10, 11–13
women
  survivors, 1965 genocide, Indonesia 94–96
  women's voices 37
  see also feminism/feminist theory; gender

Y

Yogyakarta, Indonesia, women survivors of the 1965 genocide 94–96
Young, Iris Marion 125, 135, 161, 162–163, 164, 165–167, 168, 171, 172

www.ingramcontent.com/pod-product-compliance
Lightning Source LLC
Chambersburg PA
CBHW051545020426
42333CB00016B/2106